REALIST FICTION
AND THE
STROLLING SPECTATOR

John Rignall

ROUTLEDGE

London and New York

First published 1992
by Routledge
11 New Fetter Lane, London EC4P 4EE

Simultaneously published in the USA and Canada
by Routledge
a division of Routledge, Chapman and Hall, Inc.
29 West 35th Street, New York, NY 10001

Typeset in 10 on 12 point Garamond by
Computerset, Harmondsworth, Middlesex
Printed in Great Britain by
TJ Press (Padstow) Ltd, Padstow, Cornwall

A catalogue record for this book is available from the British Library.

Library of Congress Cataloging in Publication Data
Rignall, John.
Realist fiction and the strolling spectator / John Rignall.
p.   cm.
1.   English fiction–History and criticism.   2.   American fiction–
History and criticism.   3.   French fiction–History and criticism.
4.   Point of view (Literature) 5.   Realism in literature. I.   Title.
PR830.R4R54   1992
809.3'912–dc20   91-47726

ISBN 0–415–06383–3

CONTENTS

ACKNOWLEDGEMENTS

I would like to thank the Centre for Research into Philosophy and Literature at the University of Warwick for permission to reprint chapter 2, which appeared in an earlier and shorter form as 'Benjamin's *flâneur* and the problem of realism' in A. Benjamin (ed.), *The Problems of Modernity: Adorno and Benjamin*, London and New York, Routledge, 1989. I am grateful to the editor, Andrew Benjamin, for first encouraging into print the seeds of what was to become this book. I also owe a general debt of gratitude to those colleagues and former colleagues with whom I have taught courses on the novel at Warwick and from whom I continue to learn, in particular John Goode and Michael Bell. The latter generously made time, at a busy juncture, to read a final draft of this work and to comment upon it shrewdly and helpfully. I am also conscious of what I owe to generations of students of English and related subjects at Warwick, whose alert and responsive minds have, over the years, made teaching a pleasure and an instruction. Finally I would like to thank my wife Ann for her patient support.

ILLUSTRATIONS

A NOTE ON TRANSLATIONS
AND ABBREVIATIONS

Where there is a reliable, modern, and readily accessible English translation of a primary text I have cited it alongside the original. Secondary material in foreign languages is usually presented only in translation, and all unaccredited translations are my own.

References to, and quotations from, Walter Benjamin, *Charles Baudelaire: A Lyric Poet in the Era of High Capitalism*, trans. H. Zohn, London, Verso Editions, 1983, are, after the first citation in the footnotes, given in brackets in the text, prefaced by the abbreviation *CB*.

1

INTRODUCTION
The realist spectator and the problem of vision

Framed in a sunlit doorway in the background of Velázquez's *Las Meninas* stands the figure of a man in a nonchalant pose, his right foot one step higher on a staircase than his left, and his head turned to gaze in on the room in which the painter is at work on what may be taken to be a picture of the king and queen.[1] Foucault, in his celebrated analysis of the dialectic of representation in Velázquez's painting, sees in this figure one of the three observing functions that are projected into the picture itself.[2] He is the spectator who, together with the painter himself, standing with brush poised before his canvas, and his royal subjects reflected with silvery indistinction in the mirror on the wall, makes up the triangle of representation. Less obviously important than the master painter and his sovereign patrons, who are the principal objects of Foucault's attention, he nevertheless occupies a commanding position; the eye of anyone looking at the painting is powerfully drawn to the brightly illuminated doorway and the figure which it frames.[3] The spectator's gaze comes inevitably to rest on the embodiment of his own spectating.

The figure of the spectator is, then, at once marginal and central. An apparently casual observer, he is caught on the move, just dropping in, it seems, or passing by. His relationship to the hierarchy of power implied in the painting is uncertain: his is not the sovereign gaze of the master painter that orders and organizes the scene before him, nor that of the royal couple absorbed in contemplation of their own centrality and power. His gaze is, rather, that of the visitor, curious and yet detached, not fully implicated in what he observes and yet held by its fascination. He stands on the margins and nevertheless his presence is crucial to the act of representation which is mirrored in the painting. His are, in one sense, the eyes for which the picture is being painted. Without him the reflexive exploration of mimetic art would be incomplete.

With the figure in the doorway Velázquez creates a striking visual image of the act of observing or spectating which has analogues in literary works of a mimetic nature, in particular the realist novel of the nineteenth and early twentieth centuries. From Scott's notoriously uncommitted protagonists, travelling through historical crises as 'foreigners to whom every thing . . . is strange',[4] through Flaubert's aimlessly drifting witness to the events of 1848 in *L'Education sentimentale* (*Sentimental Education*, 1869), to Ford Madox Ford's sly and devious observer of domestic tragedy in *The Good Soldier* (1915), the figure of the disengaged onlooker has been a common accomplice in the realist's project of representing the world. In one respect he constitutes, like Velázquez's figure, a reflexive element in a mimetic composition, pointing up the privileged role ascribed to seeing in the practice of literary realism. If the realist assumes the world to be a coherent and intelligible system of signs that can be understood by those who, like the novelist, have eyes to see, then the observing character is both the instrument and the emblem of the intelligent observation which thus makes sense of visible phenomena. His detached yet curious gaze duplicates that of the novelist himself, who confidently assigns meaning to details of physical appearance, dress and milieu, and reads the visible exterior as a clue to the truth or life behind it. The metonymical practice of the realist seems to be based on the assumption that seeing is equivalent to knowing – 'Voir n'est-ce pas savoir?', as one of Balzac's characters typically and tellingly puts it[5] – and the figure of the spectator or observer[6] bears witness to this epistemological premise.

What is involved here, however, is not simply an act of uncritical self-mirroring. Several recent studies have attempted to retrieve realist fiction from the limbo of naivety and bad faith to which much modern criticism and critical theory have consigned it,[7] and a study of the observing character can contribute to this rehabilitation. It may be reasonable to claim that realism is 'philosophically incurious and epistemologically naive'[8] if one is trying to distinguish it from other modes of writing, but the practice of realism is a good deal more sophisticated than its ostensible premises, and in that practice those premises may be critically questioned by ironic implication. The privileged status of vision, the equation of seeing with knowing, is one such premise,[9] and I aim to show how the act of seeing represented in the fiction does not merely duplicate the novelist's vision but, rather, poses vision as a problem – a problem that reflects critically on the practice of writing and of reading, whilst also engaging the historical world beyond the text in the way that one expects from realist fiction.

F.O. Mathiessen, writing on Henry James, once claimed that 'an interesting chapter of cultural history could be written about the nineteenth century's stress on sight',[10] and although I am using the wider and more ambiguous term 'vision' as more appropriate to the nature of fiction, it is one version of such a chapter that I am attempting here. The figure of the self-enclosed female protagonist, gazing into the mirror or out of the window like Tennyson's Lady of Shalott, has already been the subject of a recent study,[11] but the spectator that I am concerned with is male rather than female, outward-looking rather than inward, not confined but on the move. He enjoys a freedom and suggests in his gaze a masterful control which are both typically masculine, but which prove in the end to be illusory. His role approximates to that of the *flâneur*, the strolling habitué of the boulevards who observes the life around him with a lively but detached curiosity, and is apparently endowed with an instinctive ability 'to seize everything in a single glance and analyse it in passing'.[12] And it is Walter Benjamin's reflections on that figure in his own idiosyncratic chapters of cultural history, the essays on Paris and Baudelaire,[13] that provide the most suggestive insights into the fictional observer and the problematic vision that he inscribes. Benjamin does not address the novel directly, though he refers to novels and novelists in passing, but in defining the *flâneur* as a threatened species whom history is about to overtake, he makes him the representative figure of a phase of nineteenth-century culture whose characteristic literary expression is precisely the realist novel. If the *flâneur*'s existence is a precarious one, balanced as he is on the brink of the alienating system of commodity exchange into which he will eventually be absorbed, the realist mode, too, can be seen in terms of a precariously achieved equilibrium soon to be disturbed.[14] In the kind of vision that, for Benjamin, characterizes the *flâneur* the relationship with realism becomes more than simply figurative: the dialectical opposites – casual and penetrating, familiar and phantasmagoric, detached and involved – that he uses to define this way of seeing are, I shall argue, pertinent to the practice of realism. Even the parallel that he draws between the *flâneur* and the commodity, while it may look like an obscure conceit, has the power to suggest ways in which the fictional figure of the observer is not just a narrative device but can be understood in terms of a specific social and historical context. Benjamin's concept of the *flâneur* has, indeed, the merit of illuminating both the self-referential and the historical dimensions of realist fiction. It can throw light on the complex, reflexive aspect of the realist vision, enabling us to see how the texts themselves challenge the equation of seeing and knowing on which they appear to be predicated; and at the same time it suggests the conditioned nature of all seeing and points to the way in which the observer or spectator is inescapably involved in a network of material relationships.

The *flâneur* presents an image of ambiguous mastery: detached, at ease, and apparently in control, he is nevertheless neither as free nor as self-determining as he appears. He sees and yet does not see; he knows and yet does not know. The implications of this ambiguity for the realist novel run in two directions. On the one hand, the limits of the fictional *flâneur's* vision and understanding reflect back critically on the implied claims of the novelist himself, challenging the identification of seeing with knowing, 'voir' with 'savoir'. On the other, the detached observer bears a significant affinity to the reader; and, more precisely, as Benjamin's reference to the commodity may suggest, to the reader as consumer. The strolling spectator of life on the streets of the great city is the creation of the same commercial culture that produces and sustains the nineteenth-century novel; while the novel, itself a commodity, presents in the figure of this observer an image of the very consumer on whom it depends. A character like Flaubert's Frédéric Moreau in *L'Education sentimentale* is inconceivable before the developed urban culture of the nineteenth century, and, as he bears passive witness to the revolution of 1848, he seems to embody the characteristics of modern man as Nietzsche scathingly defined him in the second of his *Untimely Meditations* published five years after Flaubert's novel – modern man as a mere consumer, his personality weakened by an overdeveloped historical consciousness and the gulf between his inner life and the world of action; a 'strolling spectator' of historical events which leave him essentially untouched.[15] Nietzsche's cultural criticism is clearly a predecessor of Benjamin's, offering a more sharply critical account of the same phenomenon that Benjamin addresses with his theory of the *flâneur*; and it is one of the signal achievements of the realist novel that it explores imaginatively and critically this central aspect of contemporary culture in which it is itself so deeply implicated.

Balzac's *Illusions perdues* (*Lost Illusions*, 1837-43) is an early and trenchant account of consumer society, and one detail from the panorama of garish commercialism presented by the 'Galeries de Bois' in that novel brings together vision, charlatanism, and consumerism as the objects of a, typically realist, critical and self-critical irony. The incident is a minor but characteristic example of how the realist novel can question both its own central concern with vision and insight and the visual appetite of the onlooker or reader. Amongst the hucksters of the

'Galeries de Bois' there is one successful charlatan who makes his money by offering a gullible public the promise of superior vision:

> Là s'est établi pour la première fois un homme qui a gagné sept ou huit cent mille francs à parcourir les foires. Il avait pour enseigne un soleil tournant dans un cadre noir, autour duquel éclataient ces mots écrits en rouge: *Ici l'homme voit ce que Dieu ne saurait voir. Prix; deux sous.* L'aboyeur ne vous admettait jamais seul, ni jamais plus de deux. Une fois entré, vous vous trouviez nez à nez avec une grande glace. Tout à coup une voix, qui eût épouvanté Hoffmann le Berlinois, partait comme une mécanique dont le ressort est poussé: 'Vous voyez là, messieurs, ce que dans toute l'éternité Dieu ne saurait voir, c'est-à-dire votre semblable. Dieu n'a pas son semblable!' Vous vous en alliez honteux sans oser avouer votre stupidité.[16]

> There for the first time a man set up a concern by which he has made seven or eight thousand francs on the fair-grounds. The sign over his booth was a sun revolving in a black surround, and about it these words were inscribed in flaming red: *Here man sees what God cannot see. Price one penny.* The 'barker' never admitted one man by himself, nor ever more than two people. Once inside, you found yourself facing a large mirror. Suddenly a voice which might have terrified Hoffmann himself rang out like a mechanical contrivance when a spring is released: 'You see here, gentlemen, what through all eternity God cannot see, namely a fellow-creature. God has no fellow-creature!' You went out ashamed of yourself without daring to confess your stupidity.[17]

With his mirror and beguiling offer of transcendent vision, the tout looks like a comic parody of the writer himself, who, as Balzac puts it in the preface to *La Peau de chagrin* (*The Wild Ass's Skin*, 1831), 'must have within him some kind of concentric mirror in which, according to his fantasy, the universe comes to be reflected'.[18] Here, however, the eager consumer, in whose naive desires the reader is implicated by the use of the second person plural, gets not an image of the universe but a reflection of his or her own stupidity. The mirror, that emblem of realism, is used by Balzac to aim a casual, passing blow at the kind of spurious claims and misplaced expectations that are so often associated with realist fiction.

This incidental irony is part of a larger critical and self-critical procedure in which the figure of the fictional observer or spectator plays an important role. That role is rather different from the one assigned to him in Lukács's theory of realism, which acknowledges the central significance of the figure but fits him into a Procrustean pattern of realism's greatness and decline. In the work of the great realists like Scott, Balzac, and Tolstoy, the observing character has, for Lukács, a positive, constitutive function. Scott's neutral heroes, looking on at momentous historical conflicts in which they are never whole-heartedly involved, are, for instance, 'a perfect instrument for Scott's way of presenting the totality of certain transitional stages of history'; their function is 'to bring the extremes whose struggle fills the novel, whose clash expresses artistically a great crisis in society, into contact with one another'.[19] The key term here is totality: the central character serves as a means of getting all the essential historical and social factors into the frame of the fiction; mediating between extremes, he brings about the aesthetic unity of the novel. By contrast, the presence of characters who are no more than spectators of events in the novels of Flaubert and Zola is interpreted by Lukács as a symptom of decadence.[20] The separateness of the characters from the action they witness has the effect of reducing the reader's role to that of a mere observer, and is one aspect of that process of disintegration which leads from the organic unity of realism to the fragmentation of modernism. The weakness of Lukács's scheme is that it transforms subtle differences into stark contrasts and ignores a significant element of continuity. It is the aim of this study to show that Scott's heroes, while they do serve as instruments of a totalizing vision, are more problematic than Lukács's view of them allows, and that the separateness of Flaubert's characters continues the critical tradition of realism rather than marking its decline. To focus on the character as observer or spectator – partial in his perceptions, questionably detached, and unwittingly determined by forces beyond his understanding and control – is to become aware of the problems involved in this choice of perspective, and in the realist novel's emphasis on vision as a means of understanding. The mobile perspective of the *flâneur* both serves the realist aim of comprehensiveness and, at the same time, undermines it by questioning the very possibility of such mastery and control. Examined in this way, the novel, at once critical and self-critical, corresponds not to Lukács's but rather to Bakhtin's view of it as 'ever questing, ever examining itself and subjecting its established forms to review'.[21] Taking a cue from Bakhtin's dialogic model of competing discourses, I shall argue that the particular vision of the character often stands in an interrogative relationship to the vision of the whole.

If stress is placed on the continuing thread of criticism and self-criticism in the history of the novel, the demarcation between realism on the one hand and both naturalism and modernism on the other becomes less clear than Lukács proposes. The naturalist novelist, combining the roles of observer and experimentalist, may perform a more deliberate, systematic and theoretically self-aware act of looking *into* consumer society than the realist,[22] while the modernist may present a greater degree of creative self-consciousness and a more thorough questioning of the premises of previous fiction, but both are anticipated in the practice of realism. Instead of a radical break there is a continuing process of innovation and interrogation in which vision, 'realism's metaphor of reality and its knowledge',[23] becomes ever more overtly problematic. When Ruskin, in *Præterita*, claims that 'if you have sympathy, the aspect of humanity is more true to the depths of it than its words; and even in my own land, the things in which I have been least deceived are those which I have learned as their Spectator',[24] he defines himself as a man of the nineteenth century in privileging the sense of sight as a means of access to the truth. When Sartre, in *La Nausée* (*Nausea*, 1938), has Roquentin declare that sight is an abstract invention – 'la vue, c'est une invention abstraite, une idée nettoyée, simplifiée, une idée d'homme'[25] – he announces a typically twentieth-century challenge to the primacy of sight.[26] The development from realism to modernism can, indeed, be understood as the progressive displacement of sight, or vision, from its privileged centrality and its replacement by language; but the point that needs to be made is that the major realist novels are never unquestioning of that privileged centrality, while a modernist novel like *La Nausée*, however sceptical it may be, displays a clear continuity with its predecessors in the central role it assigns to an observer and its treatment of vision as problematic. Roquentin on the rue Tournebride stands in a direct line of descent from Balzac's Lucien de Rubempré in the Tuileries Gardens or on the Champs-Elysées. To trace that continuity is one of the concerns of this study.

Benjamin's observations on the *flâneur* suggest a way of defining more precisely the changes that take place with respect to vision in the development from realism to modernism. The precarious equilibrium which the *flâneur* embodies, and which has some affinity with realism, is easily upset: 'In the *flâneur* the joy of watching is triumphant. It can concentrate on observation; the result is the amateur detective. Or it can stagnate in the gaper; then the *flâneur* has turned into the *badaud*' (*CB*, 69). This divergence into two kinds of looking can be mapped on to the history of the novel. The confident interpretation of visual phenomena, that making-sense of the world, which characterizes realist fiction in its greatest phase is taken over late in the nineteenth century by the subgenre of the detective novel, whose archetypal hero, the amateur detective Sherlock Holmes, penetrates the obscurity of the great city with his piercing eyes. The naturalist novel, too, can be seen to deploy a more narrowly purposeful and intently focused kind of observation than its realist predecessor. The other line of succession, however, leads to the novel of early modernism where the observing character, if not exactly a gaping *badaud*, is someone, like Conrad's Marlow, groping for an ultimately elusive meaning in the spectacle of life he witnesses. The polarization of vision into, on the one hand, the narrowly intent gaze – which looks inward in Proust and Woolf and takes a sinister turn in Sartre's menacing notion of 'le regard' or Kafka's paranoid world under constant surveillance – and, on the other, the bemused wonderment occasioned by the opaqueness of the observed world, could be said to characterize the aftermath of the nineteenth-century realist novel.

The role of the fictional observer in the naturalist novel's exploration of consumer society has already been well analysed,[27] and I shall concentrate here on the nineteenth-century novel and a few of its twentieth-century successors, mainly from the early period of modernism. My principal objective is the analysis and illumination of particular texts in which the figure of the observer or spectator plays a central role and which raise, in different ways and with different emphases, the issues outlined above. What should emerge, apart from a continuing preoccupation with the problem of vision, is the variety and complexity of modes of perception in nineteenth-century fiction. The choice of texts is largely determined by the subject, but limited to the languages in which I am competent. Nietzsche's essay on history and Benjamin's writings on the *flâneur* provide the scaffolding for my argument, and I begin with a more detailed discussion of what Benjamin calls his 'theory' of the *flâneur* and its relation to realism.

2

BENJAMIN'S *FLANEUR* AND POE'S 'MAN OF THE CROWD'

The *flâneur*, strolling the streets of nineteenth-century Paris with cool but curious eye, is a stock character in the documentary genre of the *Tableaux de Paris* which flourished in the 1830s and 1840s.[1] He seemed to typify the new urban culture by appearing comfortably at home on the streets and in harmony with his world. Benjamin, however, responding to Baudelaire's use of a *flâneur* persona in his *Tableaux parisiens*, which appeared as the genre was declining, sees the element of estrangement that shadows this apparent harmony and sense of place. For him the *flâneur* is a transient phenomenon, typical only of a brief period of nineteenth-century culture, a threatened figure existing in a state of precarious balance. Still standing on the margins both of the great city and the bourgeois class, he is yet to be overwhelmed by either; but it is only a matter of time before he is swept into their alienating embrace.

The figure of the *flâneur* first appears in Benjamin's writing in 1929 in a review of Hessel's *Spazieren in Berlin* entitled 'Die Wiederkehr des Flaneurs' ('The Return of the *Flâneur*').[2] That title suggests that the *flâneur* is already a creature of the past, and it is, of course, in Benjamin's later work on nineteenth-century Paris that the figure is examined in its true habitat, playing a central part in the 1935 sketch for the Arcades Project, 'Paris – the Capital of the Nineteenth Century', and the two studies of Baudelaire, 'The Paris of the Second Empire in Baudelaire' written in 1938, and the revised and much altered version 'Some Motifs in Baudelaire', published in the *Zeitschrift für Sozialforschung* in 1939.[3] Although Benjamin refers to his 'theory' of the *flâneur*,[4] it is difficult to discern anything like a coherent single theory in the various ideas which cluster around that composite and overdetermined figure. Constituted intertextually from Baudelaire's essays and poetry, from Poe's fiction and Balzac's, from Dickens's letters about his own creative practice, from Marx's theory of commodity fetishism, and from documentary

9

and historical writings about Paris, Benjamin's *flâneur* is at once an observed historical phenomenon, a type among the inhabitants of nineteenth-century Paris, the representation of a way of experiencing metropolitan life, a literary motif, and an image of the commodity in its relation to the crowd. The aspect that is central both to Baudelaire's own use of the term and Poe's story 'The Man of the Crowd', to which Baudelaire refers and which Benjamin analyses, is the aspect of vision.

The intertextual layering of the material in the chapter entitled 'The *Flâneur*' in 'The Paris of the Second Empire in Baudelaire' points to the crucial issue of seeing. In 'Le Peintre de la vie moderne' ('The Painter of Modern Life') Baudelaire uses the term *flâneur* in an attempt to define the quality of observation that he admires in the painter of Parisian life, Constantin Guys.[5] This observer of metropolitan life is himself observed and defined with the aid of a literary text about observation, Poe's 'The Man of the Crowd'. Benjamin then observes the observer Baudelaire observing Guys. He reads Baudelaire reading Poe and defining a painter of Parisian life, and uses Baudelaire's own term *flâneur* as a lens through which to see his poetry and Baudelaire's poetry as a lens through which to see Parisian life. Paris, the object of Guys's painting, is brought again before the eyes of Benjamin's reader through a complex series of mediations. We are alerted to the way things are seen by the very disposition of the textual material, and as Benjamin proceeds to develop his notion of the *flâneur* he outlines a distinctive mode of vision. Starting from Georg Simmel's premise that 'interpersonal relationships in big cities are distinguished by a marked preponderance of the activity of the eye over the activity of the ear' (38), Benjamin presents the *flâneur* as a characteristic product of urban life in that in him 'the joy of watching is triumphant' (69). His particular kind of seeing is defined in terms of dialectically related opposites: he sees the city as 'now landscape, now a room' (170). This transformation of the street into a kind of interior is one of the ways in which he makes the alien urban world bearably familiar – 'the street becomes a dwelling for the *flâneur*; he is as much at home among the façades of the houses as a citizen is in his four walls' (37) – yet that familiarity is at the same time juxtaposed to visionary strangeness in that 'the appearance of the street as an *intérieur*' is one 'in which the phantasmagoria of the *flâneur* is concentrated' (50). Seeing the city now as open, now as enclosing, now familiar, now phantasmagoric, the *flâneur* also combines the casual eye of the stroller with the purposeful gaze of the detective. His vision is both wide-ranging and penetrating at the same time; he can read the signs of the streets and unlock their secrets.

It is not hard to perceive the affinities between this complex form of seeing in the city and the practice of nineteenth-century realism, in particular the practice of those novelists of metropolitan life like Balzac and Dickens on whom Benjamin himself draws. The city as landscape, lying either desolately or seductively open before the fictional charac- ters, and the city as a room enclosing them either protectively or oppressively; the city as familiar, as knowable and known, and the city as mysteriously alien and fantastic; these are the well-established poles of Balzac's and Dickens's urban fiction. Both writers were themselves given to a *flânerie* that seems to have played a significant role in their creative lives. The importance of nocturnal street-walking for Dickens is well documented, and it is possible to see a correlation between his ramblings through London, the persona he adopts in his documentary writings, and the narrative techniques of his novels.[6] The article on the *flâneur* in one of the documentary texts Benjamin drew upon, *Les Français peints par eux-mêmes* (1840), makes an explicit connection between *flânerie* and writing, claiming that it is 'the distinctive charac- teristic of the true man of letters'.[7] Balzac, in a well-known passage at the beginning of *Facino Cane*, presents his narrator as a *flâneur* who studies the life of the streets and is able at will to enter imaginatively into the lives of the people he observes:

> Chez moi l'observation était déjà devenue intuitive . . . elle saisissait si bien les détails extérieurs, qu'elle allait sur-le-champ au-delà; elle me donnait la faculté de vivre de la vie de l'individu sur laquelle elle s'exerçait.[8]

> Observation had already become intuitive with me . . . grasping external details so well that it immediately went beyond them; it gave me the ability to live the life of the individual on whom it was focused.

This power of empathy is another characteristic of Benjamin's *flâneur*. In the first Baudelaire essay he is described as abandoning himself to it in the crowd and, and in so doing, sharing the situation of the commodity:

> The *flâneur* is someone abandoned in the crowd. In this he shares the situation of the commodity. He is not aware of this special situation, but this does not diminish its effect on him and it permeates him blissfully like a narcotic that can compensate him for many humiliations. The intoxication to which the *flâneur* surrenders is the intoxication of the commodity around which surges the stream of customers.

If the soul of the commodity which Marx occasionally men-
tions in jest existed, it would be the most empathetic ever
encountered in the realm of souls, for it would have to see in
everyone the buyer in whose hand and house it wants to nestle.
Empathy is the nature of the intoxication to which the *flâneur*
abandons himself in the crowd. (*CB*, 55)

Empathy, the aim and achievement of the realist novelist in his representation of the inner life, is another facet of the *flâneur*'s vision, and, at
the same time, it reveals, as Benjamin suggests with typical teasing
brilliance, an unwitting involvement in the commerce of contemporary
life which he thinks to look on as a superior spectator.

The equation of the *flâneur* with the commodity signals for Benjamin
the end of the former's brief existence. The middle chapter of 'The Paris
of the Second Empire in Baudelaire' shows the freedom of the *flâneur*
giving way to the fixity of the purchasable commodity, just as Baudelaire
himself is unable to maintain his strolling detachment and ends up being
harried by creditors and jostled by the crowd. Such a process has
numerous analogues in nineteenth-century fiction – the fate of Isabel
Archer in *The Portrait of a Lady* is a classic example – but it is not the
dramatic potential of the theme that I wish to stress here but the
precarious nature of the *flâneur*'s stance which it reveals. The complex
dialectical mode of seeing figured in the *flâneur* and enacted in the
narrative practice of realism is inherently unstable, and the epistemological premises of that practice are open to question. The
privileged role ascribed to the detached individual vision of the novelist
as narrator rests on the premise that seeing is equivalent to knowing. As
in the case of the narrator of *Facino Cane* to see is to know, to observe
acutely is to penetrate to the truth. This equation is a recurrent motif in
Balzac's fiction. Those characters, such as the ubiquitous Vautrin, who
are in the know, who understand the workings of the social world, are
commonly described in terms of their lynx eyes, their penetrating gaze.
Knowledge is regularly conveyed by metaphors of vision. Similarly, the
descriptive energy expended in realist practice on appearances, clothes,
buildings, interiors, is predicated on the assumption that to see, to
observe closely the visible exterior is to gain access to the life or truth
within. Seeing is knowing; description yields meaning; representation
involves faithfully mirroring what is seen.

The equation of seeing with knowing and its implications are not
directly addressed by Benjamin, and the precariousness of the *flâneur*'s
stance is defined solely in socio-historical terms. The crisis that engulfs
him is economic not aesthetic. Nevertheless, Benjamin does indirectly

reveal the problematic nature of the aesthetic and epistemological premises of realism in his reading of Poe's story 'The Man of the Crowd' in relation to Baudelaire's comments on the work in 'Le Peintre de la vie moderne'. Approaching Poe's text in both the Baudelaire essays with a different emphasis on each occasion, he does not explicitly set out its implications for an understanding of realism, but in his reading, and in one respect misreading, of Poe in the light of Baudelaire he provides the means by which these implications may be uncovered.

The misreading lies in his interpretation of Baudelaire's reading of Poe and turns on the question of who in Poe's story is to be properly designated a *flâneur*, the narrator looking at the world through the window of a London coffee-house, or 'the man of the crowd' whom he catches sight of on the street outside and eventually follows. The latter, 'this unknown man', is for Benjamin 'the *flâneur*. That is how Baudelaire interpreted him when in his essay on Guys, he called the *flâneur* "l'homme des foules"' (*CB*, 48). The text of 'Le Peintre de la vie moderne', however, reveals nothing of the sort. Baudelaire refers to the story to define more precisely the quality of observation he admires in Guys. Describing Poe's narrator as 'a convalescent, pleasurably absorbed in gazing at the crowd', he proceeds to draw the comparison with Guys: 'Imagine an artist who was always, spiritually, in the condition of that convalescent, and you will have the key to the nature of Monsieur G'.[9] A few paragraphs later he emphatically identifies the *flâneur* with Guys as a passionate observer of the crowd: 'For the perfect *flâneur*, for the passionate spectator, it is an immense joy to set up house in the heart of the multitude, amid the ebb and flow of movement, in the midst of the fugitive and the infinite'.[10] Baudelaire clearly associates the *flâneur* with the act of seeing not with the person seen.

In his second essay on Baudelaire Benjamin partially corrects his own error when he points out that the man of the crowd is not the *flâneur*:

> Baudelaire saw fit to equate the man of the crowd, whom Poe's narrator follows throughout the length and breadth of nocturnal London, with the *flâneur*. It is hard to accept this view. The man of the crowd is no *flâneur*. In him, composure has given way to manic behaviour. (*CB*, 128)

But he still believes that he is exposing Baudelaire's misreading rather than his own. He remains trapped within his own error and never makes the step from maintaining that the man of the crowd is not the *flâneur* to stating that the narrator is.

This misreading may be understood as an example of that tendency which Adorno saw and criticized in 'The Paris of the Second Empire in Baudelaire', a tendency to relate the pragmatic contents of Baudelaire's work directly to adjacent features in the social history of his time.[11] The *flâneur* is seen here as a social phenomenon, the object of the materialist historian's gaze rather than the exponent of a certain kind of vision, the seeing subject himself. And when Benjamin partially corrects himself he is still using the figure to illustrate social and economic change: Poe's man of the crowd 'exemplifies what had to become of the *flâneur* once he was deprived of the milieu to which he belonged' (*CB*, 128-9). The precariousness of the *flâneur*'s situation is defined solely by the changing circumstances to which he is exposed. What is lacking here is, as Adorno maintains, mediation, the very mediation that the concept of the *flâneur* as representing a way of seeing provides. However, Benjamin's blindness may be our insight, indicating by omission the terms that can help make sense of Poe's story and allow it to be related to the *flâneur*'s stance in a more subtly mediated way, which takes into account not only what is represented but the very mode of its representation. Benjamin quite properly distinguishes between Poe's text and realism: 'Poe's manner of presentation cannot be called realism. It shows a purposely distorting imagination at work, one that removes the text from what is commonly advocated as the model of social realism' (*CB*, 128). But, leaving aside the romantic trappings of the story, if the gaze of the narrator and the limits of his vision are made the central issue, then it emerges as 'something like the X-ray picture' (*CB*, 48), not only of a detective story as Benjamin suggests, but also of a realist text and its epistemological assumptions. In the light of Benjamin's other pronouncements on the *flâneur* 'The Man of the Crowd' can be read not only as a mirror of changing historical circumstances but also as revealing the problematic basis of a mirror theory of representation.

At the opening of the story the narrator, convalescing from an illness, is in a state of heightened but calm awareness. Although he is seated in a coffee-house rather than strolling the streets, his calm and inquisitive interest in all about him corresponds to that of the *flâneur*, and like the latter he becomes absorbed in the spectacle of the crowd. Regarding 'with minute interest the innumerable varieties of figure, dress, air, gait, visage, and expression of countenance',[12] he begins to categorize the passers-by according to their dress and occupation. The signs are unmistakable and he reads the street scene without doubt or hesitation:

> The tribe of clerks was an obvious one . . . The division of the
> upper clerks of staunch firms, or of the 'steady old fellows', it was

not possible to mistake . . . The gamblers, of whom I descried not
a few, were still more easily recognizable. (180-1)

Thus, playing the part of the typical narrator of realist fiction, Poe's
convalescent makes sense of the world for his reader, even claiming for
himself, as night thickens and the fitful glare of the gaslamps takes over,
the same kind of omniscience and power of empathy as Balzac's narrator
in *Facino Cane*:

> And although the rapidity with which the world of light flitted
> before the window, prevented me from casting more than a glance
> upon each visage, still it seemed that, in my peculiar mental state, I
> could frequently read, even in that brief interval of a glance, the
> history of long years. (183)

At this juncture he is struck by the sight of a decrepit old man whose face
wears an expression of such absolute idiosyncrasy as to be not immediately readable. He 'struggles to form some analysis of the meaning
conveyed' but can only produce a mere catalogue of disparate and often
contradictory qualities, 'the ideas of vast mental power, of caution, of
penuriousness, of avarice, of coolness, of malice, of blood-thirstiness, of
triumph, of merriment, of excessive terror, of intense – of extreme
despair' (183-4). Instead of analysis he can offer only rhetorical
declamation.

Seized by a craving to 'keep the man in view – to know more of him'
(184), on the assumption that to see more is to know more, he sets off
after him. As Benjamin puts it in another context, 'the *flâneur* is thus
turned into an unwilling detective' (*CB*, 40). After following the man for
a whole day the narrator finally stops, 'wearied unto death', and gazes 'at
him steadfastly in the face' (187). But the gaze cannot penetrate the
surface and dispel the mystery. To see the man steadily and to see him
whole is to approach no nearer to knowledge, so that all the narrator can
offer is another rhetorical declamation, a grandiose but empty label:
'"This old man," I said at length, "is the type and the genius of deep
crime. He refuses to be alone. *He is the man of the crowd*"' (188).
Beyond that the narrator can do no more than acknowledge the limits of
his own understanding:

> It will be in vain to follow; for I shall learn no more of him, nor of
> his deeds. The worst heart of the world is a grosser book than the
> 'Hortulus Animae', and perhaps it is but one of the great mercies
> of God that *es lässt sich nicht lesen*. (188)

From reading the signs of the street and making sense of the world easily and confidently the narrator has come finally to admit that the heart of the world cannot be known. *Es lässt sich nicht lesen*; the world cannot be read, and made readable, in the manner demonstrated at the beginning of the story.

In the guise of a Romantic mystery tale, then, Poe's text reflects on the problematic nature of realist narration and its premises, both showing the *flâneur's* vision at work and prescribing its limits. The narrator, in his vain attempts to attach meanings to the unfathomable face of the man of the crowd, ends up by resembling the allegorist whom Benjamin scathingly describes in one of his notes for the Arcades Project: 'the allegorist plucks an item at random from his chaotic fund of knowledge and holds it up next to another to see whether they match: that meaning to this image, or this image to that meaning.'[13] Poe's story, too, reveals the relationship between meaning and image, between world and word, to be arbitrary and mysterious, and by implication, any mirror theory of literary representation to be without secure foundation. If Benjamin does not draw these conclusions himself in his reading of Poe and Baudelaire, he nevertheless points the way towards them. His concept of the *flâneur* becomes an instrument for the understanding of realism.

It can also help to discriminate between different kinds of writing that may seem to be broadly realist. In his discussion of Poe's story Benjamin makes a passing comparison with a somewhat earlier one by E.T.A.Hoffmann, *Des Vetters Eckfenster* (*The Cousin's Corner-Window*, 1822), and draws a contrast between the different perspectives of the two works, which he later enlarges upon in the second Baudelaire essay (*CB*, 48-9, 129-31). The cousin of Hoffmann's title is a paralysed writer who amuses himself by looking down from his window at a bustling market-square in Berlin and constructing fictions to make sense of what he sees. For Benjamin this figure is a man of leisure where Poe's narrator is a consumer; one sits at home, the other is drawn by the fascination of what he sees into the crowd; constraint characterizes the one kind of vision, penetration the other. A distinction drawn by the article on the *flâneur* in *Les Français peints par eux-mêmes* also seems to be pertinent: 'The *flâneur* has need his legs as well as his mind, and when they fail he passes to the state of being an observer; that is to another existence, another condition'.[14] This absence of mobility is crucial to the structure and effect of *Des Vetters Eckfenster*. To Benjamin the difference between the two stories and the vantage points of their characters is quite simply the difference between Berlin and

London, between different stages of social development. But whether or not Hoffmann would have written differently about city life had he ever visited London or Paris, the way that he did write about it is distinctive, and distinctively German. Seen from on high, and with the aid of opera glasses, the Berlin scene amounts to 'a multiplicity of little genre pictures which in their totality constitute an album of coloured engravings', whereas Poe's London 'would be capable of inspiring a great etcher' (*CB*, 49). The artistic metaphors effectively convey the anodyne quality of Hoffmann's story, the Biedermeier charm that comes from keeping the life of the city at a distance. What is lacking is the kind of narrative momentum that derives from the *flâneur*'s perspective of Poe's work, where the narrator descends into the crowd to be brought face to face with the inscrutable nature of metropolitan life.

The limitations of Hoffmann's story brought out by Benjamin's comparison have a wider relevance to German literature in the nineteenth century and its marginal relationship to the mainstream of European realism. It is well known that the finest works of German prose fiction in that period are to be found not in the novel but in the smaller compass of the *Novelle* and in a mode only obliquely related to realism. It could be said that it is precisely the absence of a perspective like that of Poe's *flâneur* narrator which characterizes this fiction and its reluctance to engage directly with the contemporary world in the manner of a Dickens or a Balzac. Hoffmann's view from the window is characteristic rather than idiosyncratic, and it is not until the early twentieth century that the *flâneur* has any resonance in German literature.[15]

Benjamin concludes his second comparison of Poe and Hoffmann by citing Heine as an example of a writer who experienced metropolitan life and was able to see its more disturbing aspects. Walking on the boulevards with a companion who was admiring the Parisian scene, Heine stresses '"the horror with which this centre of the world is tinged"' (*CB*, 131). Benjamin might have cited a more dramatic instance of Heine's insight as a *flâneur*, the occasion in December 1841 when, strolling past the shops with their New Year displays, he observes the crowd looking at the piles of luxury articles and reflects on the expression on the people's faces:

> The faces of these people are so horribly serious and suffering, so impatient and threatening, that they form a disturbing contrast to the objects they are gazing at, and we are struck by the fear that one day they might suddenly put their clenched fists through the

window and smash to pitiful pieces all the bright, jingling toys of the fashionable world together with the fashionable world itself.[16]

Heine the *flâneur* – and he refers to himself as such – is not 'botanising on the asphalt' (*CB*, 36), but stripping the veil from consumer society. A contemporary of Balzac, he reads the signs differently, not confidently showing how society works but, rather, foreseeing how it may soon catastrophically cease to work altogether. The insight is prophetic, and as the passage goes on it seems to predict not only the revolutionary upheavals of 1848 but even the violence of the Commune. The *flâneur* foresees the end of his own privileged existence.

Poe's story points to the future in a less dramatic way, for, as Benjamin's discussion reveals, it can be read both as a diagram of realism and as an anticipation of its end. The doubleness which Benjamin explicitly identifies in 'The Man of the Crowd' is a socio-historical one, but it has implications for literary history of a related kind. In seeing the story as prefiguring the end of the *flâneur* in the development of the department store, he points to a change that has its literary equivalent in the transition from realism to naturalism; that is, to a mode of fiction that is at once the product and the critique of fully developed consumer society. Where the street was once an interior for the *flâneur*, now in the department store the interior has become a street:

> And he roamed through the labyrinth of merchandise as he had once roamed through the labyrinth of the city. It is a magnificent touch in Poe's story that it includes along with the earliest description of the *flâneur* the figuration of his end. (*CB*, 54)

This image of the individual as a consumer in thrall to the power of the commodity implies a greater degree of social determinism than is to be found in realist fiction, where the individual and the social are held in a fine balance. It also implies a society that requires a more systematic effort to understand it than that undertaken by realism, whose more generous and less schematic vision of social life is nicely epitomized by the casual yet inquiring gaze of Benjamin's *flâneur*, strolling the arcades and the boulevards of the great city. That transient figure captures, too, the precariousness of the realist mode and, at the same time, indicates the complex process of its supersession by the different but related experimentalisms of naturalism and modernism.

Before exploring in more detail the relationship between the *flâneur* and the realist fiction of the mid nineteenth century which engages directly with the unprecedented reality of metropolitan life, I shall turn to an earlier kind of spectator, the typical protagonist of Scott's novels.

This detached and uncommitted onlooker anticipates some of the themes and narrative procedures of realism in bearing witness to the conflicts of history and responding to the dramatic spectacle which it affords.

3

SCOTT AND THE SPECTACLE OF HISTORY

Scott's evasive cultivation of anonymity throughout most of his career as a novelist, that 'passion for delitescency', or lying hidden, which he names but cannot account for in the 'General Preface' to the Waverley Novels,[1] has its counterpart within the fiction in the problematic disengagement of his notoriously neutral and uncommitted protagonists. They, too, are disposed to delitescency, to observing events from a position of security, to seeing without being seen, like Waverley spying through a nailhole in his bed in Janet's cottage, or Guy Mannering hearing the voice of Meg Merrilies in the castle of Ellangowan and finding 'an aperture through which he could observe her without being himself visible' (ch. 3). To observe while remaining invisible is to occupy a peculiarly privileged vantage-point, and this privilege is as important a quality in the constitution of the typical Waverley hero as his neutrality. In general he is permitted to see and not to suffer, so that these instances of covert spectating are simply literal illustrations of the overall position he is placed in by the dispensations of Scott's narration. Such privileged invulnerability has, of course, a distinct purpose, and the importance of the protagonist as eyewitness has been appreciated ever since Scott acknowledged 'the medium of the hero' to be a useful narrative device in his anonymous review of *Tales of My Landlord* in 1817.[2] In formal terms the eyewitness serves as a 'representative of the reader at the scene of the action'[3] and forges the crucial connection between reading present and historical past. More significantly, as Lukács has famously argued, he is a means not merely of representing the historical but also of articulating a particular understanding of history – history as moving through conflict to a balance of opposites, and as determined more by social forces than by the actions of individual historical figures.[4] For Lukács the observing central character mediates between conflicting extremes and is Scott's means of seizing the totality of an historical epoch. The price of all this is the passivity and insipidness that Scott himself noted in his heroes. However, discussions of the protagonist that restrict themselves either to his instrumental function or to his lack of dynamic moral character overlook the problematic dimension of the very spectating that is crucial to his role in the process of historical representation. Put simply, the problem is that of the aestheticisation of history. Disengaged spectating carries with it the danger of treating events as objects of a merely aesthetic contemplation, of turning history into spectacle. It is a danger that shadows the very project of the historical novel with its natural gravitation towards the condition of a romance in period fancy dress.

For an analysis of this danger, and the cultural conditions that promote it, we need to turn to Nietzsche, writing half a century after Scott and against the grain of the historical mode of thinking that had come to dominate the nineteenth century. In the second of his *Untimely Meditations*, 'On the Uses and Disadvantages of History for Life' (1874), he singles out this danger as one of the drawbacks of that historical orientation of culture that Scott himself had helped to develop. Concerned in particular with the debilitating effects of an overdeveloped historical consciousness, Nietzsche diagnoses the particular sickness of contemporary culture as the growing gulf between the inner life and the outer, between educated inwardness and the public sphere of action. This gulf creates a 'weakened personality', prone to self-irony, cynicism, and insensitivity even to barbaric behaviour in the public sphere. Thus weakened, modern man, who gets his historical artists to lay on for him what amounts to a world exhibition of history, has become merely a 'strolling spectator' of events, taking pleasure in them from a distance and remaining in a condition which even the greatest upheavals of war and revolution can scarcely alter for a moment. History, it seems, has been reduced to a spectacle: hardly is a war over before it emerges as printed matter to whet the jaded palates of those who are greedy for historical entertainment. And for Nietzsche such a development has disastrous consequences, for those who treat history as a spectacle suffer a crippling diminution of their vital forces.[5]

Nietzsche's cultural criticism seems to strike at the heart of Scott's kind of fiction, and Scott himself can undoubtedly be counted as one of those historical artists who cater to the appetite for historical entertainment. Moreover, his disengaged protagonists look like direct anticipations of Nietzsche's modern man as strolling spectator. Nevertheless, it is precisely in his handling of these figures that Scott provides the grounds for a critical reading of their perspective and its implications that anticipates Nietzsche, even to the extent of identifying the spectating protagonist as a kind of consumer. The critical light which his fiction casts on its own characteristic representational device, and hence on the treatment of history as spectacle, is a mark of the seriousness which is often denied to it by those who focus only on its romantic surface. From *Waverley* (1814) onwards, where the spectating protagonist appears in his original and archetypal form, Scott's finest novels reveal a critical awareness of the pitfalls to which the fictional representation of history is exposed.

Edward Waverley certainly resembles Nietzsche's modern man, but without the historical education that is diagnosed as the cause of the latter's debility. Initially he appears to be barely educated at all and innocent of any historical and worldly understanding. But raised as he is on the pap of family legends and literary romances, his early life is marked by a limiting inwardness about which Scott is as damning as Nietzsche. The explicit moral criticism of Waverley's 'wavering and unsettled habit of mind' (ch. 7) and his enthralment by romance give grounds for seeing the novel as a straightforward story of one man's education out of misty-eyed adolescence into a state of responsible maturity where he can see things clearly and see them whole. Most readings of *Waverley* follow these lines with varying emphasis on the degree of irony with which the hero is treated; some interpret his development as simply a chastening awakening from a misguided romantic dream; others, more persuasively, argue that the romantic vision makes an important contribution to his final maturity by giving him a capacity for imaginative sympathy.[6] Yet to see the novel as presenting the hero's steady progress towards final maturity is to ignore the discontinuities and contradictions that punctuate what development there is in this thinly drawn character. That there is some movement from error towards insight cannot be denied, but it remains tentative, uncertain, and highly qualified. It is, in particular, at moments when attention is focused on Waverley's ability to see and his mode of perception that the narrative line of development is most obviously disturbed. His vision remains problematic to the last.

The predominantly ironic tone of the opening chapters leaves no doubt about the value of the young Waverley's romantically inspired visions:

> In the corner of the large and sombre library, with no other light than was afforded by the decaying brands on its ponderous and ample hearth, he would exercise for hours that internal sorcery,

by which past or imaginary events are presented in action, as it
were, to the eye of the muser. (ch. 4)

In the dubious half-light from a 'decaying' source the eye of the muser is
turned inward, delighting in the imaginary spectacle of a fictitious past.
He is the spectator of make-believe history in the theatre of the
imagination. The library is the appropriate setting for these flights of
fancy, and through the figure of the unseeing young seer Scott seemingly
defines the temptation that the reader of his own kind of fiction may be
exposed to. 'Sorcery' strikes the critical note, and it is clear that the
'visions as brilliant and as fading as those of an evening sky' which
Waverley creates 'from the splendid yet useless imagery and emblems
with which his imagination was stored' (ch. 4) bear the mark of an
etiolated aestheticism that seems to be there only in order to be
outgrown. Yet although Waverley progresses from observing in the
mind to observing in the flesh, aestheticising distance and imperci-
pience are never fully overcome. Blindness outweighs insight in the most
crucial scenes of seeing in the novel.

Arriving in Tully-Veolan the newly commissioned Waverley is confronted with a prospect which, in its primitive squalor, affronts 'an eye
accustomed to the smiling neatness of English cottages' (ch. 8) That eye
is, presumably, his own, although the description that follows – with the
exception of the 'picturesque' sight of the girls returning from the well –
appears to issue from a consciousness that is not identical with his. The
power of judgement which, at the end of the previous chapter, he had
been described as being deficient in – 'his eye could not judge of
distance or space as well as those of his companions' (ch. 7) – is here
repeatedly on display as the narrator assumes the 'voice of Scott the
philosophical historian',[7] weighing up, measuring, and drawing conclusions from what is seen: 'The whole scene was depressing; for it argued,
at the first glance, at least a stagnation of industry, and perhaps of
intellect' (ch. 8). What is at work here is a mode of perception
characteristic of realist fiction; a way of observing and reading the signs
of the world; of interpreting, deducing, and making definitive sense of
diverse phenomena. The first glance thus leads on to a closer, more
considered scrutiny: 'Yet the physiognomy of the people, when more
closely examined, was far from exhibiting the indifference of stupidity;
their features were rough, but remarkably intelligent; grave, but the very
reverse of stupid' (ch. 8). And the description closes with a judicious
summing up: 'It seemed, upon the whole, as if poverty and indolence,
its too frequent companion, were combining to depress the natural
genius and acquired information of a hardy, intelligent, and reflecting

peasantry' (ch. 8). Waverley himself is the convenient instrument of the narration in all this, and Scott makes only the most casual and perfunctory attempt to relate the observations to the consciousness of his character: 'Some such thoughts crossed Waverley's mind as he paced his horse slowly through the rugged and flinty streets of Tully-Veolan' (ch. 8). The casualness is not simply attributable to an as yet undeveloped narrative technique, for, in stressing the imprecise relationship of Waverley to the kind of perception that has been deployed, it has the important effect of foregrounding the question of his perceptiveness and opening up an ironic gap between him and the narrator just as it seems that the exigencies of social life have rescued him from his wayward imagination. It is precisely the powers of analysis and judgement displayed in this passage that Waverley is never fully to acquire, so that the scene, while apparently launching him on his education into insight and understanding, hints at the ironic way in which that trajectory will be left uncompleted.

The curious but detached gaze of the foreign visitor is in evidence again in those scenes in which Waverley is faced by a spectacular display of the feudal forces assembling for the Jacobite march on England, and once again irony is in play. In the scene of the clans departing after the deer hunt, 'their feathers and loose plaids waving in the morning breeze, and their arms glittering in the rising sun' (ch. 24), it operates at the expense of the romantic vision. The 'moving picture upon the narrow plain' is only visible to the injured Waverley because the litter in which he is lying is raised on the shoulders of some of Mac-Ivor's men, with the result that 'the romantic effect produced by the break-up of this silvan camp' (ch. 24) is associated with physical incapacity and prostration. The colourful spectacle is explicitly an invalid vision. The related, more specifically historical, scene of the Highland army setting out from Edinburgh is exposed to irony in a different way. This 'gay and lively spectacle' (ch. 44), witnessed by the now recovered Waverley from St Leonard's Hill, is qualified not by the infirmity of the spectator but by his movement, which is the instrument of one of Scott's characteristic shifts of perspective. In hurrying to catch up with Mac-Ivor's clan at the head of the column Waverley moves from a distant perspective of this 'remarkable spectacle' to 'a nearer view' which 'rather diminished the effect impressed on the mind by the more distant appearance of the army' (ch. 44). Impressive in its leading ranks, the army tails off into a ragged train of the 'common peasantry of the Highland country . . . being indifferently accoutred, and worse armed, half naked, stunted in growth, and miserable in aspect' (ch. 44). The point Scott is making is, in the first place, a socio-historical one about poverty and backwardness, which has a significant bearing on the eventual outcome of the 1745 rising; but, in addition, what is exposed here is the misleading seductiveness of history as spectacle. The 'remarkable', 'gay and lively spectacle' seen from the privileged vantage point of the hill is largely the effect of distance, and Waverley's progress to closer engagement is one that the reader is asked to follow.

In general Waverley's relationship to the Jacobite rebellion is governed by a dialectical pattern of distance and proximity, detachment and involvement. Even when he is most deeply involved, during the campaign in England, he maintains the habits and stance of the curious tourist: 'It was Waverley's custom to ride a little apart from the main body, to look at any object of curiosity which occurred on the march' (ch. 58). That stance is both enabling and problematic; a necessary device for Scott's narration and understanding of history, it can only be maintained by the transparent manipulations of plot that are needed to ensure the hero's survival as the rebellion reaches its disastrous conclusion. But the main problem is not one of verisimilitude – from the outset the residual elements of romance plotting create the firm expectation that Waverley will survive – but the persistent problem of vision. It comes to a climax in the scene in Carlisle castle where Waverley is obliged to watch powerlessly while Fergus Mac-Ivor is taken away to be executed. Here the dialectic of detachment and involvement reaches a point of crisis. Deeply implicated by his own manifestly treasonable part in the rebellion, Waverley is yet privileged to observe, with no danger to himself, the fate of his companion. It is a moment of acute narrative awkwardness, for by what right, other than the arbitrary might of the author himself, is one man doomed and the other man saved? The disturbance is registered in the reactions of the main character himself, with a significant emphasis on his eyes:

> The last of the soldiers had now disappeared from under the vaulted archway, through which they had been filing for several minutes; the court-yard was now totally empty, but Waverley still stood there as if stupified, his eyes fixed upon the dark pass where he had so lately seen the last glimpse of his friend; – at length, a female servant of the governor, struck with surprise and compassion at the stupified misery which his countenance expressed, asked him if he would not walk into her master's house and sit down? She was obliged to repeat her question twice, ere he comprehended her, but at length it recalled him to himself, – declining the courtesy, by a hasty gesture, he pulled his hat over

his eyes, and, leaving the castle, walked as swiftly as he could through the empty streets, till he regained his inn, then threw himself into an apartment and bolted the door. (ch. 69)

Staring at the 'dark pass' of the archway he sees but at the same time cannot see. The spectator's vision has culminated in a blank non-seeing, a state of stupefaction. This moment of critical rupture in the narrative spells out the fact that history is not a spectacle to delight the eye of the observer. And, when Waverley eventually comes to himself, his guilty gesture of pulling his hat over his eyes indicates not only a desire not to be seen but also a desire not to see any more. What he is fleeing from are the implications of his own behaviour, as he has done earlier in the novel when, forced by Major Melville to see his own actions in the treasonable light that they appear to others, he takes refuge in 'a deep and heavy slumber' (ch. 31). Faced with a painful dilemma Waverley characteristically closes his eyes, and this habitual action stands in a dialectical, and critical, relationship to his role as a privileged spectator.

The conclusion of the novel is marked by a degree of deliberately sought blindness on Waverley's part. In writing to Rose he refuses to open her eyes to the horror of the events at Carlisle and, in so doing, continues to close his own, gradually familiarizing to his own mind 'the picture which he drew for her benefit' (ch. 70). Horror gives way first to melancholy and eventually to a renewed awareness of 'the prospects of peace and happiness which lay before them' (ch. 70). The metaphor of the consoling picture that makes experience bearable is then taken up literally by the painting which stands as the centrepiece of the final celebratory chapter and which presents a view of the past through, as it were, half-closed eyes:

> It was a large and spirited painting, representing Fergus Mac-Ivor and Waverley in their Highland dress, the scene a wild, rocky, and mountainous pass, down which the clan were descending in the background. It was taken from a spirited sketch, drawn while they were in Edinburgh by a young man of high genius, and had been painted on a full-length canvas by an eminent London artist. Raeburn himself, (whose Highland Chiefs do all but walk out of the canvas) could not have done more justice to the subject; and the ardent, fiery, and impetuous character of the unfortunate Chief of Glennaquoich was finely contrasted with the contemplative, fanciful, and enthusiastic expression of his happier friend. Beside this painting hung the arms which Waverley had borne in

the unfortunate civil war. The whole piece was held with admiration, and deeper feelings. (ch. 71)

This representation amounts to a re-writing of the past as a colourful and comfortable legend in which the only residue of conflict and suffering lies in the decorously muted epithet 'unfortunate'. In so far as it celebrates the friendship with Mac-Ivor, the painting can, of course, be assimilated to a positive pattern of development in Waverley's life: he is showing loyalty to his companion in arms and honouring him as a gallant leader of his clan. And that gesture is at one with Scott's general ideological aim in this novel of reconciling past and present, Jacobite and Hanoverian, Scots and English, in a justification of the Union which still manages to do justice to the values of the defeated feudal culture. Nevertheless, the painting clearly re-imagines the past to an extent that can be measured against the earlier part of the novel, and, in so doing, marks a return to the treatment of history as spectacle. Temporal distance now helps create the flattering distortion that spatial distance had created earlier, turning the historical event into an object for aesthetic contemplation, into a delight for the eye of the beholder. It is significant that the novel ends with this reminder of Waverley's questionable vision and of the danger to which any representation of history, including Scott's own, is exposed.

The painting shows history not only as aesthetic object but also, and more specifically, as commodity. Sketched in Scotland, the picture has its surplus value added in London by the eminent artist who turns it into a full-length painting. This is a matter not simply of artistic skill but also of money – the money that can hire the expertise of an artist so eminent. If the past is touched up here, the effect is achieved by the same power that restores Baron Bradwardine's house at Tully-Veolan to its former state after it has been pillaged by Cumberland's troops – the power of Waverley's capital. Money can alter the appearance of things, repair the ravages of war, help set the past at a distance, and convert it into a prized and potentially marketable aesthetic commodity. Thus the restriction of vision, the comfortable partial blindness, that Waverley seems to seek and to achieve in the closing chapters of the novel is shown to be a privilege that can be purchased.

It is characteristic of the realistic dimension of Scott's fiction that *Waverley* provides a social context for the detachment enjoyed by the central character, and does so not only at the end of the novel. From the first his role as a kind of tourist, a spectator of events, is determined by class as well as purchasing power. What distinguishes him on his arrival in Scotland is not so much money, though we are told that his purse was 'well stocked when he first went to Tully-Veolan' (ch. 61), as the prestige of his family name. It is as 'the descendant of one of the most ancient and loyal families in England' (ch. 40) that he is warmly greeted and courted by the Prince. In the terms proposed by Baillie Jarvie in *Rob Roy* (ch. 26) this kind of 'honour' – the honour that is emblazoned in the very name of Waverley's family seat – is opposed to credit, the feudal principle to the bourgeois; but, as one perceptive critic has observed, the opposed terms tend to collapse into each other.[8] Waverley's dual heritage of land-owning Tory uncle and mercantile Whig father combines the two principles, and the power of the family name is in the end indistinguishable from the power of the family purse. The freedom of movement and the protected separateness that he enjoys are thus shown to be socially determined, and his own free circulation as an English visitor to a foreign land anticipates the circulation of English capital following the end of the rebellion. In this way the novel gives a social and historical meaning to the particular perspective of the protagonist, which is, in another sense, such a convenient narrative device.

There is in all this a simultaneous adaptation and critique of the vantage point of the enlightened country gentleman, the 'equal, wide survey',[9] that informs the work of an eighteenth-century novelist like Fielding. Scott makes an issue of that perspective itself and, as we have seen, shows it to be far from synonymous with breadth of vision and generosity of understanding. The most ironic construction put on Waverley's nature, Flora's in her prophetic description of his safe and settled future at Waverley-Honour to Rose, explicitly associates membership of the landed gentry with limitation of vision:

> 'And he will refit the old library in the most exquisite Gothic taste, and garnish its shelves with the rarest and most valuable volumes; – and he will draw plans and landscapes, and write verses, and rear temples, and dig grottoes; – and he will stand in a clear summer night in the colonnade before the hall, and gaze on the deer as they stray in the moonlight, or lie shadowed by the boughs of the huge old fantastic oaks; – and he will repeat verses to his beautiful wife, who will hang upon his arm; – and he will be a happy man.' (ch. 52)

In that romantic chiaroscuro of moonlight and shadow seeing is only partly seeing. The library of Waverley's early twilit dreaming is still prominent, while its stylistic transformation hints at a further retreat from the present; and on the estate tokens of the past become mere adornments to delight the proprietorial eye. This ironic description is partial and prejudiced and cannot be taken as adequately defining Waverley's final position; yet it shares with the ending a sense that the privilege bestowed by purse and property may not always afford insight and understanding, but rather can facilitate a comfortable and convenient blindness. The painting of Waverley and Mac-Ivor would find an appropriate resting place in the Gothic library, hinting, in the 'deeper feelings' that it inspires, at all that is left unseen and unstated by the treatment of history as romantic spectacle.

The critique initiated in *Waverley* reappears in later works. In *Rob Roy* (1817), where the first-person narration excludes the possibility of overt irony at the expense of the central character, privileged spectating is once again turned back painfully on the protagonist at a moment of critical rupture in the narrative; this time by means of the nightmare that seems to prescribe an alternative, disastrous ending to Frank Osbaldistone's story. His anguished dream of 'myself and Diana in the power of MacGregor's wife, and about to be precipitated from a rock into the lake' (ch. 39) at a signal from Sir Frederick Vernon, assembles the elements of paternal hostility, Highland violence, and frustrated love that could have occasioned a fatal outcome to his adventures. The nightmare of being thrown from the rock derives from an event that he has been witness to as an unthreatened spectator, the horrific death of the exciseman Morris at the hands of Helen MacGregor and her followers, and it can be read as the trauma which that incident has left. The cost of spectating is here levied on the unconscious. It may be only a dream, but the point is forcibly made that for others the bad dream is the stuff of reality.

When Scott moves from exploring the conflicts of Scottish history to recreating the remote world of the English Middle Ages it might seem that he has succumbed to the lure of history as spectacle, but *Ivanhoe* (1819) itself continues to cast a critical light on that temptation. The scene in which Ivanhoe and Rebecca watch the attack on Torquilstone castle, where they are held captive, presents a paradigm of spectating and its role in the fictional representation of history. Ivanhoe, wounded, prostrate, unable even to crawl to the window, resembles a caricature of the passive Waverley hero, and his function as a protected spectator is delegated to Rebecca who watches the attack 'with tolerable security', 'availing herself of the protection of the large ancient shield, which she placed against the lower part of the window' (ch. 28). The two functions of romantic expectation and innocent eye that were combined in Waverley are thus separated: Ivanhoe, whose attitudes are determined by the code of chivalry to which he adheres, responds to the battle with martial excitement tempered by frustration at being unable to participate, while Rebecca, whose 'eye kindled, although the blood fled from her cheeks' looks on as one to whom all is new and strange. The description proceeds dialectically: Ivanhoe's questions, governed by his knowledge of combat and the chivalric code, prompt answers from the sharp-sighted Rebecca, so that we see the assault on Torquilstone through a double mediation:

> 'What does thou see, Rebecca?' again demanded the wounded knight.
>
> 'Nothing but the cloud of arrows flying so thick as to dazzle mine eyes, and to hide the bowmen who shoot them.'
>
> 'That cannot endure,' said Ivanhoe; 'if they press not right on to carry the castle by pure force of arms, the archery may avail but little against stone walls and bulwarks. Look for the Knight of the Fetterlock, fair Rebecca, and see how he bears himself; for as the leader is, so will his followers be.'
>
> 'I see him not,' said Rebecca.
>
> 'Foul craven!' exclaimed Ivanhoe; 'does he blench from the helm when the wind blows highest?'
>
> 'He blenches not! he blenches not!' said Rebecca, 'I see him now; he heads a body of men close under the outer barrier of the barbican.' (ch. 28)

The effect of this dialectical procedure is both to create a dramatic scene and, at the same time, to set the two mediating consciousnesses in opposition to each other so as to articulate a criticism of Ivanhoe and his values. His inability to see the battle is both literal and metaphorical. Obtusely unaware of why Rebecca is willing to court danger at the window – her unreturned love for him makes her careless of her own safety, since death would be an almost welcome release – he also fails to understand why she turns away from the battle as it reaches its violent climax:

> She turned her head from the lattice, as if unable longer to endure a sight so terrible.
>
> 'Look forth again, Rebecca,' said Ivanhoe, mistaking the cause of her retiring; 'the archery must in some degree have ceased, since they are now fighting hand to hand. – Look again, there is now less danger.' (ch. 28)

The humane sensitivity which is affronted by the sight of men slaughtering each other is beyond his comprehension. What for him is a 'brave game' and glorious exhibition of knightly prowess is for her senseless carnage and suffering; and the dialectical description of the battle culminates in a dialectical confrontation between them in a debate on chivalry. Rebecca's eloquent and pointed interrogation of Ivanhoe's values – '"What remains to you as the prize of all the blood you have spilled?"' Is glory sufficient reward '"for the sacrifice of every kindly affection, for a life spent miserably that ye may make others miserable?"' (ch. 28) – leaves him routed, only able to answer her by unworthily citing her Jewishness as the reason for her inability to understand his notions of nobility. He then, like all Scott's heroes faced with painful truths, closes his eyes in sleep. His blindness and obtuseness remain unassailable but at the same time transparent. To see warfare as a 'brave game' and glorious spectacle is a failure of vision that is shown up by the percipience and superior moral awareness of Rebecca. The privileged security of the typical Waverley hero is revealed to be a blinkered seclusion, while true insight is the prerogative of the unprivileged and vulnerable figure of the Jewess, doubly disadvantaged by her race and her gender. The chapter closes with the image of her awake to dangers internal as well as external, vulnerable both to physical suffering and the painful emotions that afflict her passionate and compassionate heart:

> She wrapped herself closely in her veil, and sat down at a distance from the couch of the wounded knight, with her back turned towards it, fortifying, or endeavouring to fortify her mind, not only against the impending evils from without, but also against those treacherous feelings which assailed her from within. (ch. 29)

The watchful, anxious, emotionally exposed woman is a truer witness of history than the secure and superior male with his convenient capacity for sleep.

Ivanhoe's limiting adherence to the questionable code of chivalry is echoed in a later and greater novel by Hugh Redgauntlet's anachronistic commitment to the feudal order. *Redgauntlet* (1824), perhaps Scott's finest and most complex work, presents the most searching critique of the treatment of history as spectacle. Returning to the Jacobite material of *Waverley* – this time the entirely fictitious plotting of a third rebellion in the 1760s, which never eventuates – Scott subjects both it and his own characteristic devices to an ironic reworking. In making *Redgauntlet* culminate in an historical non-event, Scott leaves the historical process itself out of his novel. It is merely implied rather than dramatically enacted as it was in *Waverley*. Moreover, the complex narrative structure of *Redgauntlet*, which involves epistolary as well as impersonal narration and repeatedly emphasizes the act of narration itself, points to the shaping power of the imagination in the construction of history. Historical events assume a dramatic shape in the effort of the mind to understand them, so that history is a spectacle only in the telling; while to seek to look on it as a spectator is to lay claim to a separateness that can only be illusory.

At the begining of the novel such looking is the dubious privilege of Darsie Latimer, enabled by an unearned income 'to ramble at pleasure over hill and dale, pursue every object of curiosity that presents itself, and relinquish the chase when it loses interest' (letter 1). This *flâneur*-like freedom is critically placed by one of Scott's characteristic doubling devices which contrasts it with the life of dutiful effort led by his friend and correspondent, the aspiring lawyer Alan Fairford. The juxtaposition of two kinds of existence and two ways of looking at the world seems designed to characterize Darsie's perspective as immaturely romantic in the manner of Waverley. Alan Fairford castigates Darsie's view of himself as the hero of some romantic history whose birth and connection are shrouded in a flattering mystery; describes his view of the world in terms of a 'Claude Lorraine glass which spreads its own particular hue over the whole landscape' (letter 5); and urges him to 'view things as they are, and not as they may be magnified through thy teeming fancy' (letter 5). And the course of events confirms the truth of this analysis and the cogency of this advice. Darsie is forced to change his view of things, in particular his romanticized view of 'the fruitful shores of merry England' (letter 3) from across the Solway Firth. This apparently fertile, ordered and civilized land – 'crossed and intersected by ten thousand lines of trees growing in hedge-rows, shaded with groves and woods of considerable extent, and animated by hamlets' (letter 6) – turns out to be as wild and lawless a realm as the Scottish Borders. In a typical shift of perspective Scott shows simplifying distance giving way to a puzzling experience of complexity. And it is not simply Darsie's romantic perspective that is singled out for correction in this way, since Alan, too, is obliged to undergo a similar experience. The striking parallel between the two characters' prostration and imprisonment in England suggests a rebuff to the youthful self-importance that they initially have in common despite their difference in outlook. The sense of control and centrality implied in their rather archly self-conscious correspondence, with its insistent first person singular, is exposed as an illusion as soon as they cross into England. Indeed, the narrative structure of the novel itself seems designed progressively to marginalize the initially central selves of the doubled heroes: their exchange of letters is followed by Darsie's Pamela-like journal of captivity, which yields in turn to a third-person narrative in which both characters play only a subsidiary role. If, at the beginning of the novel, *how* they see things is important, by the end it is not. Darsie at the Prince's council of war, and Darsie and Alan at the final scene of his departure are neither set apart as significant spectators nor involved as important actors in what is happening. They are simply there, absorbed into the context of events of which they are part but which they do not control, and which they witness as others witness them.

The would-be leading actor in, and stage-manager of, the historical drama, Redgauntlet himself, is, of course, ironically undermined in a similar way. It is not only his ill-conceived plans to restore the Stewarts, but his whole understanding of history that is exposed to ironic scrutiny. His peculiar fatalism involves a view of history as a drama or spectacle in which the parts have already been written by the transcendental hand of destiny: '"we play but the part allotted by Destiny, the manager of this strange drama, stand bound to act no more than is prescribed, to say no more than is set down for us; and yet we mouth about free-will, and freedom of thought and action, as if Richard must not die, or Richmond conquer, exactly where the Author has decreed it shall be so!"' (ch. 8). Destiny is a playwright, and history takes the form of a dramatic confrontation of forces, a shapely contest between heroic individuals in which one must die and the other conquer. When Redgauntlet outlines to Darsie the critical state of the nation and his proposed remedy, his ideas assume the same dramatic, indeed melodramatic, pattern:

> 'The state of this nation no more implies prosperity, than the florid colour of a feverish patient is a symptom of health. All is false and hollow . . . Many eyes, formerly cold and indifferent, are now looking towards the line of our ancient and rightful monarchs, as the only refuge in the approaching storm – the rich are alarmed – the nobles are disgusted – the populace are inflamed – and a band of patriots, whose measures are more safe in that their numbers are few, have resolved to set up King Charles's standard.' (ch. 19)

An heroic Stewart king will ride to the rescue of his people. It is the once romantic Darsie, now chastened by abduction, captivity, and humiliation into clear-sighted common sense, who puts this simplifying vision in its place:

'I look around me, and I see a settled government – an established authority – a born Briton on the throne – the very Highland mountaineers, upon whom alone the trust of the exiled family reposed, assembled into regiments, which act under the orders of the existing dynasty. France has been utterly dismayed by the tremendous lessons of the last war, and will hardly provoke another. All without and within the kingdom is adverse to encountering a hopeless struggle, and you alone, sir, seem willing to undertake a desperate enterprise.' (ch. 19)

Darsie's seeing is here equated with knowing: what he sees as he looks about him is what the novel itself proclaims to be the true state of affairs. With the bathos of its ending it refuses to turn history into the dramatic spectacle that Redgauntlet desires. Indeed, it is only in stories told by characters within the main narrative that history assumes anything like the form of a drama or spectacle: Pate-in-Peril's tale of escape from the English dragoons on Errickstone brae, for instance; or Lilias's account of how she took up the champion's gauntlet at George III's Coronation Feast. Her action, dictated by Redgauntlet, precisely expresses his view of history as the confrontation of individuals, but it remains without consequence. The offer of individual combat to the King is not taken up and it is as if the episode never occurred: '"the matter was little known,"' Lilias admits, '"and it is said that the King had commanded that it should not be further enquired into – from prudence, as I suppose, and lenity"' (ch. 18). Indeed, the story turns out to be little more than the 'idle tale' that Darsie had always considered it, and its affinities are not with the principal events of the novel but with that other legendary story, Wandering Willie's tale of Steenie Steenson's descent into hell to retrieve his rightful property by confronting the diabolical figure of his former master.

The individual confrontations that do take place in the dramatic present of the novel, Darsie's with Redgauntlet and Alan's with the Prince, are of a significantly different nature. Comparison throws light not so much on Steenie Steenson's greater integrity as on the more complex situations in which the two young men find themselves,[10] and hence on the gap between the dramatic neatness of the tale and the untidier, relatively inconsequential nature of experience in the lived history of the novel. The melodramatic rhetoric and barely contained passion with which Redgauntlet exhorts his nephew to join his planned uprising as they ride to meet the Pretender at Crackenthorp's inn continually threaten to turn verbal disagreement into violent conflict, but Darsie's politely expressed doubts and careful temporizing allow the passion to subside, and the episode never reaches its threatened dramatic climax. The novel here prefers the undulations of a continuing sense of unease to the sharp contours of outspoken, head-on collision. The encounter between Alan Fairford and the Pretender disguised as a Catholic priest takes a similar course. It is a masterly scene which renders uncomfortably real the tension between Alan's urge to treat his interlocutor as an equal and the deference that the latter's manner seems to command; and it uses it to suggest the friction between two different and incompatible cultures, the bourgeois and the feudal. That friction is subtly conveyed by the play of glances with which the interview begins:

> Fairford rose to receive him respectfully, but as he fixed his eyes on the visitor, he thought that the Father avoided his looks. His reasons for remaining incognito were cogent enough to account for this, and Fairford hastened to relieve him, by looking downwards in his turn; but when again he raised his face, he found the broad light eye of the stranger so fixed on him, that he was almost put out of countenance by the steadiness of his gaze. (ch. 16)

Alan's tactful respect for the sensibilities of the other is answered by the fixed gaze of a man accustomed to command: a respectful acknowledgement of difference between equals is confronted by an assertion of hierarchical difference in status. Alan Fairford unknowingly looks on a representative of Scotland's past whilst he himself is fixed and defined, not as the subject of a divinely ordained sovereign, but as a man who does not belong to feudal society at all. As the interview proceeds he comes to affirm his bourgeois credentials with pride: "'My father's industry has raised his family from a low and obscure situation – I have no hereditary claim to distinction of any kind'" (ch. 16). The scene, with its continuing tensions and politely circumspect definition of opposed stances, does not present a dramatic historical conflict so much as a gradual clarification of the historical changes that have taken place before the action of the novel, in the twenty years or so that have elapsed since 1745.

The ending of the novel similarly registers historical change rather than showing it acted out in a conflict between opposing forces. And, in thus avoiding the customary focus of the Waverley novels, it diminishes at the same time the importance of the observing central figure and his spectating. Alan Fairford's sensitive turning away of his eyes from the Prince is echoed at the end by General Campbell. After he has announced that the conspirators are free to leave, he turns away to the window so as not to overhear their consultation. The tactfully averted gaze suggests the reduced status of observation here. Campbell does continue to watch the faces of the Prince and his supporters as they walk to the beach, but as one who is anxious to spot any sudden change in their behaviour that may send his plans awry, rather than as one who is savouring from a safe distance the historical significance of the scene before him: 'General Campbell acompanied them with an air of apparent ease and indifference, but watching, at the same time, and no doubt with some anxiety, the changing features of those who acted in this extraordinary scene' (ch. 23). With an air of detachment that is only assumed, he is himself one of the actors in this scene rather than a spectator. Neither are Alan and Darsie set apart as privileged spectators in the Waverley mould:

> Darsie and his sister naturally followed their uncle, whose vio-
> lence they no longer feared, while his character attracted their
> respect; and Alan Fairford accompanied them from interest in
> their fate, unnoticed in a party where all were too much occupied
> with their own thoughts and feelings, as well as with the impend-
> ing crisis, to attend to his presence. (ch. 23)

Personal concern for relatives and friends is what determines the presence of these observers, and what they witness is not the grand spectacle of history in the making but a private drama of personal disappointment, leave-taking and exile. Alan Fairford, unnoticed but not disengaged, drawn by his interest in the fate of his friends, is truly the representative of the reader on this occasion – a reader who is not, like Nietzsche's strolling spectator, craving excitement, but, rather, who is intelligently absorbed in the working out of individual lives. A novel which seemed at first to promise a colourful re-enactment of the conflicts of 1745, ends by ironically mocking the expectations thus aroused. History, it suggests, also happens in less dramatic ways, and is, all about us, quietly taking its course.

Scott's subtle interrogation of his central narrative device, the un-committed onlooker, anticipates Balzac's use of observers whose gaze both imitates and questions his own. More like Benjamin's *flâneur* than Nietzsche's spectator of history, Balzac's figures confront the alluring spectacle of a commodified urban culture and provide a means of exploring the new reality of the great city. Their significance lies not only in what they see but in the alienation which is the condition of their seeing and whose implications go to the heart of Balzac's attempt at an all-encompassing vision.

4

BALZAC
The alienated gaze

Towards three o'clock on an October afternoon of 1844 an oddly dressed elderly man is walking along the Boulevard des Italiens with an expression of satisfaction on his ugly face. It is the opening of *Le Cousin Pons* (*Cousin Pons*, 1847). The idle observers lounging in the cafés are struck by the sight of this intriguing figure whose curiously outmoded dress – a nut-coloured spencer worn over a greenish coat with white metal buttons – retains traces of the fashion of as long ago as 1806. His odd appearance seems to require a special kind of attention to unlock its secrets, the analytical attention of 'les connaisseurs en flânerie',[1] 'those expert in idle observation'.[2] And it is this sort of attention that it promptly receives, and not only from the observers at the café tables. Balzac's narrator, aligning himself with those lounging connoisseurs of the life of the boulevards, proceeds to display his own analytic powers, interpreting the visual data with confident authority and claiming to recognize at first sight a well educated man in the grip of a secret vice, whose Don Quixote nose indicates the kind of devotion to great causes that can easily degenerate into gullibility. Dress and physical appearance are read as signs of the life and personality they clothe in a classic demonstration of the metonymical practice of realism by its most flamboyant exponent, whose imperial project is to reproduce the world as a coherent and intelligible system.

The curious spectacle of the old man could only be witnessed, the narrator claims with characteristic hyperbole, in Paris; and it is scenes such as these, he continues, that make of the boulevards a continuous drama. The ability to understand the details of this drama is itself a product of the life of the streets; its image is the practised eye of the *flâneur* with whom Balzac's narrator explicitly associates himself. Narration seems to be simply a matter of observation: the Parisian world reveals its meaning to the knowing and perspicacious observer.

It is observation that Balzac, in his first literary manifesto, the Preface to *La Peau de chagrin* (*The Wild Ass's Skin*, 1831), singles out as one of the two essential powers of the writer, 'that sagacious and curious genius who sees and registers everything'.[3] While he ascribes equal importance to the power of expression, it is vision which, as the argument develops, emerges as the privileged term, coming to be associated with a form of mental or magical mobility. The poet and the truly philosophical writer are endowed with 'a sort of second sight which allows them to divine the truth in all possible situations; or, better still, some power which takes them where they ought and want to be' (310). What is being elaborated here is the myth of the writer as transcendent genius, as masterful subject whose sovereign gaze commands and comprehends the totality of experience: 'Thus the writer should have analysed characters, es- poused all forms of behaviour, traversed the entire globe, experienced all the passions before writing a book' (310). Such a writer has either 'seen the world in reality, or his soul has revealed it to him intuitively' (311). It is just this kind of encompassing vision that Balzac implicitly lays claim to himself, and his grand project of representation in the *Comédie humaine* has its origin in an assumed position of mastery and subjective autonomy such as is outlined here. Yet the fiction does not collude with the myth that inspires it. Rather, it mounts a sceptical challenge. The fictional figures who most obviously embody superior powers of observation and penetrating vision – such as the antiquary in *La Peau de chagrin*, the miserly moneylender Gobseck, or the criminal Vautrin – are all subjected one way or another to a humbling irony. More interestingly, when the writer's ability to range across the globe and his familiarity with all sorts and conditions of men is translated into the localized mobility and metropolitan knowingness of the *flâneur* on the boulevards, as in the opening of *Le Cousin Pons*, the position and perspective of the observer are revealed to be distinctly problematic. Balzac's fiction, apparently predicated on the assumption of the trans- parency of phenomena to the perceptive eye, presents vision as a problem precisely at those points where it focuses closely on the figure of the observer or spectator: that is, when the kinds of observers whose analytic powers are praised in passing at the beginning of *Le Cousin Pons* are themselves made the centre of attention. The explicit or implicit claims to superior vision that Balzac makes as author or narrator are thus challenged by the texts themselves, and the implications of this challenge lead to the heart of his fiction. Paris is the context in which this can be seen most clearly and where Benjamin's ideas on the *flâneur* are most apposite and illuminating, and my argument will focus on two works which draw directly on Balzac's own early experience in Paris, *La Peau de chagrin* and *Facino Cane* (1836), and on one of his principal explorations of Parisian life, *Le Père Goriot* (*Old Goriot*, 1835), with some reference to the thematically related novels *Illusions perdues* (*Lost Illusions*, 1837–43) and *Splendeurs et misères des courtisanes* (*A Harlot High and Low*, 1838–47).

La Peau de chagrin, with its parable of the magic skin which shrinks with every wish that it grants and its figuring of society as a heartless and alluring *femme fatale*, serves as an allegorical prologue to the *Comédie humaine*, setting out the law of life in Balzac's world, the self-defeating course of sexual desire and social ambition. The central story of the skin whose gain is loss and whose power perdition calls into question the very mastery and control implied in Balzac's creative enterprise; and, in particular, the detached, superior vision celebrated in the preface is singled out for ironic scrutiny. Both Raphaël de Valentin and the antiquary from whom he receives the skin embody different kinds of detached seeing, and, although initially opposed, these two modes of vision are finally shown to be related by a detachment that is redefined not as a mark of superiority but as a sign of alienation.

The novel opens with the experience of loss – loss of money, of identity, and even the desire to live. Losing his last Napoleon on the roulette table and reduced to social nullity, 'un véritable zéro social' (14), an anonymous young man, who is not even accorded the minimal identity of his name of Raphaël until after he has taken possession of the skin, wanders the streets of Paris planning his suicide. His melancholy progress, void of interest in or desire for anything that is offered to his view, is a ghostly parody of the *flâneur's* strolling indulgence in the pleasures of the eye as he wanders past the shops examining their displays with indifference. One thing alone causes a tremor of residual desire, the sight of an attractive, manifestly wealthy young woman entering a shop to purchase lithographs. It is a vision that combines the seductions of sexuality and conspicuous consumption that are both denied to the isolated and indigent young man:

> Il contempla délicieusement cette charmante personne, dont la blanche figure était harmonieusement encadrée dans le satin d'un élégant chapeau. Il fut séduit par une taille svelte, par de jolis mouvements. La robe, légèrement relevée par le marchepied, lui laissa voir une jambe dont les fins contours étaient dessinés par un bas blanc et bien tiré. La jeune femme entra dans le magasin, y marchanda des albums, des collections de lithographies; elle en

acheta pour plusieurs pièces d'or, qui étincelèrent et sonnèrent sur le comptoir. (15)

He contemplated with delight this attractive woman, whose pale face was harmoniously framed by the satin of an elegant bonnet. He was captivated by her slender figure and pretty movements. Her dress, slightly raised as she stepped from the carriage, allowed a glimpse of a leg whose delicate lines were revealed by a well-fitting white stocking. The young woman entered the shop and bought some albums and collections of lithographs, paying for them with several gold coins which glittered and rang on the counter.

Purchasing images, she herself, with the gold coins that glitter and ring on the counter, presents a graphic image of purchasing, of the circulation of money and the system of commodity exchange in action. Cut off by poverty from participating in that system, and hence from that interest in the urban display of commodities that marks the *flâneur*, Raphaël can only look on from an undiminishable inner distance. The passionately piercing glance that he casts at the woman, as a farewell to love and femininity, is not received as a glance to be reciprocated but merely as a compliment to be pocketed. His last glance of desire thus rebuffed, Raphaël's ocular relationship to his surroundings is disturbed; his vision becomes clouded by a physical agony and he sees the buildings and people around him as though through a swirling mist. The blurring of vision implies a loss of control. The seeing subject no longer surveys the world with even the cold and melancholy detachment of the would-be suicide, but loses all sense of stability and self-containment. The opening experience of loss thus culminates in a loss, a dispersal, of the self that will only be temporarily suspended by possession of the magic skin.

It is in this state of disturbance that he enters the antiquary's shop to seek nourishment for his senses in the contemplation of 'objets d'art', as though this might restore his control and equilibrium. But, confronted with the accumulated debris of past civilizations, he is transported into an ecstatic visionary state where the universe appears to him in shapes of fire. Thus his tour of the shop takes the form of a fevered *flânerie* through the past in which he enters imaginatively into the lives of all sorts and conditions of men. Accredited by the narrator with the sensibility of a poet, he becomes himself akin to the art-objects he observes, neither quite living nor quite dead, overwhelmed by and dispersed among the debris of fifty centuries. It is from this more intensely disturbed condition, described in terms of sickness and oppression (24), that he is summoned by the commanding voice of the antiquary, a figure extravagantly defined as the apparently supernatural opposite of the young man – old but tenacious of life, desiccated but with youthful fire in his eyes, authoritative, self-contained, controlled. He is one of Balzac's men of superior vision, described in the same kind of hyperbolic terms as Gobseck and Vautrin will be later: his cold features reveal 'the lucid tranquillity of a God who sees everything, or the proud strength of a man who has seen everything'; 'la tranquillité d'un Dieu qui voit tout, ou la force orgueilleuse d'un homme qui a tout vu' (29). He is an image of the seeing subject as autonomous, masterful, authoritative, like the writer defined in the preface, but with a qualifying irony playing about him. His life, as he describes it to Raphaël,has been devoted to seeing, on the explicit assumption that seeing is the same as knowing: '"Ma seule ambition a été de voir. Voir n'est-ce pas savoir?"' (38). Avoiding all excess and all emotion, he has ranged across the whole world – '"j'ai vu le monde entier"' (37) – as a curious but passionless spectator. His unhurried, attentive, indefatigable passage has been that of a globetrotting *flâneur*, seeing everything at his leisure and without desire. And like the *flâneur* on the boulevards he is comfortably at home in the outer world, wandering through the universe as though in the garden of a house which belonged to him: '"Je me suis promené dans l'univers comme dans le jardin d'une habitation qui m'appartenait"' (38). Despite the affinity between this free-ranging, all-encompassing vision and that of the writer, the antiquary is clearly presented as a sinister and ambiguous figure whom a painter could, with two different strokes of his brush, render as either an image of the eternal Father or as the grinning mask of Mephistopheles. The terms of this comparison are more significant than the moral ambiguity, for in either case the antiquary is defined as a transcendental spectator, a stranger to all human desire and human emotion. The claimed superiority is critically placed by the gothic extravagance of the whole scene and by the old man's remoteness from the life he observes. The transcendental perspective may be instrumental in the creation of Balzac's fiction but it is itself no more than a fiction, as the antiquary's fate spells out. In the third part of the novel he succumbs to the emotions and desires he has despised, becoming erotically infatuated and turning into a grotesquely dandified doll dancing attendance on a *demi-mondaine*. The self-contained, masterful subject is exposed as a myth; yet a crucial distance remains between the observer and the world observed, figured in the absurd discrepancy between the desiccated old man and the supple beauty of the dancer he adores. It is not the distance of superior detachment but that of a fundamental estrangement which finally links the antiquary to Raphaël himself.

This conjunction of seeing and inner distance, vision and estrangement, is central to Balzac's fiction. Adorno expressed it most succinctly when he likened Balzac to a peasant coming up to town to find every door closed to him and every window shuttered, and then setting out to imagine for himself what must be going on behind them. What his novels uncover is that the alienation which caused him to write in the first place is itself the secret essence which he wanted to divine.[4] The distance that separates the spectator from the seen turns out to be the basic condition of life in Balzac's fictional world, as *La Peau de chagrin* spells out with the neatness of allegory. In tracing the career of Raphaël de Valentin from studious, celibate garret to fatal possession of the magic skin, which satisfies his every desire at the expense of his life force, the novel works variations on the theme of the alienated gaze. The narrative is punctuated by scenes of spectating that serve as points on the graph of Raphaël's decline. The nearest thing to an engrossing and fulfilling vision that he experiences is the rooftop vista of Paris from his garret, whose monotony is broken by strange and beautiful effects of light and shadow, and the occasional Baudelairean glimpse through an upper window of a young girl doing her hair(100). However, that figure in the window points to the grain of disruption in this harmonious state, for the celibate's life is riven by intense erotic fantasies, the expression of repressed desire, which make his studious existence a perpetual lie. When later he finds a real focus for his desire in the alluring but heartless *femme fatale* Fœdora, he comes no nearer to fulfilment. His relationship to her is summed up in the scene where he plays the voyeur, hidden behind the curtain in her bedroom to watch her undress. To see her beauty unveiled is to be dazzled by the physical perfection of a body which is likened to a silver statue. A prurient curiosity may be satisfied, but the human form as silver statue affords no more tangible satisfaction to the furtive lover. 'So near and yet so far' – '"Etre si près et si loin d'elle"' (162) – is his lament as he looks a little later at her sleeping form and puzzles vainly to decipher the meaning of the cry of 'Mon Dieu!' which she has mysteriously uttered before falling asleep. This laconic exclamation, which suggests an infinite range of possible meanings, none of them more definitive than the others, is an entirely ambiguous sign:

'Ce mot, insignifiant ou profond, sans substance ou plein de réalités, pouvait s'interpréter également par le bonheur ou par la souffrance, par une douleur de corps ou par des peines. Etait-ce imprécation ou prière, souvenir ou avenir, regret ou crainte? Il y avait toute une vie dans cette parole, vie d'indigence ou de richesse; il y tenait même un crime! L'énigme cachée dans ce beau semblant de femme renaissait, Fœdora pouvait être expliquée de tant de manières qu'elle devenait inexplicable.' (162–3)

'These words, insignificant or profound, without substance or full of realities, could equally well be interpreted as expressing either happiness or suffering, physical pain or mental. Was it a curse or a prayer, was it inspired by memory or anticipation, by regret or fear? There was a whole life in this exclamation, a life of poverty or of riches; or even a crime! The enigma hidden in this beautiful semblance of a woman was reborn, Fœdora could be explained in so many ways that she became inexplicable.'

The ambiguity of the linguistic sign points up the insoluble puzzle of the merely seen, and Raphaël resembles Poe's narrator in 'The Man of the Crowd', seeing infinite possibilities and sinister depths in a human figure who remains ultimately inscrutable. The voyeur's furtive contemplation, far from bringing him closer to the object of desire, has distanced him further from it, emphasizing the gap between seeing and knowing, 'voir' and 'savoir'.

Possession of the magic skin, which confers on Raphaël the ability to appropriate anything that he sets eyes on, has the ironic effect of simply confirming the distance between the subject and object of desire, since desire can only be satisfied at the expense of life. Seeing amounts not to knowing but to apprehending what may incite a fatal longing. In order to forestall such a temptation Raphaël carries a specially constructed distorting eyepiece which makes the most beautiful scenes appear hideous. The optician's art is reversed in an attempt to see less clearly, to keep the world at a distance. The third and final part of the novel describes Raphaël's increasingly desperate attempts to maintain that distance, and the inevitable infiltration of the visible and desirable world through his elaborate defences. In the end the most innocent and attractive scene can affront his alienated gaze, which, in turn, can, through his magic power, act like the distorting glass, blighting the pleasant prospect to make it conform to his inner emptiness. The lively village fête that arouses him from sleep on his final journey to Paris is instantly banished by an imprecation that he cannot stifle, so that he finds himself looking at an empty and abandoned scene. His fate is melodramatically sealed a few days later when he awakes to find the beautiful Pauline at his bedside, infinitely desirable yet at the same time infinitely remote, since to embrace her is to exhaust his shrunken stock of life. The principal chagrin that the skin creates is, indeed, the distance it sets between Raphaël and the life around him, and in that respect it symbolically and fantastically intensifies his initial predicament as an estranged spectator.

The novel, then, proposes a different and more complex answer to the antiquary's original rhetorical question about seeing being tantamount to knowing – 'Voir n'est-ce pas savoir?' – than the one that the question apparently expects. Seeing is equated, not with knowing, but with yearning and separation, desire and alienation, in such a way as to undermine the epistemological certainties implicit in Balzac's narration. Vision *in* the novel serves to question the vision of the novel.

The material implications of the symbolic skin, which transforms Raphaël into an alienated consumer tempted by the world's rich offerings that have no power to satisfy him, and which acts like a capital sum that is drawn on until exhausted, are to be worked out in the realistic social novels of the *Comédie humaine* where the material success that is so vigorously pursued consistently fails to bring fulfilment. It is that material dimension that is given greater prominence in the other work which draws directly on Balzac's early years in Paris, the short story *Facino Cane*. The narrator, like Raphaël leading a life devoted to study, finds his one distraction in observing the street life of Paris:

Une seule passion m'entraînait en dehors de mes habitudes studieuses; mais n'était-ce pas encore de l'étude? j'allais observer les mœurs du faubourg, ses habitants et leurs caractères. Aussi mal vêtu que les ouvriers, indifférent au décorum, je ne les mettais point en garde contre moi; je pouvais me mêler à leurs groupes, les voir concluant leurs marchés, et se disputant à l'heure où ils quittent le travail. Chez moi l'observation était déjà devenue intuitive, elle pénétrait l'âme sans négliger le corps; ou plutôt elle saisissait si bien les détails extérieurs, qu'elle allait sur-le-champ au-delà; elle me donnait la faculté de vivre de la vie de l'individu sur laquelle elle s'exerçait, en me permettant de me substituer à lui comme le derviche des *Mille et une Nuits* prenait le corps et l'âme des personnes sur lesquelles il prononçait certaines paroles.[5]

One passion alone drew me away from my studious habits: but wasn't that still a form of study? I walked the streets to observe the manners of the faubourg, its inhabitants and their characters. As badly dressed as the workers and indifferent to decorum, I did not put them on their guard against me; I was able to mingle with groups of them and watch them striking their bargains and arguing with each other as they were leaving work. Observation had already become intuitive with me, penetrating the soul without neglecting the body; or rather, grasping external details so well that it immediately went beyond them. It gave me the ability to live the life of the individual on whom it was focused, allowing me to substitute myself for him, like the dervish in the *Arabian Nights* who took over the body and soul of those over whom he pronounced certain words.

This is Balzac's fullest description of the narrator as *flâneur*, endowed with that intoxicating power of empathy to which Benjamin's figure abandons himself in the crowd. He follows a working-class couple, listens to their conversation about earnings and expectations, and enters imaginatively into their lives. It is generally assumed that it is Balzac himself who is talking in the person of the narrator, giving a direct insight into the imaginative gifts that made him a novelist:

Quitter ses habitudes, devenir un autre que soi par l'ivresse des facultés morales, et jouer ce jeu à volonté, telle était ma distraction. A quoi dois-je ce don? Est-ce une seconde vue? est-ce une de ces qualités dont l'abus mènerait à la folie? Je n'ai jamais re-cherché les causes de cette puissance; je la possède et m'en sers, voilà tout. (1020)

To leave my habits, to become someone other than myself by an intoxication of the moral faculties, and to play this game at will, such was my distraction. To what do I owe this gift? Is it second sight? Is it one of those qualities whose abuse will lead to madness? I have never explored the sources of this power; I possess it and make use of it, that is all.

One of Balzac's most perceptive critics, Albert Béguin, sees in this interrogation the novelist's anguished scrutiny of his own gifts of vision, his awareness of their proximity to mental derangement, which he then characteristically shrugs off in an energetic determination to make use of them.[6] However, the story itself – as opposed to the narrator – far from shrugging off this self-scrutiny, continues it in indirect fashion by bringing the narrator's penetrating gaze to bear on Facino Cane, the blind Italian clarinet-player at a working-class wedding, and setting up a dialectical relationship between them. If Balzac is interrogating his own powers of vision here, he is doing so more extensively than Béguin allows.

Initially the blind man seems to provide merely another occasion for a display of the narrator's powers of empathy and intuition. His reading of the Italian's face in melodramatically hyperbolic terms, claiming that it bore the marks of all the violent passions that make a man either a criminal or a hero, is confirmed by the man's own story of adulterous passion, murder, imprisonment, discovery of untold treasure in a vault beneath his cell, and eventual daring escape. Just as the description of the man's face, from the opening comparison with the mask of Dante to the final implied image of a volcano, involves a variety of Italian motifs, Facino Cane's tale continues the Italian theme in its operatic extravagance. But the contrast between the object of the narrator's gaze at the beginning of the story – the working people of the faubourg – and the melodramatic life at first intuited from the face and then set out in Facino Cane's narrative, is so stark that we seem to be faced with two different worlds and two different kinds of seeing, each calling into question the other. When the narrator learns that Facino Cane comes from Venice, his response, tritely maintaining that it is a beautiful city which he had always imagined visiting, expresses both received wisdom and personal ignorance: '"Venise est une belle ville, j'ai toujours eu la fantaisie d'y aller"' (p. 1024). It is then in fantasy that he does go there; as he studies the Italian's face Venice appears before him:

> Je voyais Venise et l'Adriatique, je la voyais en ruines sur cette figure ruinée. Je me promenais dans cette ville si chère à ses habitants, j'allais du Rialto au grand canal, du quai des Esclavons au Lido, je revenais à sa cathédrale, si originalement sublime . . . je contemplais ses vieux palais si riches de marbre, enfin toutes ces merveilles avec lesquelles le savant sympathise d'autant plus qu'il les colore à son gré, et ne dépoétise pas ses rêves par le spectacle de la réalité. (1025)

> I saw Venice and the Adriatic, I saw it in ruins on this ruined face. I walked through that city so dear to its inhabitants, I went from the Rialto to the Grand Canal, from the Riva degli Schiavoni to the Lido, I returned to its cathedral so original and sublime . . . I contemplated its old palaces so rich in marble, in short all those wonders which the scholar can sympathize with all the more because he colours them to his own liking and does not allow the spectacle of reality to spoil the poetry of his dreams.

This *flânerie* takes place in the mind, untouched by the spectacle of reality or the real topography of Venice, and involves not observation but dream images acquired at second hand. The obviously mediated nature of this vision casts doubt on the *flâneur* narrator's perception of the Parisian workers at the beginning of the story. The penetrative understanding of which he boasts may be, like the vision of Venice, no more than the manipulation of received ideas and conventional images. Such doubts are quickened by the connection made between his seeing and the blindness of the Italian. The latter, too, lays claim to a penetrative power, but one that is confined to intuiting the presence of gold, which he can sense so well that, despite his blindness, he always stops in front of jewellers' shops. In one sense this fixation on gold exposes as hyperbole the narrator's grandiose reading of the man's character in terms of Italian passions and despotic grandeur amid poverty: what drives him is, rather, the commonplace dream of riches that poverty customarily engenders. As Benjamin puts it, 'when it is a matter of evaluating a person's behaviour, an intimate acquaintance with [his] interests will often be much more useful than an acquaintance with his personality' (*CB*, 40). The narrator's focus on the putatively passionate personality reveals the limitation of his perception. In another sense an affinity is suggested between the narrator's perception and the blind man's unseeing fixation which further calls into question the authority of the former. At the beginning of the story he describes his power of entering into the lives and souls of other people as the dream of a man awake, 'le rêve d'un homme éveillé' (1020); at the end Facino Cane describes *his* vision of the Venetian treasure by which he is obsessed as the same whether he is waking or dreaming:

> 'Ce trésor', me dit-il, 'je le vois toujours, éveillé comme en rêve; je m'y promène, les diamants étincellent, je ne suis pas aussi aveugle que vous le croyez: l'or et les diamants éclairent ma nuit, la nuit du dernier Facino Cane, car mon titre passe aux Memmi.' (1031)

> 'This treasure,' he told me, 'I see it always, when I am awake just as when I am dreaming; I walk amongst it and the diamonds sparkle; I am not as blind as you believe. The gold and the diamonds illumine my night, the night of the last Facino Cane, for my title passes to the Memmi.'

Both narrator and character are dreamers awake, and the lurid vision of treasure is of the same order of reality as the idealistic vision of empathetic understanding.

By the end of the story the narrator has been drawn, it seems, into an ambiguous complicity with Facino Cane's material obsession. His sudden exclamation of 'We shall go to Venice' – 'Nous irons à Venise' (1031) – may be read as an attempt to humour the old man by pretending to fall in with his plans to unearth the hidden Venetian hoard, or as signalling the impecunious student's infection by the dream of wealth. But even in the former case he can be seen to have entered into a system of exchange, offering something, even if only assumed acquiescence, in return for the story that the musician has told him; and if, as Barthes has argued,[7] such an exchange is the basis of all story-telling, it is also clearly related here, through the subject of the treasure, to the larger system of exchange that governs the workings of the social world. Similarly his immediate qualification that they would set out as soon as they had some money may be taken as no more than a stalling device; but the very mention of money, and the readiness to enter, even fictitiously, into the fantasy of treasure, mark a significant change of focus in the narration. The figure who began by proclaiming his commitment to a monastic life of study has his imagination fired by a tale of treasure, and he closes his final statement in direct speech with the word money. The freedom and detachment of the *flâneur* have given way to an ambiguous involvement with extravagant material desires and with the commodity fetishism of a man obsessed with gold and diamonds. And the final reference to acquiring money suggests that the economic necessities which the narrator once observed to be the concern of a working-class couple have now come to impinge on his own existence. In a contradictory, though characteristically Balzacian way, the story moves at the same time towards complicity with the lurid inner vision and towards exposure of the material basis of social life; and in so doing it blurs the distinction between blindness and insight, and calls into question the authority and perceptiveness of a narrator whose self-proclaimed gifts of vision look so like those of Balzac himself.

When, in *Le Père Goriot*, Balzac makes more extensive use of a kind of onlooker – the ambitious student Rastignac – this character's initiation into Parisian life displays a similar movement from detachment to complicity. In the larger frame of the novel the young man on the make serves as the lens through which Balzac examines and exposes the different layers of the body social and its connecting tissue of money. Privileged by his youth, his gender, and his aristocratic name and connections, Rastignac is a singularly fortunate figure and a highly convenient narrative device. Driven by a powerful ambition for social success, he is too purposeful a figure to be a *flâneur*, but he has something of the latter's mobility and insouciance as he circulates freely between petty-bourgeois boarding-house and the salons of high society, making visible the economic, genetic and moral connections between the opposite ends of the metropolitan world. In an obvious way his initiation takes the form of a progressive extension and clarification of vision, from his first keyhole glimpse of Goriot acting mysteriously to his final encompassing view of Paris from the heights of Père Lachaise. On occasions he is cast in the role of spectator: witnessing the encounters of his cousin Madame de Beauséant first with her Portuguese lover and then with the Duchess de Langeais, he is present yet overlooked, within touching distance of the protagonists and yet as remote as if he did not exist. On others he is the disciple, benefiting from the insights of his two mentors, his aristocratic cousin and the criminally percipient Vautrin. And in all this there is a persistent emphasis on the act of seeing: his moral vision is described as lynx-like; when he realizes the effect on Monsieur de Restaud of his aristocratic connections he suddenly sees clearly into the murky atmosphere of high society; and after his first lesson at the hands of his cousin he sees the world as it really is. It would be tedious to describe each step in this visual education; suffice it to say that it raises Rastignac towards the level of insight displayed by the narrator at the beginning of the novel, so that what he sees from the cemetery – Paris stretched out along both banks of the Seine – is precisely the valley full of suffering that was evoked in the opening pages.

Rastignac's vision is in this respect unproblematically instrumental. He may not always see as clearly as he thinks he does – his moment of illumination at the Restauds' is immediately followed by the unforgivable solecism of mentioning the unmentionable Goriot – but, in general, we are not asked to doubt his perception. He functions as a lens, unflawed by irony, through which we observe the Balzacian world. It is a world composed of signs, and he is one of the means by which those signs are read. Nevertheless his seeing is not neutral, dispassionate, or unconditioned, and it is in the material implications of his privileged perceptions that irony does come into play. Like Benjamin's intellectual as *flâneur*, who thinks he is entering the market-place to observe but in fact is seeking a buyer (*CB*, 170), Rastignac is not simply looking round but actively looking *for* a source of income and a social position. Seeing is bound up with desire. Like the typical student that he is declared to be, if he begins by admiring the carriages on the Champs-Elysées he ends up by envying them. His activity is thus not simply an interpretative one, a reading of the signs, since what he sees is coloured by his social and sexual designs; and they, in turn, are inseparable from each other.

Given Rastignac's privileged status in the narrative there is never any doubt that he will get what he wants, but the inner distance that separates the seeing subject from the object of his yearning gaze in the early part of the novel is one that persists, creating an ironic subtext to his privileged progress. A dialectic of distance and proximity, detachment and involvement, characterizes the most significant scenes of seeing at both ends of the novel; the glimpse of Goriot through the keyhole and the closing panoramic survey of Paris from the cemetery. On the former occasion, returning to the boarding-house from his first venture into high society, Rastignac is induced to play the voyeur by strange sounds coming from the old man's room and catches sight of him mysteriously breaking down silver-gilt plate into ingots. The curious scene suggests a variety of possible interpretations to the onlooker, but none as strange and yet, at the same time, as near to hand as the true one. Seen through the keyhole Goriot seems to belong to an alien sphere – Rastignac immediately thinks that he is a criminal or a madman – but the truth is, of course, that the old man's destruction of his wealth is directly related to the very image that is revolving in the young man's mind after his experience that evening at a ball, the image of the rich and attractive Madame de Restaud whose attentions he has been soliciting. Seemingly a chance spectator of a scene that is remote from his own life, he is in fact deeply, if unwittingly, involved in it by the force of his desires. Those desires are made explicit when he later stumbles on the mysterious connection between Goriot and Madame de Restaud and wishes to penetrate the mystery in order to exercise sovereign power over her. What motivates him is no idle curiosity or detached spirit of inquiry, but a primitive drive for social and sexual conquest. It is this drive that makes him a singularly fitting instrument for Balzac's narrative project of clarification – a project which is fired by so strong a passion for understanding that the mystery of Goriot's connections is solved a third of the way through the novel. Mystery and mystification are only incidental to Balzac's purpose – a respect in which he differs signally from Dickens – for the point made by Le Père Goriot, and the Comédie humaine in general, is that knowledge of the social world brings no release from its binding conditions.

This is the main implication of the final scene, where Rastignac, standing alone in the cemetery after Goriot's funeral, is at last able to look down on the city both literally and figuratively, to see Parisian society for what it is and to see it whole:

Rastignac, resté seul, fit quelques pas vers le haut du cimetière et vit Paris tortueusement couché le long des deux rives de la Seine où commençaient à briller les lumières. Ses yeux s'attachèrent presque avidement entre la colonne de la place Vendôme et le dôme des Invalides, là où vivait ce beau monde dans lequel il avait voulu pénétrer. Il lança sur cette ruche bourdonnant un regard

qui semblait par avance en pomper le miel, et dit ces mots
grandioses: 'A nous deux maintenant!'

Et pour premier acte du défi qu'il portait à la Société, Rastignac
alla dîner chez madame de Nucingen.[8]

Thus left alone, Rastignac walked a few steps to the highest part of
the cemetery, and saw Paris spread out below on both banks of the
winding Seine. Lights were beginning to twinkle here and there.
His gaze fixed almost avidly upon the space that lay between the
column of the Place Vendôme and the dome of the Invalides;
there lay the splendid world that he had wished to gain. He eyed
that humming hive with a look that foretold its despoliation, as if
he already felt on his lips the sweetness of its honey, and said with
superb defiance,

'It's war between us now!'

And by way of throwing down the gauntlet to Society, Rastignac went to dine with Madame de Nucingen.[9]

The combination of detachment and involvement is as clearly discernible here as it was in the keyhole scene. Standing apart, and distanced
from Parisian society by his apparently superior insight, he is yet bound
to it by desire and ambition. The gaze that disdainfully comprehends is
also the gaze that anticipates the honeyed pleasures of the world of
fashion. So, too, the melodramatic challenge that rhetorically defines
him as the defiant opponent of society is at the same time the gesture that
reveals him to be a social creature like all the others in Balzac's world of
fiercely competing individuals. The opposition of Rastignac and the
beau monde, like all the other melodramatic opposites in the novel –
squalid Pension Vauquer and dazzling Faubourg St Germain; Goriot on
his truckle bed and his daughters in their diamonds – is taken up and
resolved in a larger encompassing unity, that of the social whole. The
challenge, in expressing a sense of difference and superiority, reveals
only blindness to his own motivations and to the common conditions of
existence. The distance that is figured in the gaze from the heights of
Père Lachaise is both the motor and the malady of social life in Balzac's
fiction; it is the distance that separates individuals from each other and
from the fulfilment of their desires. The gaze of the knowing and
ambitious provincial betrays the alienated man.

Rastignac's final action of going off to dine with Madame de
Nucingen, while opening out on to another potential narrative, achieves
a sense of closure partly by referring us back to the opening pages of the
novel and the narrator's provocative jibe at the reader; 'Après avoir lu les
secrètes infortunes du père Goriot, vous dînerez avec appetit' (6) –

'When you have read of the secret sorrows of old Goriot you will dine with unimpaired appetite' (28). Whereas *Facino Cane* turned the narrator's empathetic vision back on itself, *Le Père Goriot* interrogates the capacity for insight and empathy of the reader, who should be reminded by Rastignac's spuriously defiant gesture of the charge of callous consumerism laid at the outset. The narrator's initial emphasis on the *drama* he is about to present defines the reader as a kind of spectator, and the distance from the fictional action that this implies is then pilloried as a moral failing, as the insensitivity that allows the novel to be consumed as an armchair amusement. The reader is thus both set apart from the fictional world and at the same time identified as a creature of that world, sharing the general heartless self-interest that can only be momentarily moved to pity before the juggernaut of civilization moves on its pitiless way. The double action of the opening pages is both to point up difference and distance – it is doubtful, the narrator claims, whether the story will be understood outside Paris – and to seek to abolish it, by bringing Paris before our eyes. Likewise the aesthetic dimension of the novel is made manifest by referring to the Rue Neuve-Sainte-Geneviève as the bronze frame of the story at the same time as the narrator asserts that none of this is fiction but all is true. The most illuminating parallel with such contradictory doubleness is Brecht's theory of the 'Verfremdungseffekt', which both insists on the need for the theatre to display its own artifice and yet, as Benjamin argues, seeks to abolish the orchestra pit by stressing that the dramatic action is continuous with the historical world that the audience inhabits.[10] Rather like Brecht's theory and practice Balzac's opening in this novel can be seen as an attempt to create a properly receptive and perspicacious audience, in this case by dwelling provokingly on their likely failure to respond with insight and understanding. It is possible that these hectoring shock tactics may succeed in creating both the required responsiveness in the reader and the continuity between world and book that is characteristic of realism, but the most striking element in this self-conscious opening remains the insistence on inner distance and insensitivity, and the self-doubt that this implies. In the very act of raising the curtain on his drama Balzac betrays a self-critical awareness that the melodramatic mode he has chosen to work in may leave his reader remote and unmoved, and that the alienating conditions he is dramatizing are ones that his writing can reveal but not transcend.

Balzac's commitment to spectacle combined with his suspicion of mere spectating is related to the fundamental ambiguity of his fiction, in which explicit moral condemnation of social corruption is accompanied, and in the end outweighed, by the sheer aesthetic appeal of the drama to which such corruption gives rise. It is, notoriously, the colourful criminal Vautrin who steals the show; and both his example and his advice to Rastignac stake a claim for the superiority of acting, of doing something – however immoral – over mere spectating:

> – Mon petit, quand on ne veut pas être dupe des marionettes, il faut entrer tout à fait dans la baraque, et ne pas se contenter de regarder par les trous de la tapisserie. (97)

> 'If you don't want to be taken in by puppets, my son, you must go behind the scenes and not peep through holes in the curtain.' (107)

The argument is couched in terms of the tactics of social survival, but the castigation of the mere onlooker as furtive and uninformed has a wider significance. Rastignac's involvement in the social drama, for all the histrionic heroics and blindness to his own motives that are entailed, is not subjected to any very rigorous moral criticism, since to play an active part, however sordid, in the lurid spectacle is, on Balzac's implicit scale of values, superior to watching from the stalls or the wings. The limitations of such watching are underlined by the example of one of the most repellent figures in the novel's gallery of grotesques, Madame Vauquer, whose glassy eye is the outward sign of her impenetrable narrowmindedness. Taken, of course, entirely by surprise by Vautrin's unmasking and arrest, she revealingly and comically defines herself as an uncomprehending spectator of events:

> Et dire que toutes ces choses-là sont arrivées chez moi, dans un quartier où il ne passe pas un chat! Foi d'honnête femme, je rêve. Car, vois-tu, nous avons vu Louis XVI avoir son accident, nous avons vu tomber l'Empereur, nous l'avons vu revenir et retomber, tout cela était dans l'ordre des chose possibles; tandis qu'il n'y a point de chances contre des pensions bourgeoises: on peut se passer de roi, mais il faut toujours qu'on mange. . . (241–2)

> 'To think that all these things should happen in my house, in a district where there is never a cat stirring! Upon my word as an honest woman I must be dreamimg! For it's true we've seen Louis XVI have his accident, we've seen the Emperor fall, we've seen him come back and fall again; but that's all in the natural order of things, those are things that can easily happen, you see, whereas middle-class boarding houses are firmly settled, unchanging

things, they don't have upsets like that: you can do without a king, but you can't do without your dinner . . .' (238)

To her empty gaze history is a meaningless succession of great men that bears no relation to her own life. In the comically grotesque figure of this gaping spectator who fails to see the very connectedness that it is the project of the *Comédie humaine* to disclose, Balzac presents another image of blind indifference, of how not to respond to the spectacle he has produced.

The final scene of *Le Père Goriot* shows Rastignac abandoning the detached perspective of the spectator for a role as actor in the drama of social life. From now on in the *Comédie humaine* he is a man seen rather than seeing, performing in the spectacle of fashionable society instead of observing it. In particular he becomes an object of envy and admiration for other young men on the make, most notably Lucien de Rubempré in *Illusions perdues*. Once the reader of signs, he functions here as a sign himself in Balzac's system of social meaning. The preface to the third part of *Illusions perdues* spells it out: 'You will find in the juxtaposition of the character of Rastignac, who succeeds, and that of Lucien, who succumbs, a picture on a grand scale of a central fact of our epoch; ambition which succeeds, ambition which fails, youthful ambition, ambition at the outset of life'.[11] That contrast between the two characters informs the ironic narrative of failure that constitutes the second part of the novel 'Un grand homme de province à Paris'. When, for instance, Lucien symbolically makes the transition from spectator of Parisian life to actor by leaping from the auditorium on to the stage of Le Panorama-Dramatique at the bidding of the cynical journalist Lousteau, his move is made with an ominously insouciant disregard for the nature of the arena he is entering, menacingly figured in the darkness and squalor of the empty theatre:

> Il n'y avait plus alors dans la salle que les ouvreuses qui faisaient un singulier bruit en ôtant les petits bancs et fermant les loges. La rampe, soufflée comme une seule chandelle, répandit une odeur infecte. Le rideau se leva. Une lanterne descendit du cintre. Les pompiers commencèrent leur ronde avec les garçons de service. A la féerie de la scène, au spectacle des loges pleines de jolies femmes, aux étourdissantes lumières, à la splendide magie des décorations et des costumes neufs succédaient le froid, l'horreur, l'obscurité, le vide. Ce fut hideux.
>
> Lucien était dans une surprise indicible.

– Eh! bien, viens-tu, mon petit? dit Lousteau de dessus le
théatre.

– Saute de la loge ici.

D'un bond, Lucien se trouva sur la scène. (339)

By then the auditorium was empty save for the box-openers who
were making an inordinate chatter as they removed the small
benches and shut up the boxes. From the footlights, which had
been snuffed out like a single candle, emanated a noisome odour.
The curtain was raised. A lantern was let down from the flies. The
firemen and theatre hands started their round. The magic of the
scenery, the spectacle of pretty women filling the boxes, the
blazing lights, the resplendent enchantment of back-cloths and
new costumes gave place to coldness, desolation, darkness, emptiness. Everything looked hideous. Lucien's surprise was
indescribable.

'Well well, are you coming, my boy?' said Lousteau from the
stage. 'Jump up here from the box.'

Lucien reached the stage with one bound.[12]

This leap in the dark at another's prompting stands clearly opposed to
Rastignac's considered, if self-dramatizing, challenge from the heights
of Père Lachaise. The move from spectating to acting is, in this case,
never securely accomplished, and Lucien only succeeds in becoming
ultimately a spectacle for the disdainful amusement of others. Nevertheless, the stark and insistent contrast between Rastignac as success and
Lucien as failure barely conceals a pattern of underlying affinity that
allows us to see the narrative of failed ambition as the ironic subtext,
now brought patently to the surface, of ambition achieved. The affinity
emerges most clearly in the way that both characters are cast in the
ambiguous role of the *flâneur*. Rastignac's apparently free and sovereign
circulation through the salons of fashionable society is mimicked and
qualified by Lucien's desperate and ultimately downward spiral, while
the dark intimations of alienation and prostitution in Rastignac's *flânerie*
are made explicit in the unhappy experience of 'un grand homme de
province à Paris'.

That experience begins and ends on the boulevards, where Lucien
looks on at the spectacle of Paris from which he is excluded, at first by
poverty and obscurity, and finally by renewed poverty, grief, and failure.
The narrative of his rise and fall is framed by these views of Paris from
the perspective of the *flâneur*, albeit one who does not feel fully at home
on the streets of the capital. That perspective is both an effective
instrument of narration, making Paris visible and its system of codes and

signs transparent, and at the same time a revealing product of the urban world. The spectator's stance is not simply the mark of Lucien's exclusion; it is, more significantly, a facet of the leisured society to which he aspires to belong, so that there is only a fine line between his unhappy *flânerie* and the apparently assured perambulation of the established Parisian dandies like Rastignac and de Marsay. The difference, thrown into relief by his provincial ignorance and self-consciousness, lies in the various kinds of mastery which they exhibit:

> Plus il admirait ces jeunes gens à l'air heureux et dégagé, plus il avait conscience de son air étrange, l'air d'un homme qui ignore où aboutit le chemin qu'il suit, qui ne sait où se trouve le Palais-Royal quand il y touche, et qui demande où est le Louvre à un passant qui répond: – Vous y êtes. Lucien se voyait séparé de ce monde par un abîme, il se demandait par quel moyens il pouvait le franchir, car il voulait être semblable à cette svelte et délicate jeunesse parisienne. (178)

> The more he admired these young people with their happy, care-free air, the more conscious he grew of his uncouth appearance, that of a man who has no idea of where he is making for, wonders where the Palais-Royal is when he is standing in front of it and asks a passer-by the way to the Louvre only to be told: 'You're looking at it.' Lucien saw that a great gulf separated him from such people and was wondering how to cross it, for he wanted to be like these slim young dilettantes of Paris. (166)

His painful sense of separation sees its opposite in their nonchalant self-assurance, while his provincial ignorance is defined by his not knowing his way around in the most literal, topographical sense. They, it seems, are masters of this space, surveying and controlling it by an imperious gaze which selects Lucien as a victim:

> Un froid mortel saisit le pauvre poète quand de Marsay le lorgna; le lion parisien laissa retomber son lorgnon si singulièrement qu'il semblait à Lucien que ce fût le couteau de la guillotine. (197)

> The unhappy poet was seized with a mortal chill when he saw de Marsay staring at him through his monocle: the Parisian lion then let it fall in so singular a fashion that it seemed like the drop of the guillotine blade to Lucien. (185)

The quizzing glass is the emblem of a superior, exclusive, selective vision that can single out, scrutinize, and cut at will; an offensive weapon in the struggle for social mastery. Not only are the young men whom Lucien envies in full command of that system of signs into which he is being so painfully initiated, they seem, too, to be in full control of themselves as signifiers, projecting the particular image of elegance, wealth, and social superiority that they choose. Later, when Lucien commits the mistake of inviting his new-found socialite friends to dinner at Coralie's apartment, thereby revealing his intimate relationship with the actress, Rastignac is the first to sneer at Lucien's naive exposure of what he himself conceals. Controlling appearances, Rastignac and his like create the impression of a masterful, autonomous, self-determining subjectivity. They would appear to be the true *flâneurs*, at home on those boulevards where Lucien wanders disconsolate on his 'promenade vagabonde' (170).

Nevertheless, it is he who, in his aimless, wide-eyed wandering, brings to light the problematic nature of the *flâneur*'s relationship to his surroundings in which they, too, are implicated. In his first stroll on the boulevards he takes more notice of things than persons. To the eyes of the newcomer the distinctive feature of the Parisian scene lies in its material rather than its human characteristics; the luxury of the shops, the height of the houses, the constant juxtaposition of extreme wealth and extreme poverty. Indeed, the human is subordinated to the material, and in the face of this new environment Lucien experiences 'une immense diminution de lui-même' (170). This diminution of the self is dialectically related to an increase in the importance of objects – the gloves and canes, watches and buttons, that seize his attention as he looks enviously on the dandified young men about town. What he is confronted with is a world of commodities:

> En regardant ces jolies bagatelles que Lucien ne soupçonnait pas, le monde des superfluités nécessaires lui apparut, et il frissonna en pensant qu'il fallait un capital énorme pour exercer l'état de joli garçon. (178)

> At the sight of these fascinating trifles which were something new to Lucien, he became aware of a world in which the superfluous is indispensable, and he shuddered at the thought that he needed enormous capital if he was to play his part as a smart bachelor. (166)

The necessary superfluities inspire a fetishistic attachment to which the would-be dandy falls immediate prey. However much this is moralized as Lucien's individual weakness, his feminine susceptibility to the temptations of luxury, the novel shows him to be caught up in a whole system of socially determined desires which no one is privileged to escape. The appetite for commodities and the need for capital are insatiable; desire and envy are never laid to rest even in the most conspicuously successful social climbers. When Lucien later enjoys his brief hour of social triumph, sporting stylish canes, diamond studs, and all manner of rings and waistcoats, he becomes the object of envy for the once envied Rastignacs and de Marsays, for, we are told, men of the world are as jealous of each other as women. Lucien's susceptibility is the common currency in the society of *Illusions perdues*, 'almost infinitely permeable to the fetishism of the commodity'.[13]

Commodity fetishism is not the whole story, however, for Lucien's fate reveals a more sinister relationship between the commodity and the *flâneur*. Benjamin's observation that the *flâneur*, as 'someone abandoned in the crowd', 'shares the situation of the commodity' (*CB*, 55), is pertinent to Lucien's final appearance on the boulevards at the end of 'Un grand homme de province à Paris' as he waits for Coralie's maid Bérénice to bring him the money he needs to get home to Angoulême:

> Lucien se promena sur les boulevards, hébété de douleur, regardant les équipages, les passants, se trouvant diminué, seul, dans cette foule qui tourbillonnait fouettée par les milles intérêts parisiens . . . En flânant, il vit Bérénice endimanchée causant avec un homme, sur le boueux boulevard Bonne-Nouvelle, où elle stationnait au coin de la rue de la Lune.
>
> – Que fais-tu? dit Lucien épouvanté par les soupçons qu'il conçut à l'aspect de la Normande.
>
> – Voilà vingt francs qui peuvent coûter cher, mais vous partirez, répondit-elle en coulant quatre pièces de cent sous dans la main du poète. (538)

Lucien walked about the boulevards stupefied with grief, watching the carriages and passers-by. He felt dwarfed and isolated in this crowd swirling about him, driven along by the multifarious interests to which Parisians are inclined . . .

While he was wandering about, he saw Bérénice in her best clothes, chatting with a man in the muddy Boulevard Bonne-Nouvelle, where she had taken up her stance at the corner of the rue de la Lune.

'What are you doing?' cried Lucien, aghast at the suspicion which the sight of the Norman woman aroused in him.

'Here are twenty francs. The price may be dear, but you'll be able to go home,' she replied, slipping four five-franc coins into the poet's hand. (475–6)

The conjunction of *flânerie* and prostitution – the feminine form of *flânerie*, as it has been called[14] – is eloquent, not just of Lucien's degradation, but of the true condition of all the elegant young men of the world in Balzac's Paris. The dandified *flâneur* is not sovereign and self-determining, the impresssion of mastery is spurious. 'He goes to the market-place . . . supposedly to take a look at it, but in reality to find a buyer' (*CB*, 34). The gaze of the detached observer who takes stock of the metropolitan scene is not free and unconditioned, but implicated in the system of exchange whose rich display he admires. His circulation is inseparable from that which he observes. As Benjamin suggests and Balzac dramatizes, the fate of the *flâneur* is to become just another commodity.

Lucien's second career in Paris as the creature of Vautrin in *Splendeurs et misères des courtisanes* is a lengthy demonstration of this fate, in which the equation between *flânerie* and prostitution is further elaborated in the relationship with the courtesan Esther. Once again the narrative of Lucien's Parisian experience opens and closes with him 'en promenade', and these framing scenes are as telling as before. In the opening masked ball, which, in a typical Balzacian move, becomes a metonymic image of the social whole, Lucien is not the seeing subject but the object of the admiring gaze of others:

> En 1824, au dernier bal de l'Opéra, plusieurs masques furent frappés de la beauté d'un jeune homme qui se promenait dans les corridors et dans le foyer, avec l'allure des gens en quête d'une femme retenue au logis par des circonstances imprévues. Le secret de cette démarche, tour à tour indolente et pressée, n'est connu que des vieilles femmes et de quelques flâneurs émérites.[15]

> In 1824, at the last ball of the season at the Opera, several masks were struck by the beauty of a young man who was strolling along the corridors and through the foyer with the air of someone searching for a woman who had been delayed at home by unexpected circumstances. The secret of this gait, by turns languid and hurried, is known only to old women and some experienced *flâneurs*.

He embodies the qualities which he once envied in Rastignac and de Marsay, but the apparent detachment and cool control of the *flâneur* are no more then a mask, since the mastery involved here is, of course, Vautrin's. The perfect poise of the successful socialite has to be paid for at the highest price. If Lucien appears to have crossed the abyss which separated him from the fashionable elite at the beginning of *Illusions perdues*, it is only to be plunged into a deeper one, as his farewell letter to Vautrin finally makes clear:

> 'Vous avez voulu me faire puissant et glorieux, vous m'avez précipité dans les abîmes du suicide, voilà tout' (473).
>
> 'You wanted to make me powerful and glorious, and all you have succeeded in doing is pitching me into the abyss of suicide'.

It is as he prepares for suicide in the Conciergerie that he indulges in his last, this time imaginary, *flânerie*. Standing in his cell and wandering with his eyes alone, he sees with hallucinatory clarity the medieval palace in its original state:

> Lucien vit le Palais dans toute sa beauté primitive. La colonnade fut svelte, jeune, fraîche. La demeure de saint Louis reparut telle qu'elle fut, il en admirait les proportions babyloniennes et les fantaisies orientales. Il accepta cette vue sublime comme un poétique adieu de la création civilisée. En prenant ses mesures pour mourir, il se demandait comment cette merveille existait inconnue dans Paris. Il était deux Lucien, un Lucien poète en promenade dans le Moyen-Age, sous les arcades et sous les tourelles de saint Louis, et un Lucien apprêtant son suicide. (479)

> Lucien saw the palace in all its pristine beauty. The colonnade was slender, young, and fresh. Saint Louis's dwelling reappeared as it used to be, and he admired its Babylonian proportions and oriental extravagances. He accepted this sublime sight as a poetic farewell to civilized creation. In making his arrangements to die he wondered how this marvel could exist in Paris without anyone knowing about it. He was two Luciens; a poetic Lucien strolling through the Middle Ages, and a Lucien preparing his suicide.

The juxtaposition of past and present generates a nostalgia that is both personal and social. What Lucien admires in the colonnade – 'svelte, jeune, fraîche' – are the qualities he once admired in the gilded youth of Paris and once himself possessed. At the same time the medieval palace represents a world of art and beauty that is opposed to, and miraculously ignored by, modern Paris. Uncontaminated by the demands of commerce, it invites a purely aesthetic admiration, free from all desire to possess. There is, it seems, a nostalgia here for an ideal state of society, associated with the primitive beauty of the Middle Ages, where appearance and essence coincide and the cash nexus is unknown. This nostalgia may be Balzac's, but it stems initially from Lucien's particular perspective. It could be said of him here as it has been said of Benjamin's *flâneur* that 'his faltering gaze strives to aestheticize the city', and, in so doing, serves as a prelude to 'l'art pour l'art'.[16] If Lucien began by imitating Scott he ends by anticipating a Pre-Raphaelite or 'fin de siècle' poet; and that development implies a movement to the social margins. His elegiac vision of possibilities lost is a marginal one, achieved only on the very edge of existence and in a prison-cell that mocks the imaginative freedom involved. This is the symbolic truth of the *flâneur*'s position in Balzac's world – an apparent freedom that is synonymous with imprisonment, and an act of seeing that is inseparable from estrangement and self-estrangement. Lucien's last enjoyment of the ocular pleasures of the *flâneur* is only achieved through a splitting of the self that casts a critical light on the whole practice of such spectating. His vision beautiful is a final illustration of the alienation involved in the gaze of the *flâneur*.

Balzac's *flâneur* figures, whether knowing observers or young men on the make, all display a sense of mastery and control that proves in the end to be illusory. The next chapter explores a similar internal challenge to the kind of perspective that shapes the fiction, but a fiction which responds to urban existence in a strikingly different way.

5

BLEAK HOUSE

The *flâneur*'s perspective and the discovery
of the body

Critical couplings of Balzac and Dickens are commonplace, and invariably barren. Comparison simply quickens a sense of contrast. Balzac
aspires to a comprehensive understanding, to a vision of the whole in
which the essential and the typical are isolated and illumined by the light
of his interpreting intelligence. As Proust put it with excusable exag-
geration, Balzac's 'style does not reflect, does not suggest: it explains'.[1]
Dickens's imagination, on the other hand, moves amidst darkness and
mystery, exploring obscure corners, seizing on odd details, pursuing the
grotesque and eccentric. Its wayward energies resist integration into a
general understanding of social life even as such an understanding is
being attempted. If he possesses, in Chesterton's words, 'the key of the
street',[2] that key never entirely unlocks its secrets. A margin of mystery
remains, untouched by the interpretative impulse of the realist or the
generalizing rhetoric of moral judgement and exhortation that frames
the fiction.

The difference between the two writers can be seen in the implications of the *flânerie* to which both were disposed. When Balzac, as the
narrator of *Facino Cane*, presents himself as a *flâneur*, it is his power of
visual penetration that is stressed. When Dickens, in his letters to
Forster from Switzerland in 1846, famously insists on the importance of
street-walking for his creative life, his vision is associated with something
like hallucination. Lamenting the absence of London's streets, he makes
two contradictory claims. The first is that he needs experience of the
streets to revive his flagging imagination:

> For a week or a fortnight I can write prodigiously in a retired place
> (as at Broadstairs), and a day in London sets me up again and
> starts me. But the toil and labour of writing, day after day, without
> that magic lantern, is IMMENSE!! . . . *My* figures seem disposed
> to stagnate without crowds about them.[3]

The second claim, made a few weeks later, is that he needs streets to calm his imagination and free it from its own haunting creations:

> The absence of any accessible streets continues to worry me . . . at night I want them beyond description. I don't seem to be able to get rid of my spectres unless I can lose them in crowds.[4]

But the contradiction is resolved in the intensity of the visual experience he is describing. Whether inspiring or soothing, walking the night-time streets of London is associated not with straightforward observation but with an intense and heightened vision – a vision of spectres and magic-lantern images. If the *flâneur*'s vision embraces the dialectical opposites of, in Benjamin's terms, the familiar and the phantasmagoric, it is clear that, for Dickens in 1846, it is the latter that predominates.

It was not always so, for the earliest fruits of his *flânerie*, the *Sketches by Boz* (1836–7), are more the product of a free-ranging, sharp-eyed curiosity than of a haunted and hallucinative imagination. The narrative persona of Boz, with his taste for lounging and sauntering, combines carefully discriminating observation with speculation on the lives whose surface he only glimpses as he passes by: 'We are very fond of speculating as we walk through a street, on the character and pursuits of the people who inhabit it'.[5] This 'speculative pedestrian' (190), as he calls himself, is an uncomplicated *flâneur* who feeds his eyes and his mind on the spectacle of street life: 'What inexhaustible food for speculation do the streets of London afford!' (59). Speculation, as Hollington has suggested,[6] may here carry a residual sense of its older, obsolete meaning, defined by the *OED* as 'the faculty or power of seeing; sight, vision, *esp.* intelligent or comprehending vision'; and it is this vision, the peculiar power of seeing possessed by the strolling spectator, that is the creative source of Dickens's earliest writings. When, much later, he adopts a similar narrative persona in *The Uncommercial Traveller* (1860), it is clear that his vision has darkened and the role and perspective of the *flâneur* have become more problematic. Where Boz in 'The Streets – Night' can implicitly identify himself with 'the inquisitive novice' (58), the Uncommercial Traveller in 'Night Walks' presents himself as 'the homeless wanderer';[7] and the later documentary pieces are altogether more sombre in tone and subject, and lacking in the sharp visual clarity, the curious uncomplicated seeing, of the *Sketches by Boz*.

The difference between the earlier and later documentary writing is the same as that which separates the author of the *Sketches* from the established novelist who wrote the letters from Switzerland in 1846. A recent critic has gone so far as to see that change as exclusively for the worse: the establishment of the novelist involves 'the loss of a mode of seeing and writing which . . . could thread the complexities of an urban environment in a way that the later more strictly 'authorial' style could not'.[8] According to this argument, the power and radical energy of the *Sketches* stem from the stylistic flexibility and the mobility of point of view which Dickens achieves through his great gift for mimicry, his ability to assume a whole repertoire of identities and roles. What is lost in the creation of the homogeneous authorial vision of the mature novelist is a form of visual freedom, a 'capacity for seeing society as a massively heterogeneous and pulsatingly vital assemblage of discrete and interrelated clusters'.[9] The making of the novelist involves, it seems, surrendering the *flâneur*'s vital and mobile mode of seeing.

The argument is challenging but, although it makes a good case for the liveliness of the early writing, the implication that Dickens would have been a better writer if he had never written *Dombey* and the subsequent novels is more provocative than persuasive. The move from producing loosely connected sketches to densely plotted novels necessarily involves some loss of freedom and a tighter imaginative control, but that is not to say that the *flâneur* dimension of Dickens's creativity is ever abandoned. In the period of his mature fiction he has his Uncommercial Traveller make the pertinent observation that 'my walking is of two kinds: one, straight on end to a definite goal at a round pace; one, objectless, loitering, and purely vagabond' (95). The novelist, it could be said, incorporates that purposive movement without surrendering the vagabond other; and if, as Benjamin suggests, the *flâneur* combines the casual eye of the stroller with the purposeful gaze of the detective, then Dickens's mature novels can be seen to rely more heavily than the early writings on the latter, most obviously and literally in *Bleak House* (1852–3) where the figure of Mr Bucket plays a crucial organizing role. Dickens's vision may grow more sombre and his *flânerie* be more coloured by the mysterious and the phantasmagoric, but the *flâneur*'s mode of seeing remains a central element in his creativity. As Raymond Williams has put it, 'the decisive movement' of a Dickens novel 'is a hurrying seemingly random passing of men and women, each heard in some fixed phrase, seen in some fixed expression: a way of seeing men and women that belongs to the street'.[10] What the novels reveal is not the loss of the *flâneur*'s vision but its development, and at the same time, as I aim to show in relation to *Bleak House*, Dickens's readiness to submit that vital source of his own creativity to a searching examination.

Bleak House is the exemplary text since, in its metropolitan setting, its emphasis on observation and detection, and its double narrative structure of anonymous narrator and narrating character, it makes extensive use of the *flâneur*'s mode of seeing while at the same time exploring the implications of this kind of perspective through a number of related characters. Dickens's procedure in this respect is very different from Balzac's, which privileges the act of seeing by equating seeing with knowing, 'voir' with 'savoir', and then questions it by ironic implication. *Bleak House*, which opens famously with a brilliantly visual description of vision obscured, presents the act of seeing as troubled, limited, and problematic from the outset, and, in posing it as a problem, comes to interrogate the moral value and material conditions of the strolling spectator's perspective to which it is imaginatively indebted.

The relationship between Dickens's street-walking, his documentary writings in the *Sketches by Boz* and *The Uncommercial Traveller*, and the mode of narration he adopts in his novels has been persuasively outlined by Hollington.[11] In *Bleak House*, he suggests, the anonymous narrator can be seen as a kind of *flâneur* who possesses the key to the streets and whose freely-ranging yet penetrating gaze can make sense of the urban labyrinth which baffles and repels the innocent eye of Esther Summerson. But the point that needs to be added is that he does not simply clarify matters by exploring the fictional world of London and suggesting 'ways of reading the mystifying system of signs':[12] rather, he performs a dialectically double action of revelation and mystification. He renders the London world familiar and meaningful, and yet at the same time mysterious. If he illumines, then, like the moon that serves as the vehicle for his freely ranging movement in chapter 48 and shines down on the murder of Tulkinghorn, he illumines darkly. In this celebrated set-piece the moon acts as the agent of narration, linking the different scenes and suggesting a causal relationship between them, while bathing everything in an uncertain light. By moving from Lady Dedlock's nocturnal restlessness to the lawyer, then to the sound of the shot that disturbs the peaceful night, and finally to the prostrate body, the roaming narrator creates a web of deceptive connections by means of these moonlit juxtapositions. His function may be 'to construct causalities out of contiguities',[13] but that process cannot always be trusted as a means of access to the truth. His *flâneur*-like freedom to 'pass from the one scene to the other, as the crow flies',[14] creates both connection and confusion, meaning and mystification. Or, to put it another way, the essentially metonymical procedure that characterizes realist narration is here taken to the point where it generates 'a problematic excess of metonymy',[15] an endless proliferation of lateral connections that defies rather than promotes comprehension. The very tense of the anonymous narration suggests a process without term or direction, a senseless continuum – in contrast to Esther's comfortably end-determined narrative – and, as has often been noted, the abuses of the law and the evils of society exposed by the impersonal narrator are left untouched by the happy outcome to Esther's experience. However knowing, confident, and commanding the *voice* of the narrator may be, the *vision* that he imparts is not one of total illumination and understanding, but more like that of the 'chance people on the bridges' in the opening chapter who are shown 'peeping over the parapets into a nether sky of fog, with fog all around them, as if they were up in a balloon, and hanging in the misty clouds' (49).

That 'peeping' anticipates the diminutive act of looking that Esther characteristically attributes to herself in her part of the narrative. Her perspective is necessarily more circumscribed than that of the anonymous narrator, although her perceptions are sharp and reliable, and for the most part we are not asked to question the validity of her insights. With her 'silent way of noticing what passed before me' (63), she is a trustworthy witness and her seeing largely unproblematic. It is only with respect to herself that her vision is restricted and that her characteristic peeping comes to suggest an inability to look squarely at her own life and person. Her narrative is the story of how she overcomes this inability, or overcomes it to the extent that her position as a middle-class young woman allows. If her vision is still in some ways blinkered at the end of the novel, the blinkers are primarily those of gender.

The difference between the two narratives can, indeed, be understood in terms of gender, as the difference between a male and female voice;[16] and that distinction can be extended to their different ways of seeing the world. Curious observer of London life though she is, Esther is scarcely a *flâneur*, for the latter's roaming gaze is marked by a mobility and moral insouciance that are more typically male. Her own vision is more scrupulous and morally focused. Yet she moves amongst figures who do have something of the *flâneur* about them: her morally discerning gaze is turned upon men like Richard Carstone and Harold Skimpole whose passage through life is the leisurely stroll of the would-be gentleman, and, at the climax of the novel, it is directed by that of the strolling detective Mr Bucket. A foil to these *flâneurs* as she is to the anonymous narrator, Esther with her 'silent way of noticing' interrogates their kind of seeing and its moral implications. Dickens, unlike Balzac, both uses the *flâneur*'s vision and brings a moral perspective to bear on it.

According to Benjamin the origins of the detective novel lie in the obliteration of the individual's traces in the big-city crowd (*CB*, 43). The detective story that is Esther's life certainly has its origins in just such an obliteration: her father, gone to ground in the labyrinth of London, has erased his identity and been reduced to 'Nemo', the nobody who is anybody in the anonymity of the crowd. But another kind of obliteration has been effected, too, by the repressive, puritan upbringing that has, it seems, forced Esther into a permanent posture of self-effacement and burdened her with a diminished sense of her own worth and her legitimate claims on life. What she has to discover is not only where she comes from, but also where she is bound, what station in life she can assume and how she can fulfil herself; and the answer to the former question is no help in answering the latter. Fulfilment is harder to find than her father and mother, but the search for both has one physical common factor. Near the beginning of her narrative Esther claims with characteristically coy self-deprecation that 'my little body will soon fall into the background now' (74). Precisely the opposite is true. The detective story of Esther's experience is concerned with the discovery of the body – her mother's, of course, but in a more important sense her own. Her story involves a painful, reluctant turning of her gaze upon her own physical being and its legitimate claims.

Entering London for the first time she is confronted with a spectacle that affronts her innocent eye: 'We drove slowly through the dirtiest and darkest streets that ever were seen in the world (I thought), and in such a distracting state of confusion that I wondered how the people kept their senses . . .' (76). The nervously qualifying parenthesis betrays a figure as yet unconfident in her own generalizations, whose negative superlatives express not understanding but horrified recoil. And even when that horror has abated and her eyes have begun to respond to the rich diversity of life in the 'wonderful city' (110), admiration is not accompanied by understanding. She registers the diversity but only as a series of disconnected perceptions:

> I admired the long successions and variety of streets, the quantity
> of people already going to and fro, the number of vehicles passing
> and repassing, the busy preparations in the setting forth of shop
> windows and the sweeping out of shops, and the extraordinary
> creatures in rags, secretly groping among the swept-out rubbish
> for pins and other refuse. (97)

The connections that this novel is centrally concerned with are not here being made, the signs of street-life not being read. There is a disabling distance in Esther's observations, and it is the distance that she has to travel in the course of her story. Here she looks at the 'extraordinary creatures in rags' as at another species rather than beings of her own kind whose kinship with her will finally be revealed by the identity of the 'distressed, unsheltered, senseless creature' (868) whom she finds dressed in the rags of the poor and lying on the steps of the burial-ground at the end of the novel.

Esther's understandably limited understanding and insight in these early scenes is most tellingly in evidence when she is waiting in Kenge and Carboy's for her audience with the Chancellor:

> Everything was so strange – the stranger for its being night in the day-time, the candles burning with a white flame, and looking raw and cold – that I read the words in the newspaper without knowing what they meant, and found myself reading the same words repeatedly. As it was of no use going on in that way, I put the paper down, took a peep at my bonnet in the glass to see if it was neat, and looked at the room which was not half lighted, and at the shabby dusty tables, and at the piles of writings, and at a bookcase full of the most inexpressive-looking books that ever had anything to say for themselves. (76–7)

Experiencing a strangeness so complete that she is unable to read even the familiar linguistic signs of the newspaper, she turns for relief to what should be even more familiar, and looks at herself in the mirror. But it is significant that she peeps rather than looks, and that what she focuses on is her bonnet and not her face. Her gaze is characteristically averted from her own person. Her vision fails to connect here as it does in another sense on the streets, and her subsequent development can be read as the gradual redemption of that failure in her discovery of the body. The charge sometimes laid against Dickens that he has failed to give Esther a face and a body entirely miss the point. She has both, but only slowly and painfully does she, and hence we, come to see them.

It is, of course, disease which begins to make the connection between Esther and the creatures in rags, on the one hand, and her own body on the other. Disease strikes the high-born and slum-dweller alike, and foregrounds the body that is scarred by suffering. The scene with the looking-glass at Kenge and Carboy's is echoed after her illness on the occasion when, with solemn deliberation, she determines to look again in the mirror:

> My hair had not been cut off, though it had been in danger more than once. It was long and thick. I let it down, and shook it out, and went up to the glass upon the dressing-table. There was a little muslin curtain drawn across it. I drew it back: and stood for a

moment looking through such a veil of my own hair, that I could see nothing else. Then I put my hair aside, and looked at the reflection in the mirror, encouraged by seeing how placidly it looked at me. I was very much changed – O very, very much. At first, my face was so strange to me, that I think I should have put my hands before it and started back, but for the encouragement I have mentioned. (559)

The face is strange – stranger, one might add, for never having been examined before in the novel – and its features are left undefined. The central impression is one of distance and estrangement; her face is reified as an object external to herself, her reflection is 'the' reflection, and 'it' looks back at her like another creature. The effect of the illness is to make Esther aware of the stranger whose existence she has never fully acknowledged – her own body. Only one physical feature is given definition and texture, her hair which, 'long and thick', first obtrudes upon her vision. Her gesture of letting it down and shaking it out strikes a sensual note that is remarkably at odds with her customary demureness, and its obtrusive presence can be read as the repressed sensual dimension of her nature reasserting itself. Her body is at once estranged and reified, and yet still making its claims felt.

The same kind of tension is clearly present in the uncomfortable scene in which she reads Jarndyce's letter proposing marriage. The uncontrollable tears which it occasions are eloquent of an instinctive reluctance to accept what her genteel sense of duty and feelings of gratitude towards her guardian tell her she should accept. She is able to articulate her sense of deprivation without being able to define the reason for it, feeling 'as if something for which there was no name or distinct idea were indefinitely lost to me' (668). But what she cannot find words for is clearly identified by her actions. Standing outside herself again and looking at 'the face in the glass' (p. 568), she apostrophizes it as a separate entity; then, after instructing herself to be cheerful and suggestively kissing her housekeeping keys, she collects a book containing the pressed flowers once given to her by Woodcourt and, seeing the sleeping form of Ada as she passes the open door to her room, steals in to kiss her:

> It was weak in me, I know, and I could have no reason for crying; but I dropped a tear upon her dear face, and another, and another. Weaker than that, I took the withered flowers out, and put them for a moment to her lips. I thought about her love for Richard; though, indeed, the flowers had nothing to do with that. Then I

took them into my own room, and burned them at the candle, and they were dust in an instant. (669)

What Esther cannot see or directly say is made so abundantly clear by this elaborate pantomime that interpretation seems supererogatory. Bringing her *alter ego* Ada into association with Woodcourt and the idea of love, she is weeping over an objectified image of her own body and its lost prospects of erotic fulfilment. The nameless sense of loss is given form and meaning in the sleeping body of the young woman, while the kiss she bestows on Ada, together with the burning of the flowers, can be seen as a poignant farewell to the very possibility of love.

The basic elements of this scene – emotional disturbance, the shadowy presence of Woodcourt, and the unconscious female form – are all recapitulated at the climax of Esther's story when she makes her literal discovery of the body on the steps of the graveyard. And in the nightmare journey with Mr Bucket that leads up to that moment there are images of gazing, of faces and reflections, which both echo the earlier scenes of problematic self-scrutiny and act as a sinister premonition of what is to come:

> During the whole of this time, and during the whole search, my companion, wrapped up on the box, never relaxed in his vigilance a single moment; but, when we crossed the bridge he seemed, if possible, to be more on the alert than before. He stood up to look over the parapet; he alighted, and went back after a shadowy female figure that flitted past us; and he gazed into the profound black pit of water, with a face that made my heart die within me. The river had a fearful look, so overcast and secret, creeping away so fast between the low flat lines of shore: so heavy with indistinct and awful shapes, both of substance and shadow: so deathlike and mysterious. I have seen it many times since then, by sunlight and by moonlight, but never free from the impressions of that journey. In my memory, the lights upon the bridge are always burning dim; the cutting wind is eddying round the homeless woman whom we pass; the monotonous wheels are whirling on; and the light of the carriage-lamps reflected back, looks palely in upon me – a face, rising out of the dreaded water. (828)

Here, even more disturbingly than after her illness, Esther is coming to see her own face, to confront her own physical nature through contact with sex and death, with the shadowy female figure on the night-time street and the profound black pit of the river. When she eventually reaches the gate of the burial-ground and goes on alone to discover the body of her mother, there is, in the moment of recognition, a precise echo of her earlier gesture in relation to her own body: 'I passed on to the gate, and stooped down. I lifted the heavy head, put the long dank hair aside, and turned the face. And it was my mother, cold and dead' (869). The act of putting the hair aside which once revealed her own face, now reveals her mother's. Where own hair was 'long and thick (559) the dead woman's is 'long and dank', but the disturbing physicality is the same, hinting at a sensuality that is never openly expressed. This literal discovery of the body, significantly witnessed by the sympathetic figure of the loved and loving male, Woodcourt, can be seen as the final stage of Esther's developing awareness of her physical nature. It is the climax of the novel, both literally and metaphorically the goal of her journey. The nightmarish unreality of the search culminates in an implicit recognition of the reality not only of mortality but of the physical dimension of her own life, of the sexual love which created her, which drove the dying woman to the grave of her beloved, and which will now bring Esther and Woodcourt into each other's arms.

The importance of the scene lies, too, in the fact that Esther is forcibly pitched out of her role as onlooker, forced not only to see what her whole nature shrinks from seeing but also to touch. That bodily contact brings her own little body finally into the foreground, overcomes the distance implied in her initial experience of life and London, and graphically illustrates the interconnectedness of human lives that is the moral theme of the novel. The moral vision of *Bleak House* is, indeed, fundamentally at odds with the detached stance of the spectator. Nevertheless, in this climax we may be reminded of the problematic vision of the *flâneur*, finding one pair of Benjamin's dialectical opposites divided between Esther and Inspector Bucket. For her the city streets at night are so nightmarishly phantasmagoric 'that the stained house fronts put on human shapes and looked at me; that great water-gates seemed to be opening and closing in my head, or in the air; and that the unreal things were more substantial than the real' (867). The detective, on the other hand, maintains his 'watchful steady look' (829) and shows himself to be professionally familiar with the labyrinth of streets that Esther finds so disconcerting. This juxtaposition of the phantasmagoric and the familiar, of the emotionally engaged Esther and the coolly vigilant Bucket reproduces the duality of the novel's narrative structure at the level of character. When, at the beginning of the search for Lady Dedlock, the detective 'mounts a high tower in his mind, and looks out, far and wide' (824), he is explicitly accredited with something like the

authority and detachment of the omniscient narrator – a point supported by the earlier, ironically inflated proposition that 'time and place
cannot bind Mr. Bucket' (769). Yet his juxtaposition with Esther and
the outcome of their search for the missing woman have the effect of
questioning and undermining this authority. His perspective is, in the
end, no more privileged than hers; neither offers exclusive access to the
truth, for both are partial and imperfect, involving as much blindness as
understanding. To put it another way, London is neither the unreal city
of Esther's nightmare visions – 'I was far from sure that I was not in a
dream' (827) – nor as transparent a system of signs as Bucket's confident
vigilance presupposes. Even his knowing gaze can be deceived by
appearances, and when he finally realizes that he has been taken in by
Lady Dedlock's change of clothes, it is significant that he is shaken out
of his *flâneur*-like composure and becomes 'an excited and quite
different man' (840). Dickens's London is, it seems, more inscrutable
than Balzac's Paris, yielding its meaning less readily to the eyes of the
cool observer. But at the same time its nightmarish horrors are, as Esther
is forced to experience, not the stuff of dreams but a palpable and
painful reality.

The failed attempt to save Lady Dedlock has the effect of bringing
both Bucket and Esther down to earth, the one from the 'high tower in
his mind', the other from her genteel domesticity. However, despite his
relative failure at this climactic moment, the detective's keenness of
vision and understanding of the London labyrinth remain crucial to the
structure of the novel. 'A stoutly built, steady-looking, sharp-eyed man
in black, of about middle age' with 'nothing remarkable about him at
first sight but his ghostly manner of appearing' (361), he gives physical
form to the *flâneur*-like qualities of the anonymous narrator, moving
inconspicuously and knowingly from place to place and from the
highest social class to the lowest. In that 'he strolls about an infinity of
streets: to outward appearance rather languishing for want of an object'
(768), and yet 'has a keen eye for a crowd' (770), he is recognizably a kind
of *flâneur*, but with the important qualification that he is the *flâneur* as
professional, rather than amateur, detective. His casual strolling is
combined with an intelligence that organizes and controls; or, as
Dickens comically expresses it, 'through the placid stream of his life,
there glides an under-current of forefinger' (769). That admonishing
and authoritative forefinger indicates his central function in the novel. If
Dickens's imagination in *Bleak House* seems to be prone to a metonymic
drift, to a continuous proliferation of incident and character, then Mr
Bucket is one important means of holding that tendency in check and

bringing the disparate elements into relation with one another. His *flânerie* is strictly functional both within the fictional world of the novel and in its formal and thematic structure. He serves to make those connections between things apparently unconnected that are both a formal necessity and the central moral theme of the work. Seemingly innocent of any moral intentions himself, he none the less acts as the agent of a moral vision which stresses the interrelatedness of human lives in a society where, contrary to appearances, we are all members one of another.

Mr Bucket's striking lack of moral scruple, as evidenced by his relentless harrying of Jo the crossing-sweeper, is neither commented upon nor implicitly judged. As a character he remains an enigmatic but unexamined combination of kindliness and coldness. Character, however, is here subordinate to function, and in performimg his vital structural role of rooting out and rounding up he is left exempt from moral scrutiny. It is in the figure of Harold Skimpole that the moral implications of a *flâneur*'s existence are pursued. Skimpole flaunts his position as an idle spectator, defining his life as a self-confessed drone in terms of a leisured looking around at the world's rich spectacle, paid for by someone else:

> 'I find myself in a world in which there is so much to see, and so short a time to see it in, that I must take the liberty of looking about me, and begging to be provided for by somebody who doesn't want to look about him.' (143)

Among the many transparently false assertions of this loquacious *flâneur* is his claim to the power of empathy in relation to the objects of Mrs Jellyby's long-distance charity:

> 'I can sympathise with the objects. I can dream of them. I can lie down on the grass – in fine weather – and float along an African river, embracing all the natives I meet, as sensible of the deep silence, and sketching the dense overhanging tropical growth as accurately, as if I were there.' (120)

The artistic pretentions of this dilettante sensibility are clearly not meant to be taken seriously. The connections Skimpole makes, unlike Bucket's meaningful relations, are merely whimsical, the products of a trifling wit. He represents a petty simulacrum of the novelist's free-ranging, empathetic imagination, for nothing could be further from genuine empathy than the cold selfishness so obviously implied in his perverse banter. His flights of conversational fancy are characterized by a process of rhetorical inversion: the man presents himself as a child; the demanding guest as deserving the gratitude of his exploited host; the parasite as benefactor. The faint charm of these conceits wears steadily thinner to the morally discerning eyes of Esther, until finally the self-admiring rhetoric is revealed to be an exact and damning inversion of the truth in the one sentence of Skimpole's autobiography that she ever reads: "'Jarndyce, in common with most other men I have known, is the Incarnation of Selfishness"' (887). The accusation rebounds neatly on the accuser.

The moral case against Skimpole and his perspective is clearly made and needs no labouring. However, he is not simply an eccentric individual with a twisted moral sensibility, for his *flânerie* has a wider social and economic dimension. His marginal, bohemian existence, largely funded by Jarndyce, could be said to imply the general predicament of a precariously poised intelligentsia, forced to live off its wits by entertaining the wealthy in return for financial support. Benjamin's generalization in 'Paris – the capital of the nineteenth century' is pertinent, although couched in an idiom at odds with the comic mode in which Skimpole is presented:

> As *flâneurs*, the intelligentsia came into the market-place. As they thought, to observe it – but in reality it was already to find a buyer. In this intermediary stage, in which they still had Maecenases, but were already beginning to familiarize themselves with the market, they took the form of the *bohème*. (*CB*, 170–1)

Skimpole's looking about him is never disinterested but always involves an eye for the main chance and for a source of future income. His association with Richard Carstone is clearly inspired by the belief that the young man is going to inherit a fortune, while, as Mr Bucket's bribe reveals, he will betray anything and anyone for a five pound note. His vaunted innocence of money, which is regularly belied by the fact that, as Bucket observes, "'He takes it though!"' (831), can be seen as a rhetorical attempt to deny economic reality by an elaborate conceit and thus to veil his abject dependence. The aesthetic distance from the material conditions of life that he assumes is merely a pose that the novel is at pains to put into perspective.

One way that it does so is by juxtaposing Skimpole with his apparent opposite, Jo the crossing-sweeper, who is literally mired in those conditions that the bohemian dilettante affects to hover freely above. If Skimpole might like to be seen as a version of Benjamin's *flâneur*, 'whose way of living still bestowed a conciliatory gleam over the growing destitution of men in the great city' (*CB*, 170), he is shown up for what he really is by being squarely confronted with, and related to, one instance of such destitution. Significantly, it is in relation to Jo that his venality is brought most damningly to light by Bucket's bribe, and, when Jarndyce consults him about what to do with the sick boy, his airily callous advice is to turn him out on to the street. This uncharacteristically blunt decisiveness betrays a typically petty-bourgeois anxiety in the face of the poverty that always threatens his own precarious existence. Jo's destitution is too close to be comfortably countenanced, and in wanting to dismiss it from his sight he is once again seeking to deny the economic reality of his own position. Jo, who has neither the language nor the leisure to read the signs of the streets, is the opposite of the *flâneur*:

> It must be a strange state to be like Jo! To shuffle through the streets, unfamiliar with the shapes and in utter darkness as to the meaning, of those mysterious symbols, so abundant over the shops, and the corner of streets, and on the doors, and in the windows! (274)

He shuffles rather than strolls with sovereign detachment, and he is constantly 'hustled, and jostled, and moved on' (274), not the seeing subject but the uncomprehending object of other men's actions. Nevertheless, linked to Skimpole by the web of the plot, he gives physical form to the material dependence that the *flâneur*'s pose tries vainly to conceal.

Skimpole is altogether more the product of social conditions than he could ever admit, and he takes his place amongst a group of figures in Dickens's later novels who share the characteristics of a social type and suggest the symptoms of a social malaise. His dilettante existence bears some resemblance to that of the cynical James Harthouse in *Hard Times* (1854) and Henry Gowan in *Little Dorrit* (1855–7); and when he contrasts himself with Mrs Jellyby, whom he characterizes in terms of 'a strong will and immense power of business detail' (120), and insists upon his own lack of will, he anticipates Sydney Carton and his relationship to the bullying careerist Stryver in *A Tale of Two Cities* (1859). In that novel Dickens is more concerned to understand, rather than castigate, an apparently wasted life, and shows how Carton's aimlessly drifting existence has to be seen as a reaction to a society dominated by men like Stryver and his aggressive pursuit of personal success. Carton's inability to find any worthwhile goal in life passes an implicit judgement on prevailing circumstances and values, and the same is true of the disenchantment displayed by the bored and languid young men in *Our Mutual Friend* (1864–5), Eugene Wrayburn and Mortimer Lightwood, who abominate energy on the grounds that there is nothing worth being energetic about. The listless demeanour of these figures is only a pale echo of the 'objectless, loitering, and purely vagabond' (*The Uncommercial Traveller*, 95) movement associated with Dickens's *flâneur* narrators. The lounging and sauntering that were so positively construed in *Sketches by Boz* as a means to insight and understanding are reinterpreted in these later novels as symptoms of social decadence.

These further implications of the marginal existence are touched on in *Bleak House* in the fate of Richard Carstone, who declines into a lethargy of mind and body and listlessly haunts the Court of Chancery waiting for the inheritance that never comes. Carstone's loitering is the opposite of observant and his obsession creates a blindness that is evident in his unfounded suspicions of John Jarndyce. When the Chancery suit finally lapses, Jarndyce's consoling words to him speak appropriately of a restoration of vision: '"My dear Rick," said he, "the clouds have cleared away, and it is bright now. We can see now"' (926). The ending of the novel does not, of course, fully endorse this sanguine prospect. Richard Carstone dies, Tom-all-Alone's festers on unredeemed, Chesney Wold sinks into a dull repose; and when Esther brings her narrative to its happy conclusion there is, indeed, a stress on seeing, but it is not the unambiguously clear seeing to which Jarndyce refers. The last paragraphs of the novel once again pose vision as a problem.

Sitting on the porch in the moonlight, associated in this work with deceptive illumination, Esther admits to her husband that she has been thinking about her old looks; and this prompts the affectionate response from Woodcourt that she is prettier now than she has ever been. In this exchange the question of how Esther sees herself is raised once more:

'My dear Dame Durden,' said Allan, drawing my arm through his, 'Do you ever look in the glass?'

'You know I do; you see me do it.'

'And don't you know that you are prettier than you ever were?'

I did not know that; I am not certain that I know it now. But I know that my dearest little pets are very pretty, and that my darling is very beautiful, and that my husband is very handsome, and that my Guardian has the brightest and most benevolent face that ever was seen; and that they can very well do without much beauty in me – even supposing –. (935)

The key terms here are seeing and knowing, and both are problematic. Esther herself equates seeing with knowing: he must know because he has seen her. But Woodcourt's question in reply challenges that simple certainty by suggesting that she may not know despite the fact that she sees; that she may not realize the true nature of the face that she is looking at; indeed, that she may not really see it at all. The scene thus has to be read in relation to the earlier episodes with the looking-glass, and in that context the final paragraph appears to be not so much a characteristically coy expression of modesty, as a retreat from the painful self-scrutiny that she had achieved after her illness. Like her immediately preceding effusion of uxorial pride and love – 'The people even praise Me as the doctor's wife . . . I owe it all to him, my love, my pride!' (935) – it shows her once again averting her gaze from her own person to the loved ones around her.

The point being made here is a moral one, and this final emphasis is as typical of Dickens as the sentimental manner in which he makes it. It is far better not to see oneself clearly out of love for others than to see nothing but oneself after the fashion of Skimpole. There is a note in the 'Memorandum Book' from a slightly later period which wittily illustrates Dickens's preoccupation with the self-obsessed vision and its moral obstructiveness:

> The man whose vista is always stopped up by the image of Himself. Looks down a long walk, and can't see round himself, or over himself, or beyond himself. Is always blocking up his own way. Would be such a good thing for him, if he could knock himself down.[17]

Esther's averted gaze is the exact opposite, and it has a moral clarity that partly redeems the note of feminine self-effacement which remains so problematic, and which makes the conclusion so much narrower in insight and imagination than the rest of the novel.

The final insistence on a morally correct vision certainly marks a retreat from the morally disturbing one presented earlier in the novel, whose necessary instrument was the mobile *flâneur* perspective shared by the anonymous narrator and Mr Bucket. The latter's accompaniment of Esther on her nightmare journey to the steps of the burial-ground dramatically illustrates the complementary nature of these two modes of seeing in the overall achievement of *Bleak House*; and, in so far as Bucket conducts the operation, it shows, too, the dangerous exploratory power of his perspective, which opens on to a dark and lawless wilderness at the heart of civilization. Although in this novel the ultimate aim of the exploration is a demonstration of connectedness, the *flâneur* aspect of Dickens's imagination, in its very delight in diversity, always treads the perilous edge of more disturbing mysteries. The *flâneur*'s gaze can make connections, but it can also reveal a world of severed parts, alien and impenetrable, which the perceiving mind can neither understand nor bring together. The sombre first-person meditation which breaks into the narrative of *A Tale of Two Cities*, and arrests its momentum, eloquently expresses such a vision:

> A wonderful fact to reflect upon, that every human creature is constituted to be that profound secret and mystery to every other. A solemn consideration, when I enter a great city by night, that every one of those darkly clustered houses encloses its own secret; that every room in every one of them encloses its own secret; that every beating heart in the hundreds and thousands of breasts there, is, in some of its imaginings, a secret to the heart nearest it! Something of the awfulness, even of Death itself, is referable to this. No more can I turn the leaves of this dear book that I loved, and vainly hope in time to read it all. No more can I look into the depths of this unfathomable water, wherein, as momentary lights glanced into it, I have had glimpses of buried treasure and other things submerged. It was appointed that the book should shut with a spring, for ever and for ever, when I had read but a page. It was appointed that the water should be locked in an eternal frost, when the light was playing on its surface, and I stood in ignorance on the shore. My friend is dead, my neighbour is dead, my love, the darling of my soul, is dead; it is the inexorable consolidation and perpetuation of the secret that was always in that individuality, and which I shall carry in mine to my life's end. In any of the burial-places of this city through which I pass, is there a sleeper more inscrutable than its busy inhabitants are, in their innermost personality, to me, or than I am to them?[18]

The contrast with Balzac's *flâneur* narrator in *Facino Cane* could not be more striking: Dickens's persona, walking the nocturnal streets of the city, does not boast of his powers of visual penetration and empathy but dwells on the death-like mystery of individuality. For him seeing is knowing only in the negative sense of knowing what he can never know. The sense of mystery and the brooding melancholy mark one pole of Dickens's imagination, to which the later works notoriously gravitate. Nevertheless, the same *flâneur*'s perspective can, as we have seen, serve an inclusive vision which pursues the realist's goal of comprehensiveness, ranging across a crowded fictional world which is characterized by colourful life rather than death-like inscrutability. In the case of Dickens the gaze of the *flâneur* embraces the mysterious and the transparent, the comic and the sinister, connectedness and fragmentation. The extraordinary range and mobility of his imagination is figured in the *flânerie* to which he was inclined, and which he exploits and explores in his fiction. It is not the least of his qualities that, in this passage of brooding reflection, he can call into question the certainties implicit in so much of his writing, and in realism in general, by prescribing the limits of what can be seen and known by any observer of the human scene.

6

L'EDUCATION SENTIMENTALE
The blank gaze and the weakened personality

When Mr Bucket in *Bleak House* 'mounts a high tower in his mind, and looks out, far and wide' (824), he adopts a perspective associated with the anonymous narrator which implies that the truth about Lady Dedlock's disappearance can be ascertained, even if, as it turns out, he is unable to perceive it clearly and quickly enough to save her. The superior perspective is practical in its aims and limited in its achievement, exposed as it is to a humbling irony. When Flaubert has recourse to the same metaphor of the tower, the implications are very different. In his notebooks and correspondence it is invariably a means of expressing the insignificance of human affairs:

> Climb a tower so high that sounds are no longer heard and men appear small; if from there you see a man kill another man you will scarcely be upset, certainly less upset than if the blood were spurting on you. Imagine a higher tower and a greater indifference – a giant looking down on antlike creatures, a grain of sand at the base of a pyramid, and imagine the tiny creatures slaughtering one another and the grain of dust rising: what can any of that matter to the giant and to the pyramid? Now you can compare nature, God, in short, infinite intelligence, to that man a hundred feet high, to that pyramid a hundred thousand. Think, in these terms, of the insignificance of our crimes and our virtues, of our splendours and our miseries.[1]

This is a youthful remark but it cannot be dismissed as the posturing cynicism of adolescence, since a similar attitude is frequently struck in later years. The well-known letter written while working on *L'Education sentimentale* and expressing his unhappy sense of labouring at something worthless concludes with the same kind of desolate metaphysical vision:

The monks labour in vain, the sun is not on their side; for nothing is eternal, not even the sun when it comes down to it. And we, poor little grains of dust, feeble vibrations in the immense movement, lost atoms! . . . . What a metaphysic![2]

The only consolation to be derived from looking down on life from this pitiless height is the calmness of spirit that may come from detachment, as he seeks to persuade Louise Colet on another occasion:

Take life from higher up, mount a tower . . . then you will see nothing but the blue ether all around you. When it is not blue, it will be misty; what does it matter if everything disappears, drowned in a calm vapour. (*Corr.*, 2, 326)

Mounting a high tower in the mind is associated in Flaubert with the metaphysical perspective of a universal indifference, an all-embracing irony which questions the possibility of knowing anything for certain. Everything, including the notion of truth and Flaubert's own negative certainties, disappears into that 'calm vapour'. As he succinctly puts it in a late letter, 'Il n'y a pas de Vrai! Il n'y a que des manières de voir' – 'There is no Truth! There are only ways of seeing' (*Corr.*, 8, 370).

Flaubert is, indeed, more radical than any earlier nineteenth-century novelist in posing vision as a problem. Proust referred aptly to the 'revolution of vision' he had effected and likened him in this respect to Kant.[3] This new way of seeing and representing the world notoriously challenges conventional novelistic practice and even seems to strike at the very possibility of meaningful discourse. There is an early example at the beginning of the 1845 version of *L'Education sentimentale* (*Sentimental Education*) when a particular way of seeing is the focus of the narrative. The young protagonist Henry, newly arrived in Paris, wanders the city as a *flâneur*. His aimless movements are described at length and include climbing the towers of churches to obtain a view of Paris from on high:

Il montait sur les tours des églises et restait longtemps appuyé sur les balustrades de pierre qui les couronnent, contemplant les toits des maisons, la fumée des cheminées, et, en bas, les hommes tout petits qui rampent comme des mouches sur le pavé.[4]

He climbed the towers of churches and stood leaning for a long time on the stone balustrades at the top, looking at the roofs of the houses, the smoke from the chimneys, and, down below, the tiny figures of people crawling like flies on the pavement.

Once again, looking down on men from a great height renders them insignificant; but what is also brought into question by Flaubert's deadpan narration is the significance of such a view itself. What is the point of this description of pointless wandering and inconsequential contemplation? As Henry moves around the city he is repeatedly shown to be engaged in reading or interpreting; perusing the titles of books for sale on the quays of the Seine, or sitting in an omnibus and comparing and contrasting the people who get on and off. Yet this reading of the signs and inscriptions of the city streets is an empty activity, yielding no insight or understanding, and its pointlessness is summed up by the occasion when he enters a café and spends a whole hour reading the same line of a newspaper: 'Il entrait dans un café et restait une heure entière à lire la même ligne d'un journal' (54). This description of an act of reading that makes no headway and gets nowhere reflects critically and subversively on the reading of the passage itself. We see Henry seeing Paris, but the significance of such seeing remains uncertain. In a way that anticipates Frédéric Moreau in the definitive *L'Education sentimentale*, this *flâneur* does not make sense of the city life which he observes; and although this may be the point of the passage, it nevertheless infects it with the taint of pointlessness itself. As Jonathan Culler has put it in another context, 'it is clear that everything can be interpreted but not what is the significance of such interpretations'.[5]

The problem of pointlessness is posed most comprehensively by *L'Education sentimentale* of 1869, and not only in the ineffectual character and empty existence of its central figure Frédéric Moreau. Flaubert effects his 'revolution of vision' by installing at the centre of his novel that version of the *flâneur*'s way of seeing the world which was adumbrated in Henry's arrival in Paris. The difficulty of making sense which *L'Education sentimentale* raises is inscribed within it in the blank gaze of Frédéric. The contrast with Balzac is striking and instructive. Where Balzac equates seeing with knowing and then proceeds to question that equation by ironic implication, Flaubert severs any connection between seeing and knowing from the outset. To follow Frédéric drifting around the streets of Paris and failing to make sense of what he sees is to read a novel of failure quite unlike Balzac's *Illusions perdues*: not a novel whose meaning is failure, but a novel which fails to have that kind of Balzacian meaning. Flaubert uses his *flâneur* to undermine the conventional way of seeing embodied in the novel form; in short, to deconstruct realism.

Nevertheless deconstruction is not the whole story, and simply to demonstrate Flaubert's subversion of realist practice would be to cover ground already well ploughed by Culler and others. The nature of Flaubert's ironic discourse is such that it can be taken as conventionally 'lisible' as well as subversively deconstructive,[6] and my reading of *L'Education sentimentale* seeks to do justice to this contradictory doubleness. I want to take seriously the claim he makes in a letter that he was trying to 'depict a psychological state – an authentic one in my opinion – which has not yet been described' (*Corr., Supp.*, 2, 65). A recent study has explored in detail the psychological dimension of the novel and the unconscious forces at work in the figure of Frédéric,[7] but my focus will not be on the central character as a complex individual psyche but on his relation to the world about him as typifying a characteristically modern sensibility. Frédéric's psychological state can be understood in terms of the weakened personality that Nietzsche, writing in the same period, saw as typical of modern man – marked by a disjunction between the inner life and the outer, and reduced to the rôle of a strolling spectator in relation to historical events.[8] It is in the problematic vision of that spectator that the realistic and deconstructive dimensions of the novel come together: his stance is socially and historically determined and yet at the same time insidiously incompatible with the socially sanctioned conventions of novelistic meaning. Far from reproducing and reinforcing standardized ways of seeing, his vision questions them by its blankness. Frédéric the *flâneur* is both a creature of his times and the instrument of their ironic exposure.

On his first appearance he is standing in a pose so deliberately romantic that he seems to be set up as the object of some mild mockery:

> Un jeune homme de dix-huit ans, à longs cheveux et qui tenait un album sous son bras, restait auprès du gouvernail, immobile. A travers le brouillard, il contemplait des clochers, des édifices dont il ne savait pas les noms; puis il embrassa, dans un dernier coup d'oeil, l'île Saint Louis, la Cité, Notre-Dame; et bientôt, Paris disparaissant, il poussa un grand soupir.[9]

> A long-haired man of eighteen, holding a sketchbook under his arm, stood motionless beside the tiller. He gazed through the mist at spires and buildings whose names he did not know, and took a last look at the Ile Saint-Louis, the Cité, and Notre-Dame; and soon, as Paris was lost to view, he heaved a deep sigh.[10]

The long hair, the sketchbook, and the final sigh signal a romantic sensibility and aspirations unfulfilled in present circumstances. Leaving aside the nuances of Flaubert's irony and the problem of knowing whether its target is the character or the mode of fiction invoked by describing him in these well-worn terms, it is significant that Frédéric is seen seeing the city that is to be the principal arena of his aimless existence. In a typically disorienting move a first view is presented as a last, and the novel begins by leaving behind what is to be its main setting. Both the setting and the seeing are indicative of what is to come. Frédéric's gaze has the blankness it is never entirely to lose; his vision is imprecise – 'through the mist' – and uninformed, ignorant of the names of what he sees. It is not the familiar gaze of the true *flâneur* but rather the languishing gaze of one who aspires to such familiarity. That aspiration might seem to be Balzacian, but the analogy collapses as soon as it is suggested. Frédéric's final glance, 'embracing' the centre of the city rather in the manner of Rastignac and positing Paris as the object of his yearning, is immediately followed by a sigh which expresses the absence of precisely the self-assertive energy that defines Balzac's young men on the make. This is not going to be a Balzacian drama of ambition and sexual conquest. What the opening scene establishes is, rather, a connection between a melancholy longing and a view of Paris which is to be amplified in the story of Frédéric's love for Mme Arnoux. Later that connection will be spelt out:

> Paris se rapportait à sa personne, et la grande ville avec toutes ses voix, bruissait, comme un immense orchestre, autour d'elle. (68)
>
> Paris depended on her person, and the great city, with all its voices, thundered like an immense orchestra about her. (78)

His love for her is so bound up with Paris that it has the character of a distinctly urban phenomenon: it takes its sinuous course through the different quarters of the city and its crises are lived out on the streets. In its hesitant, meandering course it is itself a form of *flânerie*, and it is appropriate that Proust resorts to a metaphor drawn from the streets when he defines the pages in which it is inscribed as 'ce grand *Trottoir roulant*', 'that great moving pavement'.[11]

His first, fateful encounter with Mme Arnoux, for all its romantic trappings of dramatic love at first sight – 'Ce fut comme une apparition' (4); 'It was like a vision' (18) – is an experience which, in its entirely visual and wordless nature, can be related to the mobility and impersonality of contemporary urban existence. It resembles the experience of arresting eye-contact and fleeting beauty celebrated in Baudelaire's poem about a chance encounter on the street, 'A une passante' ('To a passing woman').[12] In both the emphasis falls on the effect of the woman's eyes upon the man's: Baudelaire drinks sweetness and deadly pleasure from the eyes of his passer-by, while Frédéric experiences the dazzlement that comes from Mme Arnoux's, 'l'éblouissement que lui envoyèrent ses yeux' (4). As the sociologist Georg Simmel, cited by Benjamin, observes, '"interpersonal relationships in big cities are distinguished by a marked preponderance of the activity of the eye over the activity of the ear"'. The reason Simmel advances is the development of public means of transport: '"Before the development of buses, railroads, and trams in the nineteenth century, people had never been in the position of having to look at one another for long minutes or even hours without speaking to one another"' (*CB*, 38). The means of transport in Frédéric's case is a boat and the city is being left behind for the country, but the experience remains distinctly urban. It is later re-enacted on the street when a chance meeting on the corner of the Rue Vivienne revives Frédéric's infatuation at a time when he appears to have overcome it. Once again the encounter is visual rather than verbal, without initially any exchange of words. It is another epiphany, another vision which stresses bright light and the power of her eyes: 'Le soleil l'entourait . . . Une suavité infinie s'épanchait de ses yeux' (261); 'The sunshine surrounded her . . . An infinite sweetness flowed from her lovely eyes' (259). If there is a phantasmagoric dimension to Frédéric's experience of city life, it is the private phantasmagoria constituted by Mme Arnoux.

On both these occasions he is overwhelmed by what he sees, not in control of his gaze; and this vision of external beauty stimulates an inner vision, a romantic train of daydreaming that is similarly beyond his control and without limits. His first sight of her prompts a series of questions about her life and a curiosity that knows no bounds. After he has left the boat he sees the journey again in his mind's eye with increased clarity, and then 'his eyelids half closed, his gaze directed at the clouds, he gave himself up to an infinite dreamy joy' (22). 'Infinite', which receives the final emphasis in the French – 'une joie rêveuse et infinie' (9) – is the crucial term, indicating the uncontrolled expansiveness of the romantic imagination. It may be in the nature of all reverie to know no bounds, but it has a particular significance in the context of Frédéric's drifting existence. The problem it raises can be defined in Nietzschean terms as one of horizons in relation to an individual's capacity for action. In the same essay on History in which he defines the weakened personality of modern man, Nietzsche proposes a general law: 'a living thing can be healthy, strong, and fruitful only when bounded by a horizon.'[13] The psychological state which Flaubert explores in Frédéric is one in which horizons are unbounded and unstable, shifting with the whims of the character's mobile imagination, and defining themselves in terms of different women and mutually exclusive, implausible ambitions – great painter, great poet, minister of state. A creature of moods, impulses, sudden enthusiasms and enervations, with no centre or strength of his own, he bears out Nietzsche's dictum, showing that 'because the lines of his horizon are always restlessly changing . . . he can no longer extricate himself . . . for a simple act of will and desire'.[14] Moreover, it is indicative of the deconstructive momentum of *L'Education sentimentale* that this absence of stable horizons ultimately throws into question the very notion of character itself. To talk about Frédéric at all is to be uncomfortably aware that the name does not spell out a clearly defined identity but signifies merely an empty indefiniteness.

Flaubert himself, in the 1850s, had diagnosed what he saw to be a specifically modern malaise in a way that anticipates both Nietzsche's insight and the problem of Frédéric. The term he uses is 'diffusion':

> That is the general weakness of the century: diffusion. Little streams that have overflowed their banks give themselves the airs of oceans. For that they just lack one thing: dimension. (*Corr.*, 3, 144)

Frédéric, with his grandiose ambitions and shallow incapacity for effective action, is just such a little stream. On another occasion diffusion is related to the intellectual atmosphere of the times in a way that also has a bearing on *L'Education sentimentale*:

> In what an epoch of diffusion we live! In former times the mind was a solitary sun; all around it there was the empty sky. Now, as on a winter's evening, its disc seems to have grown pale and it illumines all the human mist with its confused clarity. (*Corr.*, 3, 102)

This condition of hazy indistinction recalls the problem Flaubert experienced while writing the novel of keeping his characters from disappearing into the crowded and teeming ambience, the 'human mist', of the contemporary scene. But the diffuse illumination of which he writes also corresponds to the peculiar lighting of *L'Education sentimentale* itself, whose 'confused clarity' confounds the conventional sense-making activity of reading. This is nowhere more apparent than in the descriptions of Frédéric on the streets of Paris which play a prominent part in his first period of residence in the city, and in which his spectator's view of things is taken up in a larger, more perplexing vision which raises fundamental questions of meaning and connection.

These scenes of *flânerie*, whose emotional colouring ranges widely from despair to euphoria, are focalized through Frédéric, although they cannot be unequivocally attributed to his point of view. It is typical of Flaubert's teasing indirection that the question of 'who sees?' is left unanswerable, with the result that 'the very principle of point of view becomes meaningless'.[15] Sometimes it is made clear that Frédéric does not see anything at all, as when he is strolling arm in arm with Deslauriers or when, after hearing Mme Arnoux singing, he wanders through the night carried away by his emotions and no longer aware of his surroundings. It is tempting to argue that inwardness is always predominant in these scenes and that they can be understood as renderings of his changing emotional state. When he is happy, Paris is beautiful and pink clouds float like scarves above the rooftops: when he is melancholy there are dark clouds scudding acrosss the face of the moon, darkness, damp, and fog. But any attempt to establish the connection between character and scene in terms of the pathetic fallacy runs foul of the fact that the most prominent feature of these scenes is the profound disconnection of the character from everything around him. The earliest of them, which has been the subject of a masterly analysis by Peter Brooks,[16] is Frédéric's experience on the Champs-Elysées where, confronted by a parade of luxurious carriages bearing wealthy women, he feels completely alien:

> Les voitures devenaient plus nombreuses, et, se ralentissant à partir du Rond-Point, elles occupaient toute la voie. Les crinières étaient près des crinières, les lanternes près des lanternes; les étriers d'acier, les gourmettes d'argent, les boucles de cuivre jetaient çà et là des points lumineux entre les culottes courtes, les gants blancs et les fourrures qui retombaient sur le blason des portières. Il se sentait comme perdu dans un monde lointain. (24)

> More and more carriages appeared, slowing down beyond the Rond-Point so that they filled the entire roadway. Mane brushed against mane, lamp against lamp; steel stirrups, silver curb-chains, and brass buckles threw out points of light here and there among the knee breeches, the white gloves, and the furs hanging over the crests on the carriage doors. He felt as if he were lost in a remote world. (35)

The intertextual analogy is with Lucien de Rubempré newly arrived in Paris in *Illusions perdues*; but where the abyss which Lucien sees between himself and the fashionable world generates ambition, desire, and action, Frédéric remains inert in his sense of otherness and isolation. As Brooks has shown, there is an absence of desire and human agency in the whole scene which remains a 'world of surfaces contemplated for themselves'.[17] However, it is not only desire but knowledge and insight that are absent as well. Frédéric is not, like Lucien, an instrument of narration through which Parisian life is made intelligible as well as visible. His gaze does not penetrate or understand:

> Ses yeux erraient sur les têtes feminines; et de vagues ressemblances amenaient à sa mémoire Mme Arnoux. (24)

> His eyes wandered over the women's faces and vague resemblances reminded him of Mme Arnoux. (35)

And if there seems to be some painterly principle of composition at work here, the scene is not organized from Frédéric's perspective; he is merely one of the points in Flaubert's verbal *pointillisme*. 'Confused clarity' is an appropriate term for the effect of this proliferation of detail; there are points of light but there is no clear overall illumination or perspective. As the passage continues the scene breaks up, with the sun setting, the carriages scattering in the Place de la Concorde, and the horizon shifting to the sky above the Tuileries and the waters of the Seine. All this transcends Frédéric's perspective, but the unstable horizons of the scene are a visual rendering of his general condition; and as life is shown taking its course before his overwhelmed and uncomprehending eyes, what is made plain is his utter estrangement.

The alienation evinced in Frédéric's aimless sorties through the streets of Paris is more profound than that of Balzac's young men, for whom it is a spur to action as well as the underlying condition of all social life. Flaubert's *flâneur* scarcely resembles Benjamin's sharp-eyed observer at home in the urban world either. For Frédéric the city streets are not, and never become, familiar; on the contrary, they can take on a strangeness that can best be described as surreal:

> Quelquefois, l'espoir d'une distraction l'attirait vers les boulevards. Après de sombres ruelles exhalant des fraîcheurs humides, il arrivait sur de grandes places désertes, éblouissantes de lumière, et où les monuments dessinaient au bord du pavé des dentelures d'ombre noire. (65)

> Sometimes, in search of amusement, he was drawn towards the boulevards. From the cool, damp air of dark alleys he emerged on to empty squares, full of dazzling light, where statues cast jagged black shadows on to the edge of the pavement. (75)

Nor is he at home in the crowd, which, far from being the veil that obscures the true horrors of the great city, is itself a source of horror and repulsion:

> Mais les charrettes, les boutiques recommençaient, et la foule l'étourdissait, – le dimanche surtout, – quand, depuis la Bastille jusqu'à la Madeleine, c'était un immense flot ondulant sur l'asphalte, au milieu de la poussière, dans une rumeur continue; il se sentait tout écœuré par la bassesse des figures, la niaiserie des propos, la satisfaction imbécile transpirant sur les fronts en sueur! Cependant, la conscience de mieux valoir que ces hommes atténuait la fatigue de les regarder. (65–6)

> But soon he came upon more handcarts and shops; and the crowds made him dizzy, especially on Sundays, when, from the Bastille to the Madeleine, there was a vast torrent of humanity surging over the asphalt, in the midst of clouds of dust and a continuous din. He felt utterly nauseated by the vulgarity of their faces, the stupidity of their talk, and the imbecile satisfaction glistening on their sweating brows. However, the knowledge that he was worth more than these men lessened the fatigue of looking at them. (75)

Far from 'botanising on the asphalt' with the intelligent curiosity and empathy of Benjamin's *flâneur*, he is here harried into an aesthetic recoil which may be as much his creator's as his own, and which points forward to the demise of both the *flâneur*'s precarious existence and the mode of fiction with which he is associated. Frédéric's contempt for the crowd anticipates Roquentin's contempt for the bourgeois in Sartre's *La Nausée*, while the breakdown of a comprehensible world into dazzling emptiness or suffocating crowdedness foreshadows the nightmare strangeness of Kafka's fiction.

The one element that is distinctly unlike Kafka is the note of self-regard struck in the final sentence. This dubious point of solace and stability is one to which Frédéric is shown to return from his wanderings on more than one occasion. Walking the streets after leaving the Arnoux household one night, he stops on the Pont-Neuf and, in a sudden access of euphoria, conceives an ambition to be a great painter. This ironic discovery of an instant vocation proceeds to an ironic conclusion. He goes home and stands in front of the mirror:

> Son visage s'offrait à lui dans la glace. Il se trouva beau; – et resta une minute à se regarder. (50)

His own face presented itself to him in the mirror. He liked the look of it, and remained there for a minute gazing at himself. (61)

Narcissistic admiration is the reverse side of the estranged world, and it prescribes, for once quite clearly, the limits of Frédéric's vision. He has seen neither his surroundings nor his future, only an idealized image of himself, with which alone he is ever truly at home.

The inner realm of wish-fulfilling fantasy is not, of course, auto-nomous. Not only is it inhabited by commonplace romantic notions – Mme Arnoux looks to him like the women in romantic novels – it is also colonized by consumer daydreams dictated by the world of luxury that seemed so remote on the Champs-Elysées. The demise of the *flâneur* is intimated in the way in which, for all his spectatorial detachment, Frédéric comes to participate whole-heartedly in the commerce of contemporary life with his consumer plans and projects. At first he can do no more than mentally adorn Mme Arnoux with articles seen in shop-windows on his strolls, draping her in lace and cashmere and imagining jewels sparkling in her dark hair. Returning to Paris after the interlude in Nogent, flushed with the inheritance from his uncle, he is able to indulge in more grandiose daydreams and is described as resembling an architect designing a palace, planning his life in advance and filling it with riches and delicacies. The boundless space of reverie is piled high with consumer goods, and he is soon shown actually acquiring them as he buys and furnishes one apartment, and later rents and decorates another as a love-nest. The simile of the architect comes close to being taken literally when the prospect of even more money through marriage to the newly widowed Mme Dambreuse is imme-diately translated into plans for architectural improvements to the Dambreuse mansion. He decides which room to take as a study, considers creating a picture gallery on the second floor by knocking down three walls, and contemplates installing a Turkish bath. In all this the novel traces the transformation of a romantically minded *flâneur* into a bourgeois consumer.

Like his Balzacian counterparts Frédéric is ready to marry for money to increase his purchasing power, but, by making him a *rentier* with a comfortable unearned income, Flaubert takes the sharp edge of ambi-tion off these marriage prospects and dispels the potential for Balzacian drama. Moreover, he suggests the affinity between character and com-modity in more oblique ways than Balzac's melodramatic association of *flânerie* with prostitution. Frédéric does not venture into the market-place 'supposedly to take a look at it, but in reality to find a buyer' (*CB*, 34), but rather to pursue the consumer dreams that are inseparable from his dreams of Mme Arnoux. From his first encounter with her his infatuation takes a fetishistic form, with his longing to know all the furniture in her room and all the dresses she had ever worn. This shades progressively into a fetishism of the commodity. His first thoughts on receiving news of his inheritance are of the presents he will be able to buy her, and the luxurious interior in which he will be able to receive her, with its red leather and yellow silk, divans and cabinets, Chinese vases and carpets: 'et quelles étagères! quels vases de Chine! quels tapis!' (98). Interior design becomes the private poetry of his devotions, and nowhere more strikingly than in his preparation of the apartment in the Rue Tronchet:

> Puis il alla dans trois magasins acheter la parfumerie la plus rare; il se procura un morceau de fausse guipure pour remplacer l'affreux couvre-pieds de coton rouge, il choisit une paire de pantoufles en satin bleu; la crainte seule de paraître grossier le modéra dans ses emplettes; il revint avec elles; – et plus dévotement que ceux qui font des reposoirs, il changea les meubles de place, drapa lui-même les rideaux, mit des bruyères sur la cheminée, des violettes sur la commode; il aurait voulu paver la chambre tout en or. (277)

> Then he went to three shops to buy the rarest of scents; he bought a piece of imitation lace to replace the the horrible red cotton counterpane; and he chose a pair of blue satin slippers. Only the fear of seeming vulgar put a limit to his purchases. He brought them back, and more reverently than somebody decking out an altar of repose, he moved the furniture about, hung the curtains himself, and put heather on the mantelpiece and violets on the chest of drawers. He would have liked to pave the whole room with gold. (275)

Objects are endowed with an aura of sanctity by being associated with her and are animated with the desire that she both arouses and frustrates. There is an unmistakable suggestion of the kind of compensatory mechanism at work here that Benjamin sees in the nineteenth-century bourgeois cultivation of the domestic interior: 'Since the days of Louis-Philippe the bourgeoisie has endeavoured to compensate itself for the inconsequential nature of private life in the big city. It seeks such compensation within its four walls' (*CB*, 46). Frédéric's private life is doubly inconsequential, in the unconsummated nature of his relationship with Mme Arnoux and the general aimlessness of his *rentier* existence. The interest and emotion that the public world of Paris so signally fails to arouse in him, as in the scene on the Champs-Elysées, are

91

invested within his four walls in his actual or imaginary interior decoration. What is seen on the streets is nothing to what is seen not only in the mind's eye – for Frédéric is more than merely a romantic daydreamer – but in the private, self-created environment of the bourgeois interior.

Benjamin, with one of his characteristic metonymic shifts, associates a Second Empire taste for encasing household objects in velvet and plush covers with the function of the interior as a form of casing for the individual (*CB*, 46). Flaubert intimates as much with Frédéric, whose furniture and furnishings seem to constitute a protective shell for an enfeebled personality. A life left shapeless by passivity and unsustained by any developed relationship derives its contours from the objects which surround it. The revealing instance is the traumatic auction of the Arnoux's household effects. This, the climax and conclusion of Frédéric's obsession with interiors, suggests the extent to which his life is constituted by them. As he watches the components of Mme Arnoux's domestic world being knocked down one by one to the highest bidder, he not only experiences a sense of desecration but also feels as though he himself is disintegrating:

> Ainsi disparurent, les uns après les autres, le grand tapis bleu semé de camélias que ses pieds mignons frôlaient en venant vers lui, la petite bergère de tapisserie où il s'asseyait toujours en face d'elle quand ils étaient seuls; les deux écrans de la cheminée, dont l'ivoire était rendu plus doux par le contact de ses mains; une pelote de velours encore hérissée d'épingles. C'était comme des parties de son cœur qui s'en allaient avec ces choses: et la monotonie des mêmes voix, des mêmes gestes l'engourdissait de fatigue, lui causait une torpeur funèbre, une dissolution. (413–14)

> In this way there vanished, one after another, the big blue carpet with its pattern of camellias which her dainty feet used to touch lightly as they came towards him; the little tapestry easy-chair in which he always used to sit facing her when they were alone; the two fire-screens, whose ivory had been made smoother by the touch of her hands; and a velvet pincushion, still bristling with pins. He felt as if a part of his heart were disappearing with each article; and the monotonous effect of the same voices accompanied by the same gestures numbed him with fatigue, afflicting him with a deathly torpor, a sense of disintegration. (407)

It is not just the casing of Mme Arnoux's life that is being dismantled here, but his own, too.

The elegiac cadences, the emotional dissolution and fatigue, the 'torpeur funèbre', present this as the funeral of a love which seems more substantial to his melancholy memory than it ever did at the time. But the 'body' is only present by association with the objects to which it is metonymically related, and this displacement is more than simply another illustration of Frédéric's characteristic diffidence with respect to the physical attractions of Mme Arnoux. The scene implies an affinity between a reified vision of human relationships and a mode of representation. Flaubert's use of free indirect discourse renders ambiguous the associations made between the woman and the pieces of furniture: are they a sentimental indulgence on the part of Frédéric, or do they carry some unironic authority? In either case they demonstrate a way of seeing the world and of reading significance into it that is typical of the realist novel, and related here to a sense of terminal fatigue. The metonymical practice of realism, which presents the inner life in terms of the outer, intangible emotions in terms of concrete objects, appears to be at the end of its tether, the 'same voices' and the 'same gestures' creating a sense of numbing monotony. At this traumatic climax to Frédéric's emotional life Flaubert begins to dissolve not only the integrity of the central character but also the very mode in which he and his world have been presented. If Frédéric is bidding farewell to his past here and laying it to rest, it may not be too far-fetched to say that so, too, is the realist novel.

The disintegration of Frédéric's life and hopes in part 3 is accompanied by the political disintegration involved in the rise and fall of the Second Republic. But however many links and parallels the ingenious commentator may find between the private and the public spheres, they cannot disguise the fact of Frédéric's fundamental disconnection from the events he witnesses. He remains a distant onlooker whose life is characterized by that gulf between inner and outer that Nietzsche saw to be the typical condition of modern man. The outbreak of the revolution in February 1848 coincides with one of those crises in Frédéric's relationship to Mme Arnoux which he lives out on the street, but the coincidence of political and emotional disturbance in the same arena simply spells out the distance between them. Her failure to keep their rendezvous in the rue Tronchet leaves him anxiously pacing the pavements, not casting the *flâneur*'s cool and curious eye at his surroundings, but staring desperately at the street furniture, the cracks between the paving stones, and the numbers on the houses. They look back with pitiless indifference, and their role as the 'ironic spectators' (277) of his misery dramatizes the gap between his inner needs and the observed world. The same point is then illustrated by the reverse procedure as he himself is transformed into an ironic spectator of the revolutionary events. Furious at Mme Arnoux's rejection of him and liberated from his love, he goes out into the street, picks up Rosanette, and strolls home after dinner with her through the crowds, reacting to the sound of gunfire with a pitiless calm that demonstrates his utter detachment.

In these early days of the revolution he is precisely Nietzsche's strolling spectator, taking pleasure in the spectacle of history before his eyes; and Flaubert makes explicit the theatrical aspect of the experience:

> Frédéric, pris entre deux masses, ne bougeait pas, fasciné d'ailleurs et s'amusant extrêmement. Les blessés qui tombaient, les morts étendus, n'avaient pas l'air de vrai blessés, de vrai morts. Il lui semblait assister à un spectacle. (288)

> Frédéric, caught between two masses, did not budge; in any case, he was fascinated and enjoying himself tremendously. The wounded falling to the ground, and the dead lying stretched out, did not look as if they were really wounded or dead. (286)

Where Scott was implicitly critical of such spectating, Flaubert unsurprisingly makes no attempt to evaluate it. The detachment of the character is matched by that of the narrator and the aesthetic vision is unbroken. It may be momentarily disturbed, as when Frédéric treads on something soft which turns out to be the hand of a sergeant lying face down in the gutter, but the potential shock effect of such moments is dissipated in the deadpan narration of so many other random details of the revolutionary scene. To see what could be made of the experience and perspective of the detached spectator of history by a different kind of literary sensibility, one might turn not only to Scott but to another work which focuses on the revolutionary violence of 1848, Clough's epistolary novel in verse *Amours de Voyage* (1858). There the dilemma of privileged non-involvement is explored in the liberal conscience of Clough's English protagonist Claude, who, as a tourist in Rome, witnesses the siege of the city and the fall of Mazzini's Roman Republic to the French and Neapolitan armies. With guidebook in hand he watches the fighting, analyses his feelings, reflects on his relative safety as an Englishman, and agonizes about how he should act. By contrast, the detachment which Flaubert portrays in Frédéric, and in which his own narration is implicated, raises a suspicion of that 'complete insensibility to barbarism' which Nietzsche saw to be a feature of the weakened personality of modern man.[18]

Although contemporary history is viewed aesthetically by Frédéric as a spectacle, it loses any semblance of an aesthetic outline as the revolution develops. As he strolls the boulevards as a *flâneur*, witnesses the sack of the Tuileries, attends debating clubs, or engages in political discussion with M. Dambreuse, events seem less and less intelligible, and he is assailed by a proliferation of bizarre images, discordant ideas, and conflicting points of view. Unlike Scott's protagonists he is not used to mediate between these extremes in the service of an overall vision which makes sense of opposition and conflict. Rather, he is completely at the mercy of this moral and ideological bedlam, and ultimately overwhelmed. The only possible reaction, for author as well as character perhaps, is flight; and Frédéric runs off to Fontainebleau with Rosanette just as the violence of the June days is beginning. This sudden switch to an interlude of tranquil tourism may bring emotional respite, but thematically it reinforces the experience of revolution, making explicit the essentially tourist-like relationship to events that Frédéric has displayed in Paris.

The Fontainebleau episode focuses on history as well as tourism, but in setting the events of 1848 in the larger context of the French past, and even the geological past, it questions the very idea of historical understanding. History brings no enlightenment and the historical sense emerges as another facet of Frédéric's weakened personality. In widening his characters' historical horizons Flaubert anticipates Nietzsche's point that one can have too much of history, that 'there is a degree . . . of the historical sense which is harmful and ultimately fatal to the living thing'.[19] When Frédéric tells Rosanette that the rocks in the forest had been there since the beginning of the world and would stay there until the end, her reaction to this infinite vista – turning her head away, saying it would drive her mad, and going off to pick heather – registers the destruction of meaning that it involves. History can overwhelm Frédéric, too. Earlier in the novel the account given of his education has hinted at the kind of overdeveloped historical sensibility that Nietzsche ascribes to modern man: he reads books of memoirs, is haunted by the images they conjure up in his mind, and conceives an ambition to be the Walter Scott of France. The sense of imaginative promiscuity and typical 'diffusion' suggested there surface again at Fontainebleau, when he thinks of all the great people who had walked within the walls of the château and feels the dead so surrounding and jostling him that he feels dazed. From being jostled on the streets of Paris he has come to repeat the experience in the halls of history. Whatever quiet relief from revolutionary turmoil the interlude offers, it is hollowed out by a similar inner emptiness. Like the revolution it shows how a proliferation of new sights and an extension of horizons issue in a nihilistic sense of meaninglessness.

Frédéric's dazed condition is the common one. In a rare summing up, Flaubert concludes his account of the June days by emphasizing their stupefying effect on the public mind, which was disturbed as if by some natural disaster, so that intelligent people remained idiots for the rest of their lives: 'Des gens d'esprit en restèrent idiots pour toute leur vie' (338). The final chapter of the political upheaval which began in 1848, Louis Napoleon's coup d'état of 1851, presents a dramatic enactment of this descent into idiocy. Frédéric, having witnessed the beginning of the revolution as a *flâneur*, is once again out on the streets and, as one of a silent and terrified crowd, is watching cavalry charges on the boulevard when he sees Dussardier, recognizable by his tall stature, confronting the police:

> Un des agents qui marchait en tête, le tricorne sur les yeux, le menaça de son épée.
> L'autre, alors, s'avançant d'un pas, se mit à crier:
> – 'Vive la République!'
> Il tomba sur le dos, les bras en croix.
> Un hurlement d'horreur s'éleva de la foule. L'agent fit un cercle autour de lui avec son regard; et Frédéric, béant, reconnut Sénécal.

> One of the policemen, who was marching in front of his squad, with his three-cornered hat pulled down over his eyes, threatened him with his sword.
> Then Dussardier took a step forward and started shouting:
> 'Long live the Republic!'
> He fell on his back with his arms spread out.
> A cry of horror arose from the crowd. The policeman looked all around him, and Frédéric, open-mouthed, recognized Sénécal.

Faced with the horror of repression and treachery by the turncoat Sénécal, Frédéric stands in a posture of gaping stupefaction. The *flâneur* has been reduced to a mere *badaud*.

The famous paragraphs which follow, describing with laconic melancholy a life of foreign travel and unfulfilling social experience, imply that Frédéric's state of stupefaction persists. He travels, but there is no suggestion that what he sees and experiences is a source of knowledge or insight. He simply continues his earlier, peculiarly blank *flânerie* on a larger stage; and once again a widening of horizons merely numbs the mind. Flaubert emphasizes the stupefying, dizzying effect of so many landscapes and ruins – 'l'étourdissement des paysages et des ruines' (419). As at Fontainebleau, where proliferating images of French history had the same effect – 'une telle confusion d'images l'étourdissait' (323) – the spectacle of nature and the past creates a sense of the meaninglessness of things.

It is only with the reappearance of Mme Arnoux that Frédéric is shown drawing an horizon around his life and conferring on it a kind of meaning. The delicate combination of sentiment and irony in this final love scene is related to the pattern of repetition which informs it. They repeat their behaviour of old and go out together into the streets to walk together, neither noticing nor hearing the crowds and the noise through which they pass. And their final parting re-enacts the chaste separations of the past. Such repetition is finely suspended between irony and pathos, between an eternal recurrence of the same and a touching loyalty to established patterns of behaviour. Similarly, when they repeat the past to each other by telling stories of their shared experiences – 'ils se racontèrent leurs anciens jours' (421) – nostalgia balances on the edge of platitude. Mme Arnoux has recourse to a literary language that verges on romantic cliché, while Frédéric invokes the most conventional literary model of unfulfilled romantic love, that of Goethe's Werther for the domestic but unattainable Lotte:

> Elle s'étonnait de sa mémoire. Cependant, elle lui dit:
> – 'Quelquefois, vos paroles me reviennent comme un écho lointain, comme le son d'une cloche apporté par le vent; et il me semble que vous êtes là, quand je lis des passages d'amour dans les livres.'
> – 'Tout ce qu'on y blâme d'exagéré, vous me l'avez fait ressentir,' dit Frédéric. 'Je comprends les Werther que ne dégoûtent pas les tartines de Charlotte.' (421)

> She marvelled at his memory. But then she said:
> 'Sometimes your words come back to me like a distant echo, like the sound of a bell carried by the wind; and when I read about love in books, I feel that you are there beside me.'
> 'You have made me feel all the things in books which people criticize as exaggerated,' said Frédéric. 'I can understand Werther not being put off by Charlotte's bread and butter.'

Their memories of each other are bound up with the experience of reading, and they are to each other like characters in books. When Mme Arnoux first enters the room and looks avidly at Frédéric's furniture and possessions to imprint them on her memory, she resembles the reader of a realist novel, seeking to grasp a character through the metonymical mediation of his surroundings. There is an unmistakable air of 'Bovarysme' about all this, but Flaubert is less unambiguously mocking than in the earlier novel, for irony is softened by a sense of a necessary and understandable compensation for the failures and unfulfilment of the past.

The final repetition of the past in the novel, Frédéric's and Deslauriers' prolix recounting to each other of the tale of their abortive adolescent visit to a local brothel, is more straightforwardly ironic. The implications of this retrospective narration have been fully explored by Peter Brooks,[20] but narration is not the only important element in this conclusion. The scene is a last illustration of the gulf between inner and outer as Frédéric's eyes turn inward and backward, and the gaze which remained blankly uncomprehending when focused on the external world finds in a remembered incident a value that it did not have at the time. He is, indeed, as much a reader and consumer of the past as its narrator, and Flaubert shows how a failed attempt at illicit consumption can become a narrative delicacy to be consumed with pleasure and appreciated as the better part of life: '"C'est là que nous avons eu de meilleur!"' (427). Characteristically the novel ends by reflecting critically on its own processes as well as the weakened personality of its protagonist. Frédéric's action in factitiously conferring value and meaning on failure casts an ironic light on the writing of fiction, especially this one, and the appetite it serves. At the same time the conclusion confirms his peculiar ineffectuality. If one of the things which keeps us reading this life of aimless *flânerie* is the possibility that it might eventually take a decisive direction, the closing pages simply show it continuing on another level. In an anticipation of the inward turn of modernism, and with a subversive irony that may more readily be termed postmodern, Flaubert shows the *flâneur* who was unmoved by the spectacle of social life ending as the avid reader of his own, a strolling spectator along the paths of a memory which fails to persuade us of its plenitude.

Flaubert's ironic subversion of realist practice has no direct parallel in English fiction of the nineteenth century, but in the next chapter we shall see how George Eliot uses the figure of a privileged, and initially aimless, male spectator to widen the scope of her fiction to the point where it, too, begins to transcend the realist mode.

1 Velázquez, *Las Meninas*: the observer in the doorway catches the eye at the vanishing point of the painting.

2, 3 These two illustrations of the *flâneur* from *Les Français peints par eux-mêmes* suggest Benjamin's two kinds of observer, the sharp-eyed amateur detective and the gaping *badaud*.

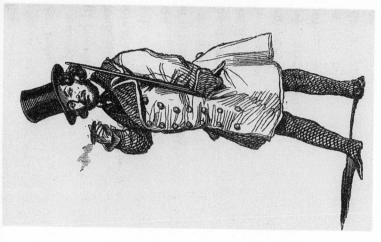

4, 5 Balzac, in stout profile, promenading with his cane, looks like a
caricature of the dandified *flâneur* illustrated in *Physiologie du flaneur* (1841).

7

VISION AND FRAME IN
MIDDLEMARCH AND *DANIEL*
DERONDA

In chapter 15 of *Middlemarch* (1871–2) George Eliot as narrator begins
by drawing a famous contrast between her own closely focused practice
and Fielding's copious digressions 'over that tempting range of relevancies called the universe',[1] and she ends by ranging as far as Paris to tell
the story of Lydgate's infatuation with an actress in his days as a medical
student. That story of romantic love, for a woman who turns out to have
murdered her husband in the course of a play, involves the kind of
sexual passion and melodramatic violence that is more commonly
associated with the French novel of the nineteenth century than the
English, and which is otherwise notably absent from Eliot's novel of life
in an English provincial town. Metropolitan life is only a lurid memory
on the margins of *Middlemarch*. Eliot, one might say, contrasts herself
explicitly with Fielding at one end of this chapter, and implicitly with a
writer like the Balzac of *Le Père Goriot* and *Illusions perdues* at the other.
These two different forms of fiction provide a frame for her own, and for
her own distinctive vision, since vision is the central issue in this chapter.

In giving an account of Lydgate's early life and education Eliot
defines a scientific way of looking at things which is in the first place his,
but clearly applies as much to the narrator. His use of the microscope
and 'longing to demonstrate the more intimate relations of living
structure' (178) correspond to her determination to concentrate all the
light that she can command on 'unravelling certain human lots and
seeing how they were woven and interwoven' (170). The 'equal wide
survey' of the eighteenth-century English country gentleman has been
replaced by a more searching, analytical, and concentrated vision which
draws its inspiration from science, and, in this chapter, from French
science in particular. In distancing herself from Fielding Eliot is, by
implication, rejecting the assumption that the English gentleman, by
virtue of his social position and unstrenuous classical education, has

privileged access to knowledge about 'that tempting range of relevancies called the universe'. The fate of the unsuccessful gentleman scholar Casaubon is to make the same point in another way. Knowledge has to be worked for, and it is significant that the principal site of such work in this chapter is Paris. Paris thus has a dual function: it is both the location of a kind of experience which has no place in Middlemarch, and the seat of scientific learning that has produced Bichat, instructed Lydgate in the aims and methods of rigorous research, and provided a model for the novelist's own practice. It is at once marginal and central. In this respect it is part of the careful framing which the novelist of *Middlemarch* shares with the scientist Lydgate: 'that arduous invention which is the very eye of research, provisionally framing its object and correcting it to more and more exactness of relation' (194). In provisionally framing the life of an English country town she includes the Paris of the study and the laboratory and excludes that of the theatre and the streets; or of the theatre of the streets such as we find in Balzac. In a novel which clearly aspires to the realist goal of comprehensiveness, she finds other ways to achieve it than through the street-level perspective of the *flâneur* which informs the urban fiction of Balzac and Dickens.

Her choice of a provincial rather than metropolitan focus for her novel can be seen as serving that extension of sympathy which she saw to be the proper purpose of art. Yet widening the scope of the fiction to embrace less familiar and fashionable forms of life creates its own problems of limiting particularity which she is at pains to overcome. In order to transcend the limitations of the provincial setting, she continually tries to place the action of the novel in a larger frame of generalization. The rhetorical effort of the narrator's commentary is to persuade us of the general truths implied in the experience of the individual characters, while the epigraphs which head each chapter, in so far as they are not Eliot's own limping verses, seek to set that experience in the wider context of world literature. The intertextual frame draws on the authority of the Bible and Bunyan, Shakespeare and Cervantes, Wordsworth and Goethe, to endorse the truth of the local particulars and present the study of English provincial life as a comprehensive account of human life at any place and in any time.

Eliot thus attempts to make the frame of *Middlemarch* as inclusive as possible; yet any frame excludes, just as all seeing is partial. The point is famously illustrated by the parable of the candle and the pier-glass, which demonstrates the distorting effect of egoism on the way any individual sees the world (297). This insistence on the relativity and partiality of all vision does not exactly undermine the novel's own project. Unlike Flaubert, with his negative conviction that there is no truth, only ways of seeing, Eliot invokes the authority of science as a model for a kind of seeing that seeks objectivity and verifiable truth. However imperfect it may be, human vision can properly aspire to objectivity, as does *Middlemarch* itself in its attempt at a typically realist comprehensiveness. Nevertheless, the central awareness of relativity does establish a problematic relationship between frame and vision; and this ultimately raises questions about the limits of realism itself.

In the fictional world of *Middlemarch* the novel's aspiration to comprehensiveness is echoed in Dorothea's desire for completeness within the narrow frame of her existence. Her impatience with Mr Brooke's 'simpering pictures', in which she can find no beauty whatsoever, derives from her awareness of all that their pastoral idealization excludes, 'the dirt and coarse ugliness of rural life' (424). Her intuitive inclination for realism corresponds to the aim and practice of *Middlemarch* itself.[2] And although her vision is subject to the partiality and fallibility of all human perception, it becomes clearer and fuller as the novel proceeds, drawing progressively closer to that of the narrator. The climax of this pilgrimage from myopia to understanding is, of course, her famous view from the window after her night of mental pain caused by the apparent intimacy of Rosamund and Will Ladislaw. The scene is all too familiar an object of discussion and interpretation, but it can still be usefully examined for the relationship between vision and frame that it presents. It is a framed vision which draws attention to the limiting frame while seeking to be as inclusive as possible:

> She opened her curtains, and looked out towards the bit of road that lay in view, with fields beyond, outside the entrance gates. On the road there was a man with a bundle on his back and a woman carrying her baby; in the field she could see the figures moving – perhaps the shepherd with his dog. Far off in the bending sky was the pearly light; and she felt the largeness of the world and the manifold wakings of men to labour and endurance. She was a part of that involuntary, palpitating life, and could neither look out on it from her luxurious shelter as a mere spectator, nor hide her eyes in selfish complaining. (846)

The chance figures who meet her gaze are significant as allegorical types rather than particular individuals: they are members of the human family, embodied images of caring and responsibility. A few deft strokes serve to characterize 'palpitating life' in general. Yet the passage also alerts us to Dorothea's own position as a spectator, even though she is not content to rest with it, and to the 'luxurious shelter' of prosperous middle-class life which makes that possible and provides the frame for her vision. In relation to that frame the figures of the man with his bundle, the woman with her child, and the possible shepherd, assume a more specific significance. They represent a world of 'labour and endurance' of which Dorothea can only ever be a spectator, the world of the rural working class. Morally she may be at one with them, but materially she remains at a distance, looking out on a life she will never have to share. With this framed vision Eliot could be said to be acknowledging the limits of her own fiction in the very act of making it inclusive. What Dorothea is looking out on is, in a sense, the world of Thomas Hardy's fiction.

It is appropriate that one of the characters that Dorothea is thinking about at this moment of enlarged moral understanding is Will Ladislaw, since his role in the novel has been precisely to widen her horizons. It is he who has encouraged her aesthetic development by extending her understanding of painting, and who has made plain to her the limitations of Mr Casaubon's scholarship. With his Polish blood, German education, and European travels, he is a citizen of a wider world than provincial Middlemarch, and he brings to bear on it a different perspective. 'Wide' is the epithet used, sarcastically but fittingly, by the painter Naumann to describe Ladislaw's interests: 'Oh, he does not mean it seriously with painting. His walk must be *belles-lettres*. That is wi-ide' (247). He is an agent of the novel's comprehensive vision; and with his ready empathy, sentimentally expressed in his fondness for children, and his tendency while in Rome 'to ramble about among the poor people' (503), he is given some of the characteristics of a *flâneur*. But although Eliot needs his mobility and rootlessness, they create a problem in this context which is both moral and formal. The other terms in which Naumann describes him are 'dilettantish and amateurish' (221), and, as Henry James perceived, 'the impression once given that he is a *dilettante* is never properly removed'.[3] In the moral climate of *Middlemarch* the *flâneur* can only appear as a dilettante.

Eliot is not, however, as dismissive of the dilettante as James, nor as Dickens is in the case of Skimpole. Ladislaw's dilettantism is a mark of potential, deriving in the first place from Goethe and anticipating Paul Bourget's positive definition of it in his *Essais de psychologie contemporaine* (1885):

It is much less a doctrine than a disposition of mind, at once very intelligent and very voluptuous, which inclines us in turn to different forms of life and induces us to lend ourselves to all those forms without giving ourselves to any of them.[4]

Eliot has sketched something like this disposition in Will Ladislaw, giving him, as has recently been suggested, some of the characteristics of the young Goethe as he appears in Lewes's biography.[5] Goethe's many-sidedness is the crucial feature, but the problem is that it cannot be adequately portrayed in a peripheral character like Ladislaw, nor, perhaps, fully explored in a novel like *Middlemarch*. All Eliot can do is gesture towards an interesting complexity, and present a perfunctory solution to Ladislaw's problem of vocation by showing him commit himself to political action out of a desire to remain close to Dorothea:

> It is undeniable that but for the desire to be where Dorothea was, Will would not at this time have been meditating on the needs of the English people or criticizing English statesmanship: he would probably have been rambling in Italy sketching plans for several dramas, trying prose and finding it too jejune, trying verse and finding it too artificial, beginning to copy 'bits' from old pictures, leaving off because they were 'no good', and observing that, after all, self-culture was the principal point; while in politics he would have been sympathizing warmly with liberty and progress in general. Our sense of duty must often wait for some work which shall take the place of dilettantism and make us feel that the quality of our action is not a matter of indifference. (501)

Just as he enlarges her horizons, so she roots him in a place and an occupation. But the problem is set out too schematically by the narrator's exposition alone and given too pat a resolution. To flesh it out fully would not only require Will to be moved from the periphery into the centre of the narrative, it would require a different kind of novel altogether – one whose principal mode would perhaps be characterized by the sort of benign irony focused on Ladislaw in this passage, and whose main concern would be the many-sidedness that is suggested here and the 'self-culture' that is explicitly referred to. In short, Will Ladislaw would be a fitting protagonist for a *Bildungsroman* in the German manner; and to the extent that he is treated with a degree of moral leniency which is at odds with Eliot's general practice in *Middlemarch*, he is already the beneficiary of the sort of 'large tolerance' that she saw to be characteristic of Goethe's *Wilhelm Meister*.[6]

Ladislaw's interesting but not fully accommodated presence in *Middlemarch* shows Eliot's imagination straining against the limited frame of a realist novel about English provincial middle-class life. It is in

Daniel Deronda (1876) that she makes her most important attempt to break free from those restrictions and comes closest to writing a *Bildungsroman* on Goethean lines, for the story of Deronda himself presents a fuller treatment of the problem of dilettantism in a way that is clearly indebted to Goethe. Deronda's initially uncommitted and un-directed existence is presented as an 'apprenticeship to life',[7] and it issues in a vocation arrived at with the aid of a wise mentor which finally takes him to a new life in another continent. Admittedly he is the object of earnest authorial idealization rather than Goethe's playful irony, but *Wilhelm Meister* and German culture in general are a deep and pervasive presence in the novel. Henry James recognized as much when he made his Pulcheria declare that 'its tone is not English, it is German', and that she 'would as soon read a German novel outright'.[8] German is the convenient label for a work which affronts the canons of English fiction by being both scathingly dismissive of English society and at the same time idealistic in its fulsome celebration of Judaism. More signifi-cantly, it is a formally innovative novel which aims at the realist goal of comprehensiveness on a higher level than *Middlemarch* by setting contemporary English society in a cultural and historical context that reaches back to the Judaic origins of Christianity. At the same time, placing the uncommitted figure at the centre of the novel has the effect of stretching the limits of conventional realist practice. Ladislaw simply widened the horizons of *Middlemarch*, but Deronda threatens to tran-scend the frame of realism altogether. His vision aspires to the visionary. In widening the scope of her fiction more radically in this respect, though not in terms of social class, than *Middlemarch*, Eliot creates a problematic relationship between the vision of her principal characters and the containing frames of social and realistic convention.

Where *Middlemarch* reached a climax in Dorothea's framed vision from the window, *Daniel Deronda* begins with an act of seeing that is disconcertingly unframed:

> Was she beautiful or not beautiful? and what was the secret of form or expression which gave the dynamic quality to her glance? Was the good or the evil genius dominant in those beams? Probably the evil; else why was the effect that of unrest rather than of undisturbed charm? Why was the wish to look again felt as coercion and not as a longing in which the whole being consents? (35)

The epigraph, which talks of the 'make-believe of a beginning', has already stressed the arbitrary nature of conventional openings, and this initial volley of questions is arrestingly unconventional. Unframed by the interpreting presence of a narrator or the mind of a clearly identified character, the initial interrogation registers a power that disturbs and evades normal categories of understanding. The unnamed woman inspires an 'unrest' which, associated as it is with 'evil', suggests the unsettling effect of sexuality on a mind unready to acknowledge it. This is a troubled and coerced seeing which challenges understanding rather than implying it, and it sets the pattern for what is to come for the two, as yet unnamed, protagonists, Deronda and Gwendolen.

In the immediately ensuing description of the casino in which Deronda is watching her gambling there is another instance of distracted seeing:

> Round two long tables were gathered two serried ranks of human beings, all save one having their faces and attention bent on the tables. The one exception was a melancholy little boy, with his knees and calves in their natural clothing of epidermis, but for the rest of his person in a fancy dress. He alone had his face turned towards the doorway, and fixing on it the blank gaze of a bedizened child stationed as a masquerading advertisement on the platform of an itinerant show, stood close behind a lady deeply engaged at the roulette table. (35-6)

The curious figure of the small boy is a gratuitous detail more typical of Flaubert than of Eliot. He has no function in the plot and is too theatrical to be seen as creating simply an effect of the real. With his face turned towards the doorway he raises expectations of some alternative focus of narrative interest; but it never eventuates, and the incident remains without consequences. If it has any significance at all, it is for the way in which the child's blank gaze is not contained by the scene at the gaming tables but looks out beyond the frame, since that announces what is to become an important motif in both halves of the double plot.

In the retrospective account of Gwendolen's life before her encounter with Deronda in Baden-Baden emphasis falls on the 'hazy largeness' (69) of her expectations by contrast with the constrictions of her position as a middle-class young woman: 'her horizon was that of the genteel romance where the heroine's soul poured out in her journal is full of vague power, originality, and general rebellion, while her life moves strictly in the sphere of fashion' (83). The way that she is confined by her social milieu is suggestively illustrated by the occasions in the early chapters when she strikes a pose, before the mirror (46) or at the piano (55), so self-consciously artistic that it seems to require a frame to complete it. The frame that actually surrounds her, even when her future is still promising and indeterminate, is that of the 'sphere of fashion'. At the dinner party at Quetcham Hall she makes an entrance that is ironically rich in promise:

> No youthful figure there was comparable to Gwendolen's as she passed through the long suite of rooms adorned with light and flowers, and, visible at first as a slim figure floating along in white drapery, approached through one wide doorway after another into fuller illumination and definiteness. (73)

Her passage here seems to presage the kind of development towards wholeness, harmony ,and definition that is Dorothea's in *Middlemarch*, but of course that sort of organic growth is denied her. The light, the flowers, and the wide doorways do not in the end represent a realm of freedom. First the luxurious shelter of affluent middle-class existence is removed by the collapse of Grapnell's bank, and then when it is restored through marriage to Grandcourt it turns out to be 'a painted, gilded prison' (651). The frame proves finally to be a cage.

This contrast, between life as she pictures it and as it is, may be the conventional stuff of realist fiction, but it is dramatized with particular power in *Daniel Deronda*. When Lydia Glasher presents Gwendolen with the tableau of Grandcourt's abandoned mistress and illegitimate children, the spectacle breaks into the narrow frame of her genteel life with terrifying visionary force: 'Gwendolen, watching Mrs Glasher's face while she spoke, felt a sort of terror: it was as if some ghastly vision had come to her in a dream and said, "I am a woman's life"' (189–90). That vision is then, in a passage of commentary at the end of the chapter, explicitly identified with reality in contrast to the images of art:

> Gwendolen's uncontrolled reading, though consisting chiefly in what are called pictures of life, had some how not prepared her for this encounter with reality. Is that surprising? . . . Perspective, as its inventor remarked, is a beautiful thing. What horrors of damp huts, where human beings languish, may not become picturesque through aerial distance! (193)

The argument presents a rationale for the melodramatic dimension of *Daniel Deronda*. What was confined to the margins of *Middlemarch* in Lydgate's experience with the actress in Paris is now a central element in Gwendolen's story, and it erupts in visions and nightmares which defy the sanitizing perspective of the picture frame. Instead of 'aerial distance' there is the powerful immediacy of images, like that of the dead face, whose origins lie close to home, in the deep recesses of the unconscious.

In her imprisoning marriage to Grandcourt a residue of her hazy largeness of expectation persists in a yearning for something beyond that socially confined selfhood. Before her marriage it was someone outside the English sphere of fashion, the German musician Klesmer, who revealed to her wider cultural horizons than her own. Now it is the fashionable but free-floating Deronda whom she casts in the role of priest to minister to her hopes of self-improvement. There is a striking combination of religiosity and sexuality in that relationship, but what is important in this context is the 'diffusive effect' (646) he has on her consciousness, the way he enlarges her view of the world by standing outside her married prison and representing 'a possible life which she had sinned herself away from' (767). His role is similar in some respects to Ladislaw's, though obviously not in its conclusion, since his decision to travel to Palestine and marry Mirah pitches Gwendolen into a frighteningly empty, lonely, and unbounded future:

> The world seemed to be getting larger around poor Gwendolen, and she more solitary and helpless in the midst. The thought that he might come back after going to the East, sank before the bewildering vision of these wide-stretching purposes in which she felt herself reduced to a mere speck. (875)

This bewildering vision has no containing frame around it, and her reduction to a mere speck stands in stark contrast to the scene at Quetcham Hall where she seemed to fill the frame of her luxurious surroundings. Her future remains uncertain, for Eliot refrains from closing the fictional frame with the kind of summarizing retrospect that concludes *Middlemarch*.

Gwendolen's painful experience of the reality of a woman's life, which is all too close to the vision proffered by Mrs Glasher, stands in striking contrast to Deronda's male life of independent means and leisured looking-around after a vocation. The difference is one not only of gender but of presentation and literary mode. Deronda, privileged in a way that owes something to the German *Bildungsroman*, largely escapes the sharply critical social realism of the Gwendolen half of the narrative. Where her dilettante trifling with the arts is put brusquely in its place by Klesmer, the spokesman of a genuinely deep and wide culture, Deronda's uncommitted existence, which could just as well be described as dilettante, is treated altogether more generously. There is, in the abstract, a distinct affinity between the unfocused aspirations with which both characters begin, but the terms in which they are described are very different. 'The hazy largeness about poor Gwendolen on the heights of her self-exultation' (83) is condescending, where Deronda's 'meditative yearning after wide knowledge' (217) is earnestly approving. The revelation that 'her horizon was that of the genteel romance' (83) implies a taint of Bovarysme and the threat of future calamity, in contrast to the suggestion of innocence eventually to be outgrown in 'his boyish love of universal history, which made him want to be at home in foreign countries and follow in imagination the travelling students of the middle ages' (220). Characterized mainly through the exposition of the narrator he benefits from a special pleading which has recourse to a Goethean model of experience and organic growth: 'He longed now to have the sort of apprenticeship to life which would not shape him too definitely, and rob him of that choice that might come from a free growth' (220). He is granted that freedom to grow, which is denied to Gwendolen, by the dispensations of a narrative which uneasily attempts to sustain an organic ideal in the unpropitious conditions of contemporary English society.

One consequence of this is Eliot's particular adaptation of the urban motif of the *flâneur*. Deronda's crucial encounter with Mirah, which leads eventually to the discovery of his origins and a saving vocation, takes place in a scene on the Thames which curiously combines the organic and the urban. For him rowing on the Thames is a form of *flânerie*, a leisured strolling which enables him to exercise his characteristic gaze, 'a very mild sort of scrutiny' (226). It allows him to indulge in his capacity for imaginative empathy and to enjoy, in the 'still seclusion which the river gave him' (225), the solitude which Benjamin's *flâneur* finds in the crowd. Deronda deliberately shuns the crowd, but it is in the most crowded part of the river by Kew Bridge, where 'the river was no solitude' and 'several persons were sauntering on the towing path' (227), that he first sees the figure of Mirah in her 'immovable, statue-like despair'. The meeting of their eyes – as in that other ocular, urban encounter between Frédéric Moreau and Mme Arnoux – is momentary but decisive, arousing the empathy of this idealized and romantically sensitive *flâneur*. As he rows away he cannot stop 'speculating on the probable romance that lay behind that loneliness and look of desolation' (228). The incident has the fleeting quality of a street encounter such as Baudelaire celebrates in 'A une passante', but here it is transposed to a semi-rural setting.

When he catches sight of Mirah again later in his outing it is as he is absorbed in a form of universal empathy, 'a half-speculative, half-involuntary identification of himself with the objects he was looking at, thinking how far it might be possible to shift his centre till his own personality would be no less outside him than the landscape' (229). It is such an escape from the limitations of his own selfhood, a transcendence of the limited frame of his own existence towards a 'passionate vision' (229) that is now offered him. This *flâneur*'s chance encounter leads not to a crime, but to a life's mission which takes him from lingering on the brink of English society to abandoning it altogether.

This adaptation of the urban phenomenon of the *flâneur* to idealistic and visionary ends is related to the double significance of the river. On the one hand it is simply the unexceptional setting for the recreation of a privileged young man, 'rowing on the Thames in a very ordinary equipment for a young Englishman at leisure, and passing under Kew Bridge with no thought of an adventure . . .' (226). In this respect it suggests the drifting nature of his undecided existence and is the appropriate location for his thoughtful mood as well as his idleness. But the commentary takes a surprising turn:

> Not that he was in a sentimental stage; but he was in a contemplative mood perhaps more common in the young men of our day – that of questioning whether it were worth while to take part in the battle of the world: I mean, of course, the young men in whom the unproductive labour of questioning is sustained by three or five per cent on capital which somebody else has battled for. (225)

The sharply realistic insight into the basis of Deronda's privileged existence, which allows him to indulge in the luxury of indecision, strikes a rare and discordant note in Eliot's idealizing presentation of him; and it is at odds with the other implied significance of the river as the beneficent stream of life, as a metaphor for the process of organic development to which he is entrusted. The metaphor is reminiscent of Goethe, and, more precisely, of how Eliot herself describes him in her essay on *Wilhelm Meister*: 'Goethe quietly follows the stream of fact and of life; and waits patiently for the moral processes of nature as we all do for her material processes.'[9] The description could apply to her own procedure with Daniel Deronda just as well as to Goethe's with Wilhelm Meister. It is just such a patient waiting that Deronda is engaged in on the literal stream of the Thames, and the processes of nature do not fail him. The insight into the material basis of his free-floating existence is simply left behind in the stream of the narrative.

It is once again on the Thames, in a meeting of glances which repeats the encounter with Mirah, that Deronda is both the subject and the object of the climactic visionary experience in the novel. Looking up from the wherry, he sees the face of his spiritual mentor Mordecai looking down from Blackfriars Bridge, 'brought out by the western light into startling distinctness and brilliancy – an illuminated type of bodily emaciation and spiritual eagerness' (549). The latter in turn sees in Deronda 'the face of his visions', the Messianic fulfilment of his inward prophecy: 'The prefigured friend had come from the golden background, and had signalled to him: this actually was: the rest was to be' (550). The setting for this vision is the working river of contemporary London and a transfiguring sunset sky:

> it was half-past four, and the grey day was dying gloriously, its western clouds all broken into narrowing purple strata before a wide-spreading saffron clearness, which in the sky had a monumental calm, but on the river, with its changing objects, was reflected as a luminous movement, the alternate flash of ripples or currents, the sudden glow of the brown sail, the passage of laden barges from blackness into colour, making an active response to that brooding glory. (549)

This transmutation of the commonplace into an ethereal beauty which forms the golden background of a vision gives the act of seeing in *Daniel Deronda* a dimension which transcends the frame of contemporary society and social realism. Like the shift from the material basis of Deronda's leisured life to the perceptual possibilities thus created, it signals the general direction of the novel and typifies its odd and uneasy achievement.

The dramatic power of this revelation cannot disguise the problems involved in the way that Deronda finds the solution to his dilettante existence in the discovery of his Jewish origins and his Zionist mission. The visionary experience and the implied metaphor of the stream of life seek to suggest that the vocation which they will lead to is an organic one, yet that suggestion remains questionable. Sunset is a time when, the narrator tells us, 'thinking and desiring melt together imperceptibly, and what in other hours may have seemed argument takes the quality of passionate vision' (229). If that passionate vision is resolved back into argument, it seems far less powerful and persuasive. In the crucial conversation with Joseph Kalonymos which precipitates his decision to make Jewishness his vocation, the issues involved in Deronda's life are made explicit and related firstly to his grandfather Daniel Charisi, and then to the predicament of the Jews in general. Kalonymos presents Charisi as a man who, with his dictum of 'Better a wrong will than a wavering' (790), combined breadth of knowledge and experience with decisiveness, thus avoiding the danger of indecision and unfocused activity that threatens his grandson. It was a similar and related danger, that of 'losing themselves among the Gentiles' (791), that was seen by Charisi as threatening the Jews of the diaspora – a danger of their identity being diffused. His insistence on the Jews remaining a distinct people, in the belief that 'the strength and wealth of mankind depended on the balance of separateness and communication' (791), not only provides Deronda with a cause worth devoting his life to but also offers a model for that life. The achievement of the Jewish people is to have been dispersed and yet to have remained homogeneous, to have combined diversity of experience with unity of faith and purpose. As a people and a culture they have solved the problem that besets Deronda of uniting breadth of experience with a definite sense of purpose and direction; and in committing himself to them he explicitly embraces the principle of their existence in a way that lends it a personal rather than exclusively national significance: '"But I think I can maintain my grandfather's notion of separateness and communication"' (792). The personal dilemma is taken up and resolved in the challenge facing a whole culture. This is Eliot's solution to the problem of horizons which Nietzsche defined in the same period, and which Flaubert explored in *L'Education sentimentale*. Just as, according to Nietzsche, every creature needs to be bounded by definite horizons in order to flourish, Deronda experiences 'the imaginative need of some far-reaching relation to make the horizon of his immediate, daily acts' (815), and finds it in his Jewishness, pointing out that '"our fathers themselves changed the horizon of their belief"' (792), as he changes and chooses his own.

There is an abstract logic in all this, along the lines of a passage from *Wilhelm Meisters Wanderjahre* which Eliot knew well and copied into her notebook for the second time when she must have been working on *Daniel Deronda*. 'Manysidedness,' Goethe writes, 'really only prepares the element in which the onesided man, having now sufficient room, can be effective.'[10] The manysidedness bestowed on Deronda by his privileged position as a wealthy young Englishman provides room for the cultivation of his Jewishness. It seems to be implied that he will be able to preserve his separateness as a Jew while maintaining communication with the wider world through his membership of upper-class English society. Nevertheless, when set out in these terms the argument looks thin and unpersuasive. There is something like a sleight of hand involved in presenting Jewishness as the solution to an individual existential dilemma. Deronda's ethnic origin is given not chosen, bestowed not earned, and in one sense he is permitted to compound his privileged existence as an upper-class Englishman with the moral privilege of belonging to what is, in this context, an idealized ethnic and cultural minority.

Deronda's discovery of his Jewish origins raises again a problem of vision and perspective:

> It was as if he had found an added soul in finding his ancestry – his judgement no longer wandering in the mazes of impartial sympathy, but choosing with the noble partiality which is man's best strength, the closer fellowship that makes sympathy practical – exchanging that bird's-eye reasonableness which soars to avoid preference and loses all sense of quality, for the generous reasonableness of drawing shoulder to shoulder with men of like inheritance. (814)

In arguing the superiority of active sympathy over detached, the passage expresses Eliot's characteristic moral position – the scene of Dorothea looking out of the window makes a similar point – but here the bird's-eye view is given the dignified gloss of reasonableness, whereas earlier in the novel it had simply been that 'aerial distance' (193) which deceives the eye and makes the squalid appear picturesque. There is only the mildest criticism of Deronda's lofty impartial sympathy, the kind of sympathy visible in the openness of his dilettante disposition and the universal empathy he indulged in while rowing on the Thames. As in the case of Ladislaw his dilettante existence and *flâneur*-like perspective have been the agents of Eliot's comprehensive vision, but the privileging of the observer has gone even further and is not qualified by the insistence to be found in *Middlemarch* that knowledge and insight are not the unearned prerogative of the English gentleman, but have to be worked for. The 'bird's-eye reasonableness' ascribed to Deronda is very close to the 'equal wide survey' associated with Fielding, from whom Eliot explicitly distances herself in the earlier novel. This time the qualifying criticism is almost incidental and the conclusion of *Daniel Deronda* itself seems to reinstate the lofty view. In looking beyond the frame of realist and social convention the novel effectively 'soars' to adopt a bird's-eye perspective from which preferences may be clearly seen but all else appears insubstantial. The journey of the Jewish trio to the East, which is being prepared in the closing pages, is elided into Ezra's journey to the next world with Deronda's and Mirah's arms around him and 'an ocean of peace beneath him' (882). The final note is, indeed, one of otherworldliness. As Deronda embarks on what is supposed to be an historical mission, the historical world drops out of sight; and, in an anticipation of the mythic patternings of modernism, he is transformed into a hero of Messianic stature.

There is, of course, a necessary vagueness about the ending, for Deronda's mission could not, by its very nature, be realized in specific detail. Nevertheless, the transcendence of a densely realized historical world, whose last claims are felt in the dramatic scene of his parting from Gwendolen, remains distinctly problematic. In Eliot's attempt to 'widen the English vision a little'[11] and achieve comprehensiveness on a higher level than *Middlemarch*, she has adapted the perspective of the *flâneur* to visionary ends; but rather in the way that the narrator's wry comment on the material basis of Deronda's leisured life broke into his *flânerie* on the river, the social and historical dimension of his privileged dilettante existence cannot be entirely dispelled from the visionary conclusion. The solution he finds to the problem of vocation is a case in point. In the final chapter of *The Impressions of Theophrastus Such* (1879) Eliot likens the Jewish national consciousness to the English, with the signal difference that the Jews have been the victims of imperial expansion whereas the English 'have been on the whole a prosperous people, rather continuing the plan of invading and spoiling other lands than being forced to beg for shelter in them'.[12] Yet in showing an upper-class Englishman escaping an aimless life of idleness at home by finding a vocation abroad and entering another culture in full confidence of playing a role of 'social captainship' (819), she presents a pattern of experience that has an uncomfortable affinity to contemporary forms of imperial adventurism. That other Englishman of the leisured upper class, Grandcourt – another dilettante, though of the opposite moral complexion to Deronda – might, we are told, have won a 'reputation among his contemporaries' if he 'had been sent to govern a difficult colony' (655). The possible parallel with less savoury foreign adventures casts a faint but discernible shadow over Deronda's saving vocation and Eliot's visionary ending. The wider vision she achieves in the conclusion of *Daniel Deronda* is problematic not only in its abstraction but also in the troubling residue of that social and historical reality she has sought to transcend.

The final separation of Deronda from England and Europe both suggests Eliot's critical distance from English upper-class society and signals a move beyond the realist mode. In the two novels to be discussed in the next chapter the separation of the principal characters from European life is implied in their status as foreigners and constitutes the starting point of the fiction. James and Ford exploit that perspective to present a critical understanding of a class and a culture, but one mediated through the consciousness of a single character for whom that culture has something of the nature of a commodity. A continuing engagement with the social in the manner of realism thus begins to assume the inward direction and ironic complexity associated with modernism, and the distance of the observer from the world observed becomes itself a central issue.

8

THE AMBASSADORS AND *THE GOOD SOLDIER*

American observers and the commodity of European life

In Henry James's *The Ambassadors* (1903) and Ford Madox Ford's *The Good Soldier* (1915) the wealthy and leisured American visitor to Europe, looking on its customs and culture with a mixture of bafflement and curiosity, is a *flâneur* figure who announces the epistemological uncertainties of modernism. For James's centre of consciousness, Lambert Strether, and Ford's narrator Dowell, seeing is not always the same as knowing, and the process of coming to know is arduous and uncertain. In different ways and with their different modes of narration the two novels present the sinuous, hesitant movement of minds groping after an elusive understanding of human behaviour. The emphasis on cerebration and foreignness marks the retreat of the *flâneur* from the popular street-life of realism to the rarefied interior realm of modernism. The representative realist figure is here co-opted for high culture, whereas, in that divergence that characterizes the breakdown of realism, the other line of descent leads to the popular fiction of Conan Doyle and Sherlock Holmes's ocular mastery of the city streets. Strether may often be shown *on* the streets but he is never *of* them, and both his and Dowell's visual experience is profoundly distanced, often diminishing the observed world to a comically mechanical miniature. Strether in the Tuileries Gardens, noting 'the deep references of a straight-pacing priest or the sharp ones of a white-gaitered red-legged soldier', 'watched little brisk figures, figures whose movement was the tick of the great Paris clock, take their smooth diagonal from point to point'.[1] Dowell enjoys a similar experience from the window of a German railway train:

> It is so pleasant to be drawn along in front of the spectacular towns with the peaked castles and the many double spires. In the sunlight gleams come from the city – gleams from the glass of windows; from the gilt signs of apothecaries; from the ensigns of the student corps high up in the mountains; from the helmets of

the funny little soldiers moving their stiff little legs in white linen
trousers.[2]

Such a perspective implies the freedom as well as the distance of the
visitor, but, in both these novels, freedom and distance are qualified by a
material connectedness that shows the residual traces of realism. Behind
the apparent freedom and beneath the subtle shiftings of consciousness
there is something simpler and cruder at work: the power of money and
the alluring power of the commodity in a culture which seems to offer
itself as an object for consumption. Elements of a realist melodrama of
money thus merge with a modernist questioning of knowledge and
character in works which stand equivocally on the border between two
modes of fiction.

James's own understanding of *The Ambassadors*, as expressed in his
preface to the New York edition of the novel, centres on Strether's
vision, his coming to see the truth about his own life and the lives about
him: 'the business of my tale and the march of my action, not to say the
precious moral of everything, is just my demonstration of this process of
vision' (xxx). By the end he has given Little Bilham the benefit of his
mature insight, arrived at a clear perception of Chad's relationship to
Madame de Vionnet, and come to understand his own relationship to
the dominant figure of Mrs Newsome. As he says to Maria Gostrey in
their final conversation: 'She's the same. She's more than ever the same.
But I do what I didn't before – I *see* her' (436). The emphasis makes
seeing a cognitive act, and this equation of seeing and understanding is
an habitual reflex in the novel: '"I see, I see" – she had easily understood' (236). Yet Strether's 'process of vision' is not simply a matter of
coming to understand, however slowly and with whatever difficulty. Not
only are there unresolved elements of uncertainty, but it also involves
other kinds of seeing that cannot be so readily equated with cognition.

A recent incisive article by William Greenslade on '*The Ambassadors*
and the power of advertising' has shown how the civilized art of display
which Chad learns in Paris is finally put to practical use in his embrace of
advertising.[3] It is also clear that, as the chief witness of this development,
Strether himself is exposed to this display not as a future practitioner but
as a potential, though ambivalent, customer. To see him in this way is to
answer Leavis's critical questions as to whether anything is 'adequately
realized' in *The Ambassadors* and whether we are asked to take Paris too
much at the 'glamorous face-value it has for Strether'.[4] What is realized is
the complex relationship of a foreign observer to a culture which has
both the tempting glamour and the essential unreality of a window-
display. From his first walks in Europe through the streets of Chester,

which the narrator identifies as 'a finely lurid intimation' (27) of what is to come, we see a man of modest means and habits, schooled to hard work and self-denial, now assailed by new temptations:

> Do what he might, in any case, his previous virtue was still there, and it seemed fairly to stare at him out of the windows of shops that were not as the shops of Woollett, fairly to make him want things that he shouldn't know what to do with. It was by the oddest, the least admissible of laws demoralising him now; and the way it boldly took him was to want more wants. (27)

The strolling *flâneur* is threatened by a wave of unfamiliar and barely controllable consumer desires. This is one aspect of the visual delights of Europe, but it merges with others that are not so demoralising. In the quickening of the senses and of the intellect which Strether experiences in Paris there is no clear distinction to be drawn between aesthetic and intellectual appetites on the one hand, and more sensuous consumer desires on the other. Glances into bookshops become 'hungry gazes through clear plates behind which lemon-coloured volumes were as fresh as fruit on a tree' (60). And the same imagery of appetite and consumption colours his browsing among the open-air bookstalls of the Odéon:

> He found the effect of tone and tint, in the long charged tables and shelves, delicate and appetising; the impression – substituting one kind of low-priced *consommation* for another – might have been that of one of the pleasant cafés that overlapped, under an awning, to the pavement; but he edged along, grazing the tables, with his hands firmly behind him. He wasn't there to dip, to consume – he was there to reconstruct. (66)

The metaphorical substitution of café for bookstall blurs the distinction between intellectual and physical appetites, and the passage powerfully conveys the sensuous appeal of the book as commodity. Strether intuitively finds something suspect in mere consumption, at the same time as he anticipates the pleasure of a future indulgence, grazing along the bookstalls with a *flâneur*'s appreciative gaze. He lingers here on the brink of involvement as a purchaser.

The visual appeal of Paris is, then, a complex one, and James's celebrated image of the city as a jewel spells this out:

> It hung before him this morning, the vast bright Babylon, like some huge iridescent object, a jewel brilliant and hard, in which parts were not to be discriminated nor differences comfortably

marked. It twinkled and trembled and melted together, and what seemed all surface one moment seemed all depth the next. (63)

The image succinctly expresses the general difficulty Strether is to have in getting his Parisian experience into focus, and the perplexing alternation between depth and surface is to characterize the way Chad and Madame de Vionnet appear to him. But the jewel, with its dual status as aesthetic object and luxury commodity, also points to the ambivalent nature of the attraction exercised by Parisian life. Reminding him of the intellectual excitement of his first visit as a young man, it invites his aesthetic admiration and touches off his 'odd spurts of the historic sense'; it represents not only a holiday from the cares of Woollett but a liberation, a world of imaginative and intellectual freedom as well as leisure. At the same time, luring him to 'want more wants', offering him the pleasures of mere consumption, it threatens to entangle and entrap him in an alien role. Strether the *flâneur* is always on the brink, enjoying his freedom to roam and gaze and speculate, but, as the gesture of keeping his hands behind him by the bookstall implies, always in danger of reaching out to buy. In danger, because to buy would be to change his relationship to the observed world, making him a consumer and in some sense a victim of the display. And this is what almost happens when he so nearly 'buys' the proffered image of the platonic relationship between Chad and Madame de Vionnet.

His stroll through Paris on the second morning of his visit, after picking up his letters from the bank in the Rue Scribe, characteristically links freedom with deferred commitment. He walks restlessly through the heart of the city anticipating the moment when he must sit down to read the letters from Woollett. To saunter through the streets, linger in the Tuileries, and pause before the bookstalls is as much a means of putting off the act of reading as a way of finding the ideal place to start it. *Flânerie* is loosely associated with reading, but not the empty reading of Flaubert's Henry in the first *Education sentimentale*, rather a deferred reading, a reluctance to get to the point, a hesitation on the brink such as mark his whole adventure in Paris. Postponing the reading of his letters he is free to read the characteristic signs and scenes of the city's life 'in the type of ancient thrifty persons basking betimes where terrace-walls were warm, in the blue-frocked brass-labelled officialism of humble rakers and scrapers . . .' (55). This is the visitor's perspective, discerning broad types of foreignness rather than making more precise and knowing discriminations. The reference to 'type' here and in the London theatre, which is seen as 'a world of types' (36), may recall Lukács's use of the term as the central criterion of realist literature, an organic synthesis of the general and the particular.[5] Strether, it could be said, attempts to read the world as if it were a classic realist text. However, James's Paris is a text of another order which refuses such organic meaningfulness and is not susceptible to straightforward categorization. Its inorganic, jewelled surface dazzles and deceives with a shifting play of light. Strether does better not to categorize but simply to receive impressions, as he does on his penny chair in the Luxembourg Gardens 'from which terraces, alleys, vistas, fountains, little trees in green tubs, little women in white caps and shrill little girls at play all sunnily "composed" together' (56). The composition is the artistic picture he makes of it, but such an art has too sensuous an appeal to be clearly distinguished from a consumer delicacy, and James links the two with a descriptive flourish: 'the air had a taste of something mixed with art, something that presented nature as a white-capped master-chef' (55).

When he finally does get down to his deferred reading what emerges from the contrast between Mrs Newsome's prose and his Parisian surroundings, between his letters and his impressions, is a liberating sense of difference: 'It was the difference, the difference of being just where he was and *as* he was, that formed the escape – this difference was so much greater than he had dreamed it would be' (57). Difference, as the precipitate of a deferred reading, carries something of the sense of Derridean *différance*; but if Strether's experience involves a constant deferment of the signified, it is not language in general but the particular language of Parisian life, its codes and conventions, that is responsible. In Paris Strether enters a world of equivocal and elusive meanings, in contrast to cut-and-dried Woollett – in contrast, too, to the world of nineteenth-century realism through whose classic terrain he strolls, his *flânerie* both continuing a realist tradition and extending it into the sceptical and self-conscious domain of modernism.

For Strether experience of Paris is mediated by an historical awareness that is both general and personal: an awareness of the history of France, including its literature, and an awareness of his own earlier visit and of Chad's first years in the city. For the reader Strether's experience is mediated by the intertextual implications of his Christian names, Lewis Lambert, and it is clothed in reminders of the French novel and of Balzac in particular. The middle-aged man from the New World retraces the steps of the Young Man from the Provinces, and, although he does not claim any analogy for himself, he certainly sees Chad in relation to that nineteenth-century type:

Old imaginations of the Latin Quarter had played their part for him, and he had duly recalled its having been with this scene of rather ominous legend that, like so many young men in fiction as well as in fact, Chad had begun. (63–4)

Recalling Chad's early career, James has him evoke more precise comparisons: Chad's left-bank associates, 'young painters, sculptors, architects, medical students' (64), form a Balzacian cast, a version of Lucien de Rubempré's 'cénacle'. And the central relationship with Madame de Vionnet, which is prefigured with ironic inaccuracy in the London theatre by the melodramatic pairing of the 'bad woman in a yellow frock' and the 'pleasant weak good-looking young man in perpetual evening dress' (36), places Chad in the position of Balzac's young men on the make profiting from the experience and affection of an older woman. Even the theatre itself, that 'world of types . . . in which the figures and faces in the stalls were interchangeable with those on the stage' (36), presents a Balzacian device for social display raised to the level of consciousness of the central character himself. Strether moves amongst echoes and allusions, poignantly aware of his own unlived life in a landscape rich in reminders of lives, both fictional and historical, fully and colourfully lived.

As a visiting spectator of the Parisian scene Strether is not an instrument of social analysis or of comprehensive understanding of the metropolitan labyrinth in the manner of his realist predecessors. The patterns he perceives are those created by his own historically attuned sensibility, as when he looks back at Madame de Vionnet's apartment as 'a vista, which he found high melancholy and sweet – full, once more, of dim historic shades, of the faint far-away cannon-roar of the great Empire' (293–4). Such romancing betrays his perpetual preference for the patterns of art, for picturesquely distanced vistas, rather than the messy proximity of recalcitrant life – 'he held off from that, he held off from everything' (61). This may be interpreted as a defence mechanism creating an illusion of control over the uncontrollable, and what it is a defence against can best be understood if he is seen as a *flâneur*, fastidiously treading the margin of that 'empire of "things"' which he encounters in Maria Gostrey's apartment:

The life of the occupant struck him of a sudden as more charged with possession even than Chad's or than Miss Barrace's; wide as his glimpse had lately become of the empire of 'things', what was before him still enlarged it; the lust of the eyes and the pride of life had indeed thus their temple. It was the innermost nook of the shrine – as brown as a pirate's cave. In the brownness were glints of gold; patches of purple were in the gloom; objects all that caught, through the muslin, with their high rarity, the light of the low windows. (83)

The 'lust of the eyes' that was first fired in Chester and then fanned by the sensuous appeal of Paris is bound up with the desire for possession enshrined here. Benjamin identifies the connexion between art and materialism in the phantasmagoria of interiors such as Maria Gostrey's:

> The interior was the place of refuge of Art. The collector was the true inhabitant of the interior. He made the glorification of things his concern. To him fell the task of Sisyphus which consisted in stripping things of their commodity character by means of his possession of them. But he conferred upon them only a fancier's value, rather than use-value. (*CB*, 168)

James's ironical image of the pirate's cave hints at a mild unease on Strether's part in the face of this careful accumulation of objects; and his sense of their precious rarity suggests their commodity character, their exchange-value, as well as what Benjamin calls their fancier's value. This becomes an explicit issue on a later visit to Madame de Vionnet's apartment. As Strether attempts to make a distinction between Maria Gostrey's interior and Madme de Vionnet's, we can see him, as an onlooker, at pains to strip the latter's possessions of their commodity character:

> He had never before, to his knowledge, had present to him relics, of any special dignity, of a private order – little old miniatures, medallions, pictures, books; books in leather bindings, pinkish and greenish, with gilt garlands on the back, ranged, together with other promiscuous properties, under the glass of brass-mounted cabinets. His attention took them all tenderly into account. They were among the matters that marked Madame de Vionnet's apartment as something quite different from Miss Gostrey's little museum of bargains and from Chad's lovely home; he recognised it as founded much more on old accumulations that had possibly from time to time shrunken than on any contemporary method of acquisition or form of curiosity. Chad and Miss Gostrey had rummaged and purchased and picked up and exchanged, sifting, selecting, comparing; whereas the mistress of the scene before him, beautifully passive under the spell of transmission – transmission from her father's line, he quite made up his mind – had only received, accepted and been quiet. (172)

The distinction is discreetly evaluative. Madame de Vionnet's 'beautifully passive' acceptance of family heirlooms emerges as somehow superior to the energetic rummaging and purchasing which Miss Gostrey shares with Chad. In its deference to patriarchal power it seems, too, more properly feminine in Strether's eyes, as if a woman's role were simply to receive, accept, and be quiet. Madame de Vionnet remains exquisitely aloof from both mannish activity and contemporary methods of acquisition, free from the taint of trade and bargain-hunting: Strether could not suspect her forebears 'of having sold old pieces to get "better" ones' (172). Any such obeisance to the market and to exchange-values would be incompatible with Strether's idealized view of aristocratic European culture, which colours his response to Madame de Vionnet from the beginning: 'He seemed at the very outset to see her, in the midst of possessions not vulgarly numerous, but hereditary cherished charming' (171). To such a vision possessions are only charming if inherited, rather than purchased as commodities; and Strether concludes by finding here not the suggestion of piratical booty, but rather 'the air of supreme respectability, the consciousness, small, still, reserved, but none the less distinct and diffused, of private honour' (173). The Sisyphean task Strether is engaged in at Madame de Vionnet's is to find ways of attributing to the empire of things this air of respectability.

To Strether's eyes Madame de Vionnet stands for 'the ancient Paris that he was always looking for' (171), and her person implies the history of a culture: 'he found himself making out, as a background of the occupant, some glory, some prosperity of the First Empire, some Napoleonic glamour, some dim lustre of the great legend' (172). A typically realist symbiosis of character and setting is given an added dimension by his romantically historicizing sensibility, and, ironically, Napoleon's thoroughly *parvenu* empire is accorded the dignity of ancient lineage. It is a case of historical distance lending enchantment to the view. What Strether cannot see but the text makes clear is that the 'prosperity of the First Empire' is not distinct from that of the present, and that aristocratic elegance has a commercial value, too. Madame de Vionnet's daughter Jeanne is disposed of on the marriage market – '"We're marrying Jeanne"' (295) – and although this arranged marriage is presented as 'founded on a *vieille sagesse*' and experienced by Strether as having 'something ancient and cold in it' (297), it also has elements of a contemporary commercial transaction. It is Chad who is responsible for bringing it about, and Chad himself, as Greenslade has shown, reveals the commercial potential of the old culture in finally adapting its art of self-display to the business of advertising. He is, too, given added value, as it were, by his experience in Paris: 'It had cleared his eyes and settled his colour and polished his fine square teeth . . . it had given him a form and a surface, almost a design . . .' (107). The terms in which this process are summed up could serve just as well to describe production of the unnamed article at Woollett: 'It was as if in short he had really, copious perhaps but shapeless, been put in a firm mould and turned successfully out' (107). 'Ancient Paris' is able to manufacture a very modern product.

Strether's historical romancing is thus put firmly in perspective, and in the end Madame de Vionnet's air of supreme respectability is shown up to be window-dressing to seduce the none too penetrating gaze of this impressionable observer. The scene by the river in which she and Chad are exposed can be read in terms of Strether's role as a *flâneur* lingering on the brink of the system of commodity exchange. The Lambinet painting which inspires his stroll in the country in the first place and accompanies it as a point of reference, as the 'oblong gilt frame' (385) through which he sees the landscape, is also significant for its status as a commodity that he has been tempted to buy. His near purchase of it in Boston is as important as its aesthetic appeal in what ensues. Not having bought it, he preserves the vision it afforded him untainted by possession and unexposed to any 'drop' or 'shock' that might have come from subsequent viewing. 'The little Lambinet abode with him as the picture he *would* have bought' (381), and the occasion of 'the only adventure of his life in connexion with the purchase of a work of art' (380). The different elements of that experience, at whose 'restoration to nature' (381) he now wishes to assist, include Boston as well as France, interior as well as exterior, the commodity status of the picture as well as its artistic vision: 'the dusty day in Boston, the background of the Fitchburg Depot, of the maroon-coloured sanctum, the special-green vision, the ridiculous price, the willows, the rushes, the river, the sunny silvery sky, the shady woody horizon' (381). And when miraculously he steps into the frame and rediscovers in nature the remembered landscape, the composition brings together Boston past and French present:

> The oblong gilt frame disposed its enclosing lines; the poplars and willows, the reeds and river . . . fell into a composition, full of felicity, within them; the village on the left was white and the church on the right was grey; it was all there in short – it was what he wanted: it was Tremont Street, it was France, it was Lambinet. (381)

Such privileged moments, in which life's disparate phenomena are brought harmoniously together, are to play a central part in modernist fiction, though here the presence of the frame and the Boston street provide a containing irony and hint at the limitations of Strether's vision in a realist manner. This is France seen through the mediation of art and from the point of view of a visitor; and, unsurprisingly, he wishes to round off his expedition with a typically French dinner in 'just the right little rustic inn' (382). The consummation is to be an act of consumption. Just as, in the Tuileries Gardens, something 'presented nature as a white-capped master-chef', the Lambinet landscape presents him with the hostess of the Cheval Blanc, and 'the picture and the play seemed supremely to melt together in the good woman's broad sketch of what she could do for her visitor's appetite' (387). The artistically mediated vision of France resolves into something that can be purchased and consumed.

In the end the detail, which seems designed to complete the picture, destroys it. The couple in the boat, revealed as Chad and Madame de Vionnet, deprive Strether of the comfortable dinner that he was expecting. He has his dinner but in most uncomfortable circumstances. Having tried to take possession of French life on his own terms, experiencing that possession as a luxurious freedom, he is painfully reminded of limits and constraints. The price he would have to pay for the perfect picture would be a wilful blindness to the real identity and intimacy of the couple in the boat, and it is too high. What follows is a process of withdrawal from commitment and the urge to possess and a return to the uncompromised detachment of the uncommitted though curious *flâneur*. At first the encounter with the couple seems to pitch him back awkwardly into 'the mainstream of his drama' (386); but if we attend to the implications of the shifting theatrical metaphors, it is clear that he is, rather, manoeuvred off the stage into the auditorium. The picture of French ruralism through which he strolls is at first 'more than anything else a scene and a stage' (386), but one in which he, too, is moving about as one of the cast. When the coincidence of meeting Chad and Madame de Vionnet is described as 'queer as fiction, as farce' (389), there is a suggestion of looking at the drama from outside, which is then confirmed by his impression that the pair 'had something to put a face upon, to carry off and make the best of' (392). With Madame de Vionnet's manner labelled a 'performance' (394) and the whole episode a 'show' (396), Strether is clearly positioned as a member of the audience. No longer the subject of a modernist epiphany, he is back in the social theatre of realism with its dramatic role-playing and moral deception.

The point is driven home in the next chapter by one uncomfortable and expressive scene in that theatre, a Parisian post and telegraph office. 'The something in the air of these establishments' is unlike the something in the air of the Tuileries or the countryside; it is 'common and constant pressure' and 'the vibration of the vast strange life of the town' (398). Deception and disturbance are all around, with 'the performers concocting their messages' and 'the little prompt Paris women, arranging, pretexting goodness knew what' (398). Strether has finally come to register the urgency of the life of the streets, as distinct from the tranquillity of the Parisian parks and the country, even if he does not participate in it. That 'vast strange life' shows up the limited and partial nature of the Lambinet image of France. Back now in the domain of the *flâneur* he fills the rest of the day, before his final interview with Madame de Vionnet, in indulgent *flânerie*, 'only idling, lounging, sitting in the shade, drinking lemonade and consuming ices' (400). *Flânerie* is again associated with deferment, with pleasurably filling the time before an awkward duty; but there is also a renewed intimation of release, this time from his commitment to Chad and Madame de Vionnet. In withdrawing from that tie he seems tacitly to accept the distance which has all along characterized his relationship to the Parisian world and which he is now no longer tempted to bridge.

Looking back at Chad's affair in the company of Maria Gostrey he concedes that 'it was all phantasmagoric' and 'none of my business' (420). In place of his bedazzled vision of Madame de Vionnet's elegant beauty, he ends with an empathetic understanding of her vulnerability: 'he could see her there as vulgarly troubled, in very truth, as a maidservant crying for her young man' (409). His disenchanted gaze has come back down to the level of the street. It is on the street, too, that he takes his leave of Chad and has a last impression of him as though dancing 'an irrelevant hornpipe or jig' – an impression created by Chad's histrionic gesture of kicking away the possibility of ever giving up Madame de Vionnet for money. Their street-level conversation has finally got down to basics, to the brute power of money which sustains the elegant life that Strether has so admired; and, in the very act of dismissing it, Chad seems to reveal himself as the puppet of that power, dancing as though to its tune in a manner both comical and absurd.

Inwardly distanced from Chad at this moment, Strether appears to see him more clearly than before; and generally in the closing chapters of the novel there is an implied connection between clarity of vision and detachment. It is not that Strether deliberately steps back in order to see more clearly, since the crucial first stage in the process of distancing is involuntary. When he recognizes the couple in the boat, seeing amounts to knowing all that he has hitherto failed to understand, 'the deep, deep truth of the intimacy revealed' (396). But such insight, like the similar revelation to Isabel Archer of the intimacy between Gilbert Osmond and Madame Merle in *Portrait of a Lady*, is not sought and it casts the seer in the role of unwitting eavesdropper rather than purposeful seeker after truth. And instead of involuntarily ordering the world like the modernist epiphany, it simply rearranges it in a disturbing, even destructive fashion. James's fictional world is more treacherous in this respect than Balzac's, which yields its secrets to the keen and steady gaze; and the treachery in this case lies in the seductive veneer that wealth and European culture supply. In his responses to the dazzling surface of European life Strether has shown that seeing is not always a matter of knowing, but rather of wanting and admiring, of appreciating aesthetically and consuming imaginatively, of romantically adorning and vicariously participating. As a foreign *flâneur* he has trod the margins of the 'empire of things', of a world of commodities and a world as commodity, and registered their appeal. Too old, as he declares to Little Bilham, for what he sees, he nevertheless sees in a variety of ways that reveal the problematic complexity of seeing in the rich arena of Paris.

The clear-sightedness that may come from detachment is, then, not the whole story of that 'process of vision' which *The Ambassadors* demonstrates. Even the deliberate act of detachment which Strether performs at the end of the novel in deciding to return to America raises questions rather than resolving them in the clear light of understanding. Is it that, 'having attained a comprehensive vision, he has no home', and stands at the end as an image of the solitary and percipient artist?[6] Or does his rejection of Paris and Maria Gostrey's offer of exquisite service amount to a betrayal of his experience and a return to the renunciatory protestant spirit of Woollett?[7] His role as a *flâneur* suggests something more equivocal than either of these certainties of progress or regression. Having been stopped on the brink of 'buying' a charming pastoral image of France and an innocent image of Chad and Madame de Vionnet, he now seems positively to accept his position on the margins. What had been the enduring predicament of a man who felt that his life had been unlived is now a stance willingly adopted. His determination 'not, out of the whole affair, to have got anything for myself' (438), is not so much a gesture of puritan self-denial as a final refusal of the temptation 'to want things that he shouldn't know what to do with' (27), the temptation to consume and covet, that Europe has presented. In his parting from Paris and Maria Gostrey there is a cheerful air of release and a serene acceptance of uncertainty. Returning, as they agree, 'to a great difference' (437), he rejects the spurious certainties of possession for a future whose meaning is infinitely deferred; yet in that deferment, as the novel has shown, may lie the only freedom available to this *flâneur*.

The 'saddest story' that Ford's narrator tells in *The Good Soldier* is announced in the subtitle to be 'a tale of passion'. It is as much a tale of possession. Dowell, another 'ageing American with very little knowledge of life' (219), looks upon European upper-class life from the margins, but, unlike Strether, ends up in empty possession of a portion of that life, an English gentleman's country estate. The discrepancy between narrative means and attained end is striking: proclaiming his ignorance, disclaiming authority in his judgements, denying any mastery or even control, Dowell finally establishes himself in a position of authority as master in the house of his late friend and rival Edward Ashburnham, and as guardian of the latter's last love, the now demented Nancy Rufford. This may seem suspicious enough to generate discussion of the unreliable narrator, but all such discussions tend to be fruitless. In a novel where the relationship between surface and depth is as unstable and shifting as in James's Paris, it remains impossible to decide whether Dowell's act of possession is superficial or substantial, merely coincidental or deeply sinister. Unreliability and epistemological uncertainty are the basic premises of a text which cannot be forced to yield definitive answers, but which sets the tale of passion and the tale of possession in a relationship of mutual interrogation.

Near the beginning of his narrative Dowell draws a significant contrast between his own mode of vision and that of his wife Florence in their peripatetic existence in Europe:

> No, we never did go back anywhere. Not to Heidelberg, not to Hamelin, not to Verona, not to Mont Majour – not so much as to Carcassone itself. We talked of it, of course, but I guess Florence got all she wanted out of one look at a place. She had the seeing eye.
>
> I haven't, unfortunately, so that the world is full of places to which I want to return – towns with the blinding white sun upon them; stone pines against the blue of the sky; corners of gables, all carved and painted with stags and scarlet flowers and crowstepped gables with the little saint at the top; and grey and

pink palazzi and walled towns a mile or so back from the sea, on the Mediterranean, between Leghorn and Naples. Not one of them did we see more than once, so that the whole world for me is like spots of colour in an immense canvas. Perhaps if it weren't so I should have something to catch hold of now. (20)

The gaze that takes swift possession is contrasted with an eye for aesthetically appealing but uncomposed details. The world for Dowell, the *flâneur* as perpetual tourist, is the world of Baudelaire's modernity, characterized by 'the ephemeral, the fugitive, the contingent'.[8] His unconnected glimpses and the metaphor of the spots of colour on the canvas may remind us of a central article of faith in Ford's and Conrad's novelistic creed: 'We saw that Life did not narrate, but made impressions on our brains.'[9] The writer's task of turning such impressions into narrative is enacted in the hesitant progress, the shifting back and forth in time, the revisions and contradictions of Dowell's narration. What he says of Florence's suicide – 'I pieced it together afterwards' (104) – could be applied to his whole story.

Given the limited nature of his own seeing, that piecing together involves recreating events at which he was either not present, or which he was too blind or dim to see. It is language which turns the unseen into the seen, and in the conversational flow of the narration vivid moments emerge, like Florence's fatal eavesdropping on Edward and Nancy, which are both starkly visual and highly rhetorical at the same time:

Anyhow, there you have the picture, the immensely tall trees, elms most of them, towering and feathering away up into the black mistiness that trees seem to gather about them at night; the silhouettes of those two upon the seat; the beams of light coming from the Casino, the woman all in black peeping with fear behind the tree-trunk. It is melodrama; but I can't help it. (105)

The self-conscious allusion to melodrama highlights the verbal artifice and literary convention at work in the composition of this 'picture', and the implied subordination of vision to language indicates the modernist dimension of Ford's novel. Vision no longer holds the central position it had occupied even in *The Ambassadors*. Dowell begins by claiming that 'this is the saddest story I have ever heard' (11) – heard rather than seen or witnessed – and hearing and speaking seem to be more important than sight in *The Good Soldier*. It is a novel dominated by talk. Dowell conceives of his own narration as a form of conversation, imagining himself not as writing but as talking at one side of the fireplace of a country cottage with a sympathetic soul opposite him. This phonocentric emphasis does not, however, ascribe a uniform authenticity to the spoken word. Speech can obfuscate as well as inform, as in the case of Florence's tireless loquaciousness, or when Leonora and Nancy talk and talk over the silent, suffering body of Edward. And where speech does have the accent of truth it may be mysteriously so. At different junctures in the novel characters are, as it were, ambushed by speech, blurting out words that they had never consciously considered before or intended to utter. Such outbursts, like Dowell's '"Now I can marry the girl"' (99) on hearing of Florence's death, point to the power of repression and the discrepancy between civilized surface and underlying depths that is both a psychological and a social phenomenon here. As Dowell comes to realize, there is more to upper-class English life and to his own existence than meets the eye; and in different ways the novel challenges the significance of the merely seen.

Cast in the role of attendant and observer, yet endowed with questionable powers of perception, Dowell is a *flâneur*-figure who embodies more intensely than his realist predecessors the problematic nature of vision. The two extremes to which, for Benjamin, the *flâneur*'s joy of watching can incline – the concentrated gaze of the detective and the open-mouthed gaping of the *badaud* – are disconcertingly combined in a character who, on the one hand, seems blind to the infidelities his wife is committing under his nose, while on the other is accustomed to snooping on his fellow guests in the German hotel where they regularly stay, being permitted 'by the courtesy of Monsieur Schontz, the proprietor, to inspect the little police reports that each guest was expected to sign upon taking a room' (29). Is he dim or deceitful, a dupe or a spy? The contradiction in his behaviour, while hinting at the wilful rather than unwitting nature of his blindness, remains unresolved, leaving the precise extent of his seeing an open question. By contrast Florence with her 'seeing eye', who gets 'all she wanted out of one look at a place' (20), is credited with an imperious and penetrating gaze which seems as unproblematic as that of any Balzacian seer. For her, seeing is a matter of taking possession, and the same is true of Edward Ashburnham who, 'coming into a room, snapped up the gaze of any woman in it, as dexterously as a conjurer pockets billiard balls' (33). With his 'perfectly level and perfectly direct and perfectly unchanging' gaze, he looks on women and on land with an expression 'of pride, of satisfaction, of the possessor' (33). Yet for both characters the mastery implied in their gaze is belied by events. Edward falls victim to feelings he cannot control, while Florence, seeing more than she bargained for, loses command of her life and runs to her death with a final eloquent gesture: 'She stuck her hands over her face as if she wished to push her eyes out' (96). In both cases the possessive gaze is the one that finally falters. However, the apparent certainty and assurance of their seeing is only ever a surmise, a point that is signalled in the text by Dowell's habit of qualifying his pronouncements with a demotically American 'I guess': 'I guess he could see in my eyes that I didn't intend to hinder him' (229). The primary significance of their gaze is, indeed, as the object of Dowell's, so that what at first appears to be straightforward leads eventually into the problematic question of character and characterization.

'For who in this world can give anyone a character?' (144), Dowell asks at one stage, and yet his task of turning impressions into coherent narrative involves a continual attempt to do precisely this. *The Good Soldier* presents both the necessity and the impossibility of characterization in the conventional realist fashion. In order to understand his experience he has to make intelligible the behaviour of others, in particular Edward, and he does so in the metonymical manner of realism, describing his appearance, his dress, and his accoutrements. But this unexceptional concentration on the visible and external yields no sure insight, and the descriptive process takes on a distinct air of parody:

> And that was absolutely all that I knew of him until a month ago – that and the profusion of his cases, all of pigskin and stamped with his initials, E.F.A. There were gun-cases, and collar cases, and shirt cases, and letter cases and cases each containing four bottles of medicine; and hat cases and helmet cases. It must have needed a whole herd of the Gadarene swine to make up his outfit. And, if I ever penetrated into his private room it would be to see him standing, with his coat and waistcoat off and the immensely long line of his perfectly elegant trousers from waist to boot heel. And he would have a slightly reflective air and he would be just opening one kind of case and just closing another.
>
> Good God, what did they all see in him? for I swear there was all there was of him, inside and out; though they said he was a good soldier. (30–1)

The note of impatience and mockery here goes beyond the figure of Edward to implicate the metonymical mode of realism and its description of character in terms of contiguities. Described by way of his appearance and accoutrements Edward remains an enigma, a handsome exterior behind which lies something unknown or even nothing at all – indeed, very much like one of his pigskin cases. The metonymy, suggesting a container for any number of unverifiable hypotheses, rebounds upon itself. Later Dowell reveals that the cases 'were not Edward's at all; they were Leonora's manifestations' (154): 'all that pigskin was her idea of a reward to him for putting her up to a little speculation by which she made eleven hundred pounds' (154–5). Even the way Edward appears is not a manifestation of his own nature but of someone else's, a social construct in which factors other than his own inclinations play a part.

However, to dwell on the social dimension of the man is no more rewarding:

> Have I conveyed to you the splendid fellow that he was – the fine soldier, the excellent landlord, the extraordinarily kind, careful and industrious magistrate, the upright, honest, fair-dealing, fair-thinking, public character? I suppose I have not conveyed it to you. (89)

Such a catalogue of stock characters conveys next to nothing, and the individual Edward never emerges from behind the various public roles. Despite Dowell's attempts to make him intelligible, he remains a puzzlingly blank figure; and although, from a traditional point of view, this might be construed as a damaging weakness of the novel, it is more profitably seen as a critical exploration of the problem of character. Edward's manysidedness and contradictoriness could be said to challenge the very notion of a unified subject; but, more importantly, Dowell's contradictory and self-defeating attempts at definition make plain the extent to which character is a verbal construct, a rhetorical effort at making intelligible what remains stubbornly elusive. Dowell is a long way removed from the *flâneur* narrator of Balzac's *Facino Cane* with his vaunted power of entering the lives of people he encounters with a single glance. Where Balzac implicitly questions this power of penetrating vision in the working out of his story, Ford's *flâneur* narrator never presumes to such authority in the first place and progressively reveals the limits of the onlooker's understanding in his self-dismantling characterization of Edward.

If Dowell's problems in defining Edward are those of a man attempting to write, his relationship to that figure also resembles on occasions that of a reader. Thinking of Edward's many acts of kindness towards his social inferiors, Dowell observes that 'I was rather apt to take these things for granted' (89). He then goes on to reflect further: 'They made me feel comfortable with him, good towards him; they made me trust him. But I guess I thought it was part of the character of any English gentleman' (89). Regarding his behaviour as typical of an English gentleman, Dowell takes it for granted and feels comfortable. The conventional category or type is reassuring, offering ready-made explanation and keeping awkward questions at bay. This readiness to settle for the undisturbing reading of behaviour is an habitual reflex. This *flâneur* is always unwilling to be jostled out of the strolling pace of his comfortable *rentier* existence. When Leonora threatens to do so in the castle at M— by reacting violently to Florence's provocative remarks about the Irish and her suggestive finger on Edward's wrist, his reaction is panic followed by 'the greatest relief I have ever had in my life' (48) when she declares herself to be an Irish catholic, thus placing herself in a category that provides an unthreatening explanation of her outraged behaviour. An offended national and religious sensibility can be appeased by apology, whereas jealousy and adultery could not be so easily despatched.

In this scene Dowell is the spectator of a drama whose real meaning he is unwilling, or too scared, to grasp. And in general it may seem that the true meaning of his narration eludes him. Near the end he makes what appears to be perhaps his most signally deluded observation:

> For I can't conceal from myself the fact that I loved Edward Ashburnham – and that I love him because he was just myself. If I had had the courage and virility and possibly also the physique of Edward Ashburnham I should, I fancy, have done much what he did. (227)

The far-fetched identification of 'he was just myself', which is immediately reduced to absurdity by the next sentence, can, however, be understood if it is taken as the expression of Dowell's empathy both as narrator and as reader of his own narrative. In telling his tale he has created in Edward a character who stands for all that he, the passionless, passive onlooker, would ideally wish to be. He has taken imaginative possession of him, and in doing so has come to identify with Edward in the way that readers of fiction may loosely talk of identifying with a character in a novel. Ford's exploration of the problem of character extends here to the affective mechanics of reader response.

The characterization of Florence leads in a different direction. She arouses no empathy and prompts no admission of love or even affection from the narrator as he attempts to recall her: 'when for the purpose of these writings I have tried to figure her out, I have thought about her as I might do about a problem in algebra' (113). Denying her any depth of feeling, he presents her as a creature of mere surface with the aid of a striking and significant simile: 'she represented a real human being with a heart, with feelings, with sympathies and with emotions only as a bank-note represents a certain quantity of gold' (114). This view of her as a facsimile of a human being, a mere 'scrap of paper' (114), may again suggest something about the literary representation of character, but the simile of the bank-note also leads into the financial subtext of the novel and its aspect as a tale of possession as well as passion. The image comes naturally enough from the pen of a figure whose most salient social characteristic is his wealth. For all his professions of ignorance about the human heart and the ways of the world, the one thing he does appear to know about is money. It is the one point on which he feels superior to Edward. The bank-note is, too, a fitting epitaph for the promiscuous Florence who circulates from man to man with commercial and heartless self-interest. But it is money itself which circulates most significantly in *The Good Soldier*, enabling or inducing the peripatetic existence of the two principal couples and determining the course of their lives. The Dowells travel the world because they have money, the Ashburnhams because they do not have enough. Leonora is married off to Edward to relieve her hard-pressed family, and her talent for economizing is employed in mitigating the effects of Edward's spontaneous generosity and expensive extra-marital affairs. His adulteries even seem to be chiefly objectionable to her as adulterations of the family fortune. And at one point in his narration Dowell attributes Edward's suicide to her outraged reaction to his expenditure of money, time, and trouble on getting a gardener's daughter acquitted of murdering her baby: 'She threatened to take his banking account away from him. I guess that made him cut his throat' (177). Here the financial subtext surfaces to challenge the main interpretation that Dowell offers of events in his tale of passion. The brutal simplicity of financial constraint cuts momentarily through the protracted discussion of passionate personalities and powerful emotions in a way that seems to confirm Benjamin's argument that 'when it is a matter of evaluating a person's behaviour, an intimate acquaintance with [his] interests will often be much more useful than an acquaintance with his personality' (*CB*, 40).

Florence cultivates her interests by marrying the moneyed Dowell, while her affair with Edward Ashburnham reveals her designs on his country estate. Even her historical and intellectual interests are marked by the kind of possessiveness that is attributed to her gaze: she makes herself at home in the past, able to find her way 'with the sole help of Baedeker, as easily about any old monument as she could about any American city where the blocks are all squares and the streets all numbered' (41). This American knowingness seeks to propagate itself in her self-imposed task of enlightening the less well informed. Her attempts to educate Edward in particular are described by an image whose intertextuality is ironically telling: 'It was Florence clearing up one of the dark places of the earth, leaving the world a little lighter than she found it' (43). The Conradian 'dark places of the earth' associates Florence's civilizing mission with imperialism's unsavoury scramble for loot, and although this simply serves in one sense as a comic hyperbole to expose her pretensions, it also suggests the material relationship in which Ford's Americans stand to European culture. What Florence desires and Dowell, perhaps unwittingly, achieves, is ownership of a portion of that culture in the estate of Branshaw Teleragh. Behind the tale of personal passion there can thus be discerned the larger movement of history, in the spectacle of American capital buying its way into the life of the English upper class.

Such history remains subtextual, for although Dowell likens his writing to historiography (13),and occasionally draws historical parallels, he makes no attempt to situate the life of his little coterie in the context of contemporary history. However, the novel's well-known insistence on the same date, 4 August, in a series of years, the next of which would be 1914, draws attention to what is missing and invites the reader to supply the absent historical dimension to this tale of individual lives. Dowell's rhetoric often points in the same direction. In presenting a rationale for his writing he invokes violent historical upheavals on a grand scale:

> For it is not unusual in human beings who have witnessed the sack of a city or the falling to pieces of a people to desire to set down what they have witnessed for the benefit of unknown heirs or of generations infinitely remote. . . (13)

And the equation he draws between the possible break-up of his little circle and the 'sack of Rome by the Goths' (13) strikes the same apocalyptic note. This emphasis on decline and fall casts Dowell in the role of a chronicler of events that yield no positive pattern of meaning. The established order of English upper-class life appears to be in terminal decline; and the incursion of American money brings no new vitality but simply reduces the form of that life to the mockery of a museum piece. Thus the final tableau of Dowell in possession of the former Ashburnham estate is empty to the point of absurdity:

> I am that absurd figure, an American millionaire, who has bought one of the ancient haunts of English peace. I sit here in Edward's

gun-room, all day and all day in a house that is absolutely quiet. No one visits me, for I visit no one. No one is interested in me, for I have no interests. In twenty minutes or so I shall walk down to the village, beneath my own oaks, to get the American mail. My tenants, the village boys and the tradesmen will touch their hats to me. So life peters out. (227)

The life is an empty parody of an English country gentleman's. The haunt of peace has become in effect a home for madness, and the concluding image of the demented Nancy sums up the absurdity of Dowell's existence:

It is very extraordinary to see the perfect flush of health on her cheeks, to see the lustre of her coiled black hair, the poise of the head upon the neck, the grace of the white hands – and to think that it all means nothing – that it is a picture without a meaning. (228)

He has taken possession of the form of beauty only, for the spirit has departed.

The spots of colour on the canvas that defined his earlier fragmented vision have here been composed into a picture, but to no purpose. In a novel that has repeatedly dwelt on the discrepancy between ordered surface and tormented depth – for instance in the juxtaposed images of the stately minuet and the carriage full of screaming hysterics (14) – this meaningless picture is the final challenge to seeing as a means of understanding. Ford shared Conrad's belief that the aim of art was above all to 'make you see', on the grounds that 'seeing is believing for all the doubters of this planet, from Thomas to the end', and that 'if you can make humanity see the few very simple things upon which this temporal world rests you will make mankind believe such eternal truths as are universal'.[10] But his practice in this novel relativizes all such certainties. What Dowell sees is always questionable, and what he makes the reader see incites doubts and questions rather than belief. The very idea of eternal truth is submerged in a universal scepticism. This scepticism focuses specifically on the kind of life this novel presents and its principal character buys into. In his *Critical Study* of Henry James, written shortly before *The Good Soldier*, Ford reflects on the privileged world that James portrays in a way that has a direct bearing on his own work:

If in short, this life is not worth having – this life of the West End, of the country house, of the drawing room, possibly of the studio and of the garden party – if this life, which is the best that our civilisation has to show, is not worth the living, then indeed western civilisation is not worth going on with, and we had better scrap the whole of it so as to begin again.[11]

The certainty implied here that western civilization is synonymous with the life of a privileged class is one that *The Good Soldier* challenges. In showing Dowell taking possession of what James's Strether admired but finally kept at a distance, it demystifies both that privileged world and the apparently privileged position of the detached observer. Dowell's distance from the world he looks on is, in the end, not that of a visitor who can admire the foreign culture with some justification and depart in freedom; it is the alienated distance of a man for whom that culture is a commodity he has purchased and one patently 'not worth having'. The effect of Ford's novel is thus to strike at what he saw to be the very heart of civilization, by exposing the 'life of the country house' to be so clearly 'not worth going on with'.

9

THE SECRET AGENT
Metropolitan life and the problem of form

James's and Ford's leisured and privileged observers, distanced by foreignness and wealth, are the means of articulating an ironic vision which announces the dominant mode of modernist fiction. While these versions of the *flâneur* belong to high culture and its subtle scepticism, popular fiction in the same period transforms his alert gaze into the piercingly assured vision of Conan Doyle's amateur detective. But there is another strand of early modernist writing around the turn of the century which eschews both the privileged distance of the former and the mechanical certainties of the latter. Conrad's *The Secret Agent* (1907), with its symbiosis of squalid, lounging revolutionaries and purposeful policemen, presents an ironic and sceptical vision operating at the level of the streets. The irony is at the same time subversive and self-reflexive, for Conrad both engages closely with the street-life of the metropolis and displays a characteristically modernist preoccupation with the problem of form. In his 1920 preface to the novel he maintains that its germ lay in his 'vision of an enormous town . . . a cruel devourer of the world's light',[1] and that, when he had reduced to manageable proportions the 'endless vistas' this offered by devising the story of Mrs Verloc, he was faced with the difficult task of disengaging that story from 'its obscurity in that immense town' (11). The metropolitan setting poses a particular problem of composition, threatening to overwhelm any attempted shape or outline with its obscure immensity. Benjamin, writing about the middle years of the nineteenth century, made the obvious point that the literature which concerned itself with the disquieting and threatening aspects of urban life was to have a great future (*CB*, 40), but one thing that distinguishes *The Secret Agent* from earlier fiction such as Dickens's, and from the great volume of contemporary writing about London which stressed its mystery and menace, is this awareness of Conrad's that the metropolis both inspires and

137

threatens his shaping power as an artist. The awareness is not confined to the preface but makes itself felt within the fiction in the experience of the characters. Where James's and Ford's observing protagonists resemble readers of a complex and deceptive social text, Conrad's various variations on the *flâneur* throw into relief a problem of form that pertains to the writer.

This association of London with the problem of literary creation is interestingly prefigured in the previous decade by Gissing's portrayal of the struggling writer Reardon in *New Grub Street* (1891). The implied point of reference, and contrast, for both Conrad and Gissing is Dickens, whose 'habit of mind', in Gissing's words, 'led him to discover infinite romance in the obscure life of London' and who was 'filled with the perception of marvellous possibilities'.[2] It is Dickens's power of perception that Gissing singles out in his critical study as the source of his creativity: 'but assuredly few men have known so well how to use their eyes . . . Keen they were in no ordinary sense; for they pierced beneath the surface, and (in Lamb's phrase) discerned the quiddity of common objects.'[3] For Gissing Dickens was the novelist of London, but a London of another time and seen by a gaze he could not seek to emulate.[4] In the figure of Reardon he dramatically renders the predicament of a latter-day novelist of the city, beset by a terminal fatigue of the creative faculty and unable to respond with Dickens's perception of marvellous possibilities. On Reardon's first appearance in the novel creative paralysis is tellingly juxtaposed to glimpses of London life:

> One evening he sat at his desk with a slip of manuscript paper before him. It was the hour of sunset. His outlook was upon backs of certain large houses skirting Regent's Park, and lights had begun to show here and there in the windows: in one room a man was discoverable dressing for dinner, he had not thought it worth while to lower the blind; in another, some people were playing billiards. The higher windows reflected a rich glow from the western sky.
>
> For two or three hours Reardon had been seated in much the same attitude. Occasionally he dipped his pen into the ink, and seemed about to write: but each time the effort was abortive.[5]

In the literature of metropolitan life such glimpses as these from the window of a garret are traditionally a spur to creativity. They inspire Balzac's would-be writer Raphaël in *La Peau de chagrin* and are transformed by Baudelaire into poems such as 'Paysage'. Here there is only blankness, and the rich glow of sunset as a poignant reminder of beauty

138

unachieved. For Reardon fluent creativity is a thing of the past and an object of nostalgia. It is significant that, when he looks back on the excitement and ease with which he wrote his first novel, he describes a creative process which has a distinct affinity with Dickens's:

> 'Very often I wrote till after midnight, but occasionally I got my quantum finished much earlier, and then I used to treat myself to a ramble about the streets. I can recall exactly the places where some of my best ideas came to me. You remember the scene in Prendergast's lodgings? That flashed on me late one night as I was turning out of Leicester Square in to the slum that leads to Clare Market; ah, how well I remember! And I went home to my garret in a state of delightful fever, and scribbled notes furiously before going to bed.' (234)

The flash of creative insight occurs during a nocturnal *flânerie* at a precisely remembered location on the streets. The fluency, the precision, and the creative encounter with street life define what has been lost: an imagination that responds with excitement to the stimulus of the urban environment. In the fictional present of *New Grub Street* writing is associated with a dulled gaze, with a fog that is as much in the head as in the streets. The *flâneur*'s perception of marvellous possibilities, the Dickensian 'glance which missed no minutest feature of what he saw',[6] have gone, and in Gissing, as Raymond Williams has put it, 'the lonely figure walking the streets is overwhelmed by the crowds and the ugliness'.[7]

Reardon's backward glance at creative *flânerie* bears some resemblance to Henry James's retrospective account of the origin of *The Princess Casamassima* (1886) in his preface to the New York edition, written about the time of the publication of *The Secret Agent*. Claiming that the novel 'proceeded quite directly, during the first year of a long residence in London, from the habit and the interest of walking the streets' and that its prime idea was 'the ripe round fruit of perambulation', James stresses the stimulating effect of the metropolis on the imagination of his younger self, who 'walked of course with [his] eyes greatly open'.[8] To a perceptive gaze and a curious mind 'the great grey Babylon' affords rich material for fiction: 'Possible stories, presentable figures, rise from the thick jungle as the observer moves, fluttering up like startled game, and before he knows it indeed he has fairly to guard himself against the brush of importunate wings' (7). For the younger James London was 'the London of the habitual observer, the preoccupied painter, the pedestrian prowler' (22), and such a figure, whose inclination was 'to haunt the great city and by this habit to penetrate it imaginatively' (22), seems to stand in a direct line of descent from Balzac's *flâneur* narrator in *Facino Cane*. Yet James no sooner claims a Balzacian power of penetration than he denies it, for he immediately declares that he was content in *The Princess Casamassima* with a vision that did not go deeper than appearances: 'My vision of the aspects I more or less fortunately rendered *was*, exactly, my knowledge. If I made my appearances live, what was this but the utmost one could do with them?' (22). Vision is knowledge, but only a knowledge of surfaces. And, as Adrian Poole has pointed out,[9] James strangely attributes value to *not* knowing in a way that seems to align him with the very complacency that he is taking to task:

> the value I wished most to render and the effect I wished most to produce were precisely those of our not knowing, of society's not knowing, but only guessing and suspecting and trying to ignore, what 'goes on' irreconcilably, subversively, beneath the vast smug surface. (22)

Thus for all the imaginative stimulus that London's streets afforded the younger James – and in which respect they are now in 1907 'dreadfully changed for the worse' (7–8) – there is a clear indication in this retrospect of how they resisted as well as excited the gaze of a *flâneur* who could no longer lay claim to the knowing penetration of a Balzac or a Dickens. If Gissing's London has been drained of the 'epistemological excitement' of Dickens's,[10] James's preface suggests the loss of epistemological confidence in the face of the city, which is another characteristic of the late nineteenth century.

Conrad's preface to *The Secret Agent*, again written retrospectively, also ascribes a crucial role in the origin of the novel to London and relates writing to the experience of walking the city streets. In both cases the danger of being overwhelmed is alluded to, but Conrad's emphasis is rather different. Where James's precious metaphor of 'importunate wings' suggests a distracting richness of potential material, Conrad dwells on the difficulty of wresting Mrs Verloc's story from the enveloping obscurity and making it credible with respect to her surroundings and her humanity:

> For the surroundings hints were not lacking. I had to fight hard to keep at arm's length the memories of my solitary and nocturnal walks all over London in my early days, lest they should rush in and overwhelm each page of the story as these emerged one after

another from a mood as serious in feeling and thought as any in which I ever wrote a line. (11)

The problem is that of keeping the chosen theme in focus, of retaining its outline in the face of the remembered city's overwhelming presence. Conrad's 'vision of an enormous town . . . a monstrous town' (10), his insistence on its obscurity, his experience of walking its streets in solitude and darkness, all suggest a difficulty of definition rather than a Dickensian delight in diversity; and the 'ironic treatment' (11) of his subject which he refers to can be seen as a solution to the problem, a way of keeping the material at arm's length and within bounds. The ironic angle of vision gives him a different purchase on London life from James: rather than resting content with appearances, he probes beneath the 'vast smug surface' to what is subversively going on in the seedy depths. His irony is penetrating as well as distancing, but what it penetrates to, in 'telling Winnie Verloc's story to its anarchistic end of utter desolation, madness, and despair' (12), is not certain knowledge but rather, in James's phrase, 'mysteries abysmal' (22) where all is uncertain and inchoate.

Conrad's solitary, nocturnal walks of the preface, together with the formal problem posed by their memory, find their way into the novel itself in the numerous scenes in which solitary figures are shown walking the streets and facing a challenge to their powers of understanding and control. Conrad's walkers are versions of the realist *flâneur*, but ones whose seeing openly mocks, rather than implicitly questions, the sense-making activity of the realist novelist. From Verloc strolling to the embassy at the beginning of the novel to Ossipon walking unseeing in the gutter and the Professor passing on 'like a pest in the street full of men' (249) at the end, these figures experience the threat of being overwhelmed and dramatize the difficulty of composing experience into meaning except in terms of absolute negation.

The description of Verloc's stately progress 'westward through a town without shadows in an atmosphere of powdered old gold' combines a Whistlerish aesthetic impressionism with orotund irony. Sharp visual details alternate with mocking and mock-pompous commentary in a way that sets a pattern for the rest of the novel. Conrad's ponderous ironic prose, which dwells on darknesses physical, mental, and meta-physical, is to lift momentarily now and then to give brilliant glimpses of urban life. Here, under a blood-shot sun whose old-gold tinge suggests the beauty of decay, what is glimpsed are random features of life in London's prosperous West End: 'a victoria with the skin of some wild beast inside and a woman's face and hat emerging above the folded hood' (19); a milk cart rattling noisily across the end of a street; 'a butcher boy, driving with the noble recklessness of a charioteer at Olympic Games, . . . sitting high above a pair of red wheels' (21); 'a thick police constable . . . surging apparently out of a lamp-post' (21). Highlighted by their inconsequential and isolated appearance these details may seem to invite symbolic interpretation, but their main significance is that they are random and resist recuperation into any general pattern of meaning. They are glimpses which do not quite add up to a coherent vision.

Verloc provides the occasion for these perceptions but they cannot be clearly ascribed to him, since he too is an object of the gaze which makes them. 'His big prominent eyes' are 'rather of the sort that closes solemnly in slumber with majestic effect' (20), and the most they can rise to are 'glances of comparative alertness' (19). As a spectator of the street-life around him Verloc has 'a dull effect of rustiness' (19), going through the motions of a *flâneur* but with powers of perception so dulled that he is little more than an open-mouthed *badaud*. His understanding of what lies before his eyes is limited to his function as an embassy spy and tool of the established order: 'He surveyed through the park railings the evidences of the town's opulence and luxury with an approving eye. All these people had to be protected. Protection is the first necessity of opulence and luxury' (20). His approving eye is without any power to penetrate, but is itself penetrated by Conrad's irony, with the disquieting effect that is characteristic of *The Secret Agent* as a whole. The passage is a typical instance of the way in which the novel raises fundamental questions of meaning and perspective. If the sense that Verloc makes of the scene is to be taken ironically, what truer meaning can be implied? To interpret Verloc's reflections as an ironic inversion of the true sense of the scene would be to side with the anarchists in their belief that prosperous bourgeois London is not worth protecting. Poised between blinkered complacency and comprehensive nihilism the novel bears the mark of a fundamental contradiction – a contradiction between, as Eagleton has put it, 'its unswerving commitment to bourgeois "normality" and its dissentient "metaphysical" impulse to reject such "false consciousness" for a "deeper" insight into the "human condition"'.[11] Just as Verloc here walks the reassuringly normal streets of the West End on his way to being thrust into the destructive madness of Mr Vladimir's bomb-plot, Conrad's street-walking figures all tread the dangerous edge between a limited bourgeois normality and a frightening abyss where nothing has value or meaning.

Hardy, writing about London in the late 1880s, described a problem of vision in an atomized metropolitan world which anticipates Conrad in an illuminating fashion:

'London appears not to *see itself*. Each individual is conscious of *himself*, but nobody conscious of themselves collectively, except perhaps some poor gaper who stares round with a half-idiotic aspect.
    'There is no consciousness here of where anything comes from or goes to – only that it is present.'[12]

A consciousness limited to registering presence, rather than reflecting on origin and end, is what most of the characters display as they walk, often without goal or purpose, through a London where a street can appear monumentally superior to time and change, evincing 'the majesty of inorganic nature, of matter that never dies' (21). But, more importantly, the figures who walk the streets – Verloc and Winnie, Inspector Heat and the Assistant Commissioner, the Professor and Ossipon – are only really conscious of themselves and their own problems. No one rises to a collective consciousness of the urban world, with the possible exception of Stevie. He, with his universal charity, struggles 'to fit all the words he could remember to his sentiments in order to get some sort of corresponding idea', and finally comes out with a lapidary general truth: '"Bad world for poor people"'(143). And Stevie, 'easily diverted . . . by the comedies of the streets, which he contemplated open-mouthed' (17), is precisely Hardy's 'poor gaper who stares round with a half-idiotic aspect'. Hardy was trying to define the peculiar blindness of London life, and *The Secret Agent* largely confirms his diagnosis in presenting characters whose visual perceptions are divorced from any larger understanding of their condition. But this absence of wider understanding is also a measure of this novel's scepticism about general truths and theories. The only character who is able to register the pitiful plight of humanity at large is an idiot, while the proponent of the opposite moral position, the Professor with his universal contempt for the human race, is a manifest maniac. What seems to be discounted by Conrad's even-handed irony is any pronouncement on human life which goes beyond the comprehensive scepticism expressed in the narrator's comment that 'true wisdom is not certain of anything in this world of contradictions' (76).

Stevie's laborious attempt to rise to a general understanding of the world is most brutally mocked by the fate he suffers, shattered by the bomb into a 'heap of nameless fragments' (78). The life that he struggles to compose into meaning is literally and definitively fragmented, and in such a way that the distinction between the human and the non-human is sickeningly elided, 'a heap of rags, scorched and bloodstained, half concealing what might have been an accumulation of raw material for a cannibal feast' (77). The same violent disintegration of forms characterizes Ossipon's horrified vision of a bomb-blast in the Silenus Restaurant, as he imagines 'the overlighted place changed into a dreadful black hole belching horrible fumes choked with ghastly rubbish of smashed brickwork and mutilated corpses' (63). These explosions, actual and imagined, are the most pointed expressions of an apprehension of the world which is central to *The Secret Agent* and which most of the principal characters experience, gazing like Ossipon into a black hole where categories are confused, forms dissolve into each other, and the human threatens to merge with the non-human. Verloc, leaning his forehead against the cold window-pane of his bedroom, is separated by this 'fragile film of glass' from 'the enormity of cold, black, wet, muddy, inhospitable accumulation of bricks, slates, and stones' (54), which threaten to engulf him. Repeatedly London is experienced as a kind of elemental confusion where forms are slipping back into a primeval slime. The Assistant Commissioner advances 'into an immensity of greasy slime and damp plaster interspersed with lamps, and enveloped, oppressed, penetrated, choked, and suffocated by the blackness of a wet London night' (126); and Winnie Verloc, after murdering her husband, anticipates her end as she steps out into the street: 'This entrance into the open air had a foretaste of drowning; a slimy dampness enveloped her, entered her nostrils, clung to her hair' (217). The formal problem alluded to in the preface is here given an existential dimension as characters face being overwhelmed by the sodden obscurity of the monstrous town from which Conrad struggled to disengage his story. And on one occasion, as Ossipon and the Professor leave the Silenus Restaurant, the relationship between writing and the city streets becomes itself a focus of attention:

> In front of the great doorway a dismal row of newspaper sellers standing clear of the pavement dealt out their wares from the gutter. It was a raw, gloomy day of the early spring; and the grimy sky, the mud of the streets, the rags of the dirty men harmonized excellently with the eruption of the damp, rubbishy sheets of paper soiled with printers' ink. The posters, maculated with filth, garnished like tapestry the sweep of the kerbstone. The trade in afternoon papers was brisk, yet, in comparison with the swift,

constant march of foot traffic, the effect was of indifference, of a disregarded distribution. (72)

Posters, print, writing itself, are all part of the uniform squalor. Writing does not transcend the confusion of forms and the general dissolution into primeval mud and slime. Sheets of paper are equivalent to rags, posters are beginning to merge with the mud of the streets, and printers' ink is just another kind of dirt. The writing of newspapers does not invest the urban world with meaning and is powerless to affect it. And the act of walking the streets is not here a means of comprehending the urban labyrinth, for the movement of men in the mass, 'the constant march of foot traffic', obliterates all meaning in a grand indifference.

Streets seen in this uniformly negative light as 'things in themselves unlovely and unfriendly to man' (54) are not ones in which any *flâneur* can feel at home, and *The Secret Agent* seems openly to mock the possibility of perceiving the street as a familiar interior. That simile is brought ironically to life when the Professor turns into a narrow alley where he is to encounter Chief Inspector Heat:

> On one side the low brick houses had in their dusty windows the sightless, moribund look of incurable decay – empty shells awaiting demolition. From the other side life had not departed wholly as yet. Facing the only gas-lamp yawned the cavern of a second-hand-furniture dealer, where, deep in the gloom of a sort of narrow avenue winding through a bizarre forest of wardrobes, with an undergrowth tangle of table legs, a tall pier-glass glimmered like a pool of water in a wood. An unhappy, homeless couch, accompanied by two unrelated chairs, stood in the open. (74)

Overlooked by the empty shells of human habitation this alley parodies a domestic interior and mocks the very idea of a dwelling. In another blurring of categories and distinctions, exterior and interior merge, but in a way that creates the opposite of a sense of homely familiarity. The second-hand furniture is 'unhappy, homeless', like the solitary anarchist himself; and man and accoutrements share the status of outcast. Like these pathetic domestic remnants exposed in the open, interiors in this novel afford no refuge from the alien wilderness of the streets. The same metaphors of untamed nature are later used to describe both the Home Secretary's office, which has 'something of a forest's deep gloom' (177) about it, and the Verloc's home, which seems to Winnie to be 'as lonely and unsafe as though it had been situated in the midst of a forest' (165). And in a set-piece narrative of exposure, Winnie's mother's worldly goods are hauled through the London streets to the almshouses in a cab which itself 'seemed cast out into the gutter on account of irremediable decay' (142). There is no room here for a Jamesian cultivation of the private life and the domestic interior, nor for any collector's fetishism of the commodity. Homes are no refuge, furnishings are rudimentary, and almost the only commodities shown to be circulating are the seedy wares and rubber goods peddled by the Verlocs in furtive transactions over the counter of their backstreet shop. There is nothing, it seems, to redeem an urban world which is in every sense at the end of its tether.

Amidst this accumulation of deadly negations the character whose ideological negation is the most violent and comprehensive has an odd sprightliness and vitality in his maniacal single-mindedness. There is, as has often been noted, an obscure and covert affinity between the Professor's nihilism and Conrad's own corrosive vision, 'as if the only imaginative commitment [Conrad] can make is to the Professor's dream of total annihilation'.[13] However, the affinity is one not so much of ideology as of form. In his preface Conrad likens himself to the revolutionists on the grounds of his 'concentrated purpose' (11) rather than his beliefs; and in a fictional world inhabited by the fat and the fleshy – the fat-pig Verloc and the obese Michaelis – and characterized by sliminess, greasiness, and a slithering confusion of forms, the Professor's spare figure and singleness of purpose have a salutary clarity of outline. 'All his movements,' we are told, 'had a firmness, an assured precision' (59). This, however, does nothing to lessen the pathetic figure he cuts or the repulsiveness of the views he holds, both of which are kept firmly in focus.

The key to this set of contradictions may be provided by Nietzsche. Although there is no direct evidence that Conrad had read Nietzsche, it is clear from his correspondence that he had read Edward Garnett's article on the philosopher in *The Outlook* in July 1899, and he seems to have been acquainted with the broad outlines of Nietzsche's thinking. In a letter of July 1899 he refers to 'the mad individualism of Niet[z]sche' and its opposite, 'exaggerated altruism', contrasting both with true and enduring faith.[14] Leaving aside the pronouncements on faith and the Church in this letter, which may anyway have been tailored to appeal to his correspondent, the pairing of rebarbative extremes can be seen to anticipate *The Secret Agent* and the antinomies represented by the Professor and Stevie. The Professor's mad individualism has, indeed, unmistakably Nietzschean characteristics. With his belief in 'the force of personality' and the power of his will; in the superiority he claims to all whose 'character is built upon conventional morality' (63);

in his inversion of Christian ethics and his desire to exterminate 'our sinister masters . . . the weak, the flabby, the silly, the cowardly, the faint of heart, and the slavish of mind' (243), he looks like a mocking caricature of Nietzsche's *Uebermensch*, or 'overman' to use the term Conrad himself employs in a letter of July 1901.[15] Conrad's irony concedes nothing to this Nietzschean ideology; yet at the same time there is in the novel a more positive affinity – ironic still, but not mocking – with the aesthetic Nietzsche sets out in *The Birth of Tragedy*. The novel repudiates the values of the mad individualism, but in its pursuit of form in the face of threatening formlessness it echoes with curious reminders of Nietzsche's complementary aesthetic principles, the Apollonian and Dionysiac.

The Secret Agent does not aspire to the condition of tragedy, but it does dramatize what Nietzsche refers to as 'a Dionysiac condition, tending towards the shattering of the individual and his fusion with the original Oneness'.[16] The fusion is here appalling rather than ecstatic, but the bleak vision of the novel is thoroughly Dionysiac in its insistence on, to use Nietzsche's words, 'the terrors and horrors of existence' (29). Such bleakness characterized for Nietzsche the wisdom of Silenus:

> An old legend has it that King Midas hunted a long time in the woods for the wise Silenus, companion of Dionysos, without being able to catch him. When he had finally caught him the king asked him what he considered man's greatest good. The daemon remained sullen and uncommunicative until finally, forced by the king, he broke into a shrill laugh and spoke: 'What would be the best for you is quite beyond your reach: not to have been born, not to *be*, to be *nothing*. But the second best is to die soon.' (29)

Significantly, it is in the Silenus beer-hall that Conrad's Professor expounds *his* nihilistic doctrines to the increasingly drunken and despairing Ossipon. And in the scene of Winnie's mother's removal to the almshouse the cabman, with 'his fierce little eyes that seemed to smart in a clear and corroding liquid' (139), is likened to Silenus as he talks to Stevie 'of domestic matters and the affairs of men whose sufferings are great and immortality by no means assured', and delivers himself of his own bleak wisdom: '"This ain't an easy world . . . 'Ard on 'osses, but dam' sight 'arder on poor chaps like me"' (139). What Nietzsche sets against the 'terrible wisdom of Silenus' is the 'fair world of Apollo' (33), the god who represents the principle of individuation; and to the extent that the Professor stands out in contrast to a world of shattered individuals, merging forms, and enveloping obscurity, he resembles an ironically etiolated embodiment of that principle, stripped of the beauty associated with Apollo. Solitary, controlled, fenced off from other men by the explosive device in his pocket, he fears only one thing, 'the mass of mankind mighty in its numbers' (74), the Dionysiac oneness of the anonymous multitude: 'The resisting power of numbers, the unattackable stolidity of a great multitude, was the sinister fear of his loneliness' (85). In his lonely individualism, embittered theorizing, and opposition to the crowds of people about him, he mimics Nietzsche's 'Apollonian artist with his thin, monotonous harp music . . . beside the demoniac chant of the multitude' (35). These shadowy parallels with Nietzsche's aesthetic help to elucidate the oddly ambiguous and contradictory status of the Professor. Repellent though his views are, they have the one virtue of clarity and consistency; and in a fictional world where the lives of individuals, and the life of society itself, seem to be slipping out of control into madness and despair, anarchy, and corruption, he represents the power of control through negation. He is, as it were, the Apollonian element in the form of the thin, monotonous music of irony; an embodiment of the device which Conrad needed to give his story its outline and disengage it from the Dionysiac obscurity of the monstrous town. It is, appropriately, with the Professor, 'terrible in the simplicity of his idea', in contrast to the Dionysiac Ossipon 'beginning to drink with pleasure, with anticipation, with hope' (249), that the novel closes.

The last page of the novel presents these two characters walking the streets blindly, disregarded, and without direction: 'Comrade Ossipon walked without looking where he put his feet, feeling no fatigue, feeling nothing, seeing nothing, hearing not a sound . . . And the incorruptible Professor walked, too, averting his eyes from the odious multitude of mankind' (249). Their aimless, unseeing progress looks like a parody of the *flâneur*'s leisurely gait and alert gaze, and it is a final illustration of the distance that separates Conrad from a writer like Dickens in his treatment of metropolitan life. Conrad's narration has none of the flamboyant, *flâneur*-like mobility and delight in diversity displayed by Dickens's anonymous narrator in *Bleak House*. In the Professor's contempt for the mass of mankind, 'impervious to sentiment, to logic, to terror, too, perhaps', and his consequent 'dreadful and sane mistrust' – 'What if nothing could move them' (74) – there are the fingerprints of a writer who did not enjoy Dickens's close relationship to either his subject or his public. Conrad's imagination does not so much inhabit the city as recoil from it. And although his eyes are not, like the Professor's, averted from its spectacle, his vision tends to focus on the single detail, leaving it isolated amid the surrounding obscurity. The scene in which the Assistant Commissioner – the strolling spectator with the keenest eye in the novel – approaches Brett Street epitomizes this procedure:

> Brett Street was not very far away. It branches off, narrow, from the side of an open triangular space surrounded by dark and mysterious houses, temples of petty commerce emptied of traders for the night. Only a fruiterer's stall at the corner made a violent blaze of light and colour. Beyond all was black, and the few people passing in that direction vanished at one stride beyond the glowing heaps of oranges and lemons. No footsteps echoed. They would never be heard of again. The adventurous head of the Special Crimes Department watched these disappearances from a distance with an interested eye. (126)

The passage brilliantly fulfils Conrad's artistic intention, as expressed in the preface to *The Nigger of the Narcissus*, 'to make you *see*',[17] but the illuminated detail is a single spot of light in a darkness which is typically given the dimension of a mysterious metaphysical absolute. On other occasions what is here a gesture towards an encompassing negative meaning takes the form of an emphatic and disruptive generalization. The Assistant Commissioner, looking out of the window before his excursion to Brett Street, beholds a scene of desolation:

> The panes streamed with rain, and the short street he looked down into lay wet and empty, as if swept suddenly clear by a great flood. It was a very trying day, choked in raw fog to begin with, and now drowned in cold rain. The flickering, blurred flames of gas-lamps seemed to be dissolving in a watery atmosphere. And the lofty pretensions of a mankind oppressed by the miserable indignities of the weather appeared as a colossal and hopeless vanity deserving of scorn, wonder and compassion. (88)

The concluding generalization, which seems to go beyond the consciousness of the character, offers a meaning only in terms of all-embracing irony and negation. It is so sweeping and dismissive, and so ponderously out of proportion to the view of the street, that it overwhelms the visual detail. Irony may be the means by which Conrad controls his material, but at moments like this it has the effect of obliterating it.

This leap into dismissive generalization is a form of imaginative recoil from the city, and it seems as though the problem of form and meaning that the subject posed for Conrad could only be resolved through negation. That negation becomes increasingly insistent towards the end of the novel. Shortly before the final images of aimless walking, and anticipating them, there is a comprehensive vision of London as it is traversed from end to end by the desperate Ossipon after he has abandoned Winnie Verloc on the boat train:

> And again Comrade Ossipon walked. His robust form was seen that night in distant parts of the enormous town slumbering monstrously on a carpet of mud under a veil of raw mist. It was seen crossing the streets without life and sound, or diminishing in the interminable straight perspectives of shadowy houses bordering empty roadways lined by strings of gas-lamps. He walked through Squares, Places, Ovals, Commons, through monotonous streets with unknown names where the dust of humanity settles inert and hopeless out of the stream of life. He walked. (241)

The walking is again aimless, only a means of distraction, and Ossipon is another parodic inversion of the *flâneur* as a means of penetrating and understanding the labyrinth of the city. He is the agent of a vision which refuses to concede any positive meaning or value to the enormous town. Slumbering on its carpet of mud in a raw mist it scarcely resembles a man-made creation at all; it is as though it has barely struggled free from the primeval slime. The urban world is defined by absences – no life, no sound, no distinguishing features. These monotonous streets with unknown names betray an imagination that is unable, or refuses, to be aroused by the spectacle of the city and can only conceive of its inhabitants as an inert and hopeless mass unworthy of closer attention. This dismissive and nihilistic vision cannot properly be read as a projection of Ossipon's disturbed mental condition, for he, too, is one of its objects, reduced to a mere form to which the neuter pronoun 'it' threatens to deny a last trace of humanity.

Conrad's London in these closing scenes of *The Secret Agent* marks a terminal point in realism's engagement with the city. The street-walking figures are still the agents of a totalizing vision, but it is a vision that achieves comprehensiveness only through rejection. The relationship of Ossipon and the Professor to the London whose streets they pace is no longer animated by the realist dialectic of individual and collective; the one may be losing control and the other maniacally retaining it, but both are shown receding into the inert and hopeless mass of humanity. Unseeing, they have none of the spectator's detachment or curiosity, and with them Conrad seems, as it were, to be closing his own eyes to the metropolitan world in a final gesture of negation. In its pervasive irony and thematic preoccupation with a problem of form *The Secret Agent* may mark the beginning of modernism, but in other respects it looks more like the dead end of realism. By contrast, the great modernist novels of urban life are to reinvent the spectator by integrating what Conrad here keeps firmly apart – the complex psychic life of the individual, brilliantly suggested but not explored in Ossipon's descent into madness, and the life of the city. Modernist fiction maps the mind and the city in the same narrative movement; the diverse phenomena of urban life mark the contours of consciousness, so that the fictional city is also a landscape of the mind. A *flâneur* like Leopold Bloom in *Ulysses* is not so much a means of exploring the urban labyrinth as an important part of the labyrinth to be explored.

10

MODERN METAMORPHOSES OF THE *FLANEUR*

To move from Conrad's London in *The Secret Agent* (1907) to Virginia Woolf's in *Mrs Dalloway* (1925), or Joyce's Dublin in *Ulysses* (1922), is to move from darkness into light. The sodden murk or rusty sunshine of a barely discernible spring give way to the high summer of modernism: 'For it was the middle of June'.[1] The change of season is an appropriate metaphor for the emergence of a fully developed modernist mode of fiction which combines elements of continuity with the realist past and new emphases to present a different kind of vision. Down the sunlit streets of Woolf's and Joyce's midsummer cities stroll figures who see and are seen in a new way. My aim in this concluding chapter is to sketch out the principal features of this new vision in the light of its realist antecedents. The full range and diversity of modernist practice lies beyond the scope of this study, but they may be sufficiently suggested by an examination of the modern metamorphoses of the *flâneur*.

The great city is not the only locus of modernist fiction, but it is a central one. Works as diverse as Gide's *Les Faux-Monnayeurs* (1925), Döblin's *Berlin Alexanderplatz* (1929), and the first volume of Musil's *Der Mann ohne Eigenschaften* (*The Man Without Qualities*, 1930) all open like *Mrs Dalloway* on the streets of the metropolis; and there are obvious ways in which novels like Döblin's and Joyce's have been decisively shaped by the very rhythms of life in a modern, mechanized urban culture. As Hugh Kenner maintains, the practitioners of modernism 'encountered the modern big city as a sudden novelty'.[2] Nevertheless the originality of that encounter can be overstated for, as we have seen, writers like Balzac and Dickens responded intensely to what was new and disturbing in the Paris and London of their day. There is a clear continuity here between the modernists and their realist predecessors, and it extends to their use of a strolling witness to life on the streets. Woolf's Peter Walsh and Joyce's Leopold Bloom are descendants of the realist *flâneur*, agents of a vision that once again aspires to inclusiveness, but, as a few examples will illustrate, an inclusiveness of a different order and achieved on a different level.

In the evening of Woolf's June day Peter Walsh makes his way through the London streets to Clarissa Dalloway's party, 'with the belief upon him that he was about to have an experience' (180). The question of what kind of experience is raised, and immediately answered:

> Beauty anyhow. Not the crude beauty of the eye. It was not beauty pure and simple – Bedford Place leading into Russell Square. It was straightness and emptiness of course; the symmetry of a corridor; but it was also windows lit up, a piano, a gramophone sounding; a sense of pleasure-making hidden, but now and again emerging when, through the uncurtained window, the window left open, one saw parties sitting over tables, young people slowly circling, conversations between men and women, maids idly looking out (a strange comment theirs, when work was done), stockings drying on top ledges, a parrot, a few plants. Absorbing, mysterious, of infinite richness, this life.

Woolf's characteristic use of free indirect discourse gives this meditation a more than purely personal significance. The beauty of the visible is crude and limited; what is seen in these glimpses through uncurtained windows hints at a larger, richer, and more mysterious beauty for which the only word is the inclusive but inadequate 'life'. That withheld substantive assembles the random details perceived by the mobile gaze of the stroller under a single rubric, but one so bland that it both turns attention back to those same details and, at the same time, indicates the ineffable nature of the whole. Life, that 'luminous halo' and 'semi-transparent envelope' famously invoked in Woolf's essay on 'Modern Fiction',[3] assumes a numinous quality that is the constant challenge to her imagination. Typically the passage proceeds from the visible to the metaphysical, registering on the way the kind of social details and distinctions that would have excited the realist – the commenting maids and the drying stockings – but assimilating them to life's 'infinite richness' with an unquestioning assurance in which the complacency of privileged Bloomsbury is hard to distinguish from the higher commit-ment of the modernist artist.

As the episode continues, Peter Walsh begins to look more and more like a keen-eyed *flâneur*: 'His light overcoat blew open, he stepped with indescribable idiosyncrasy, leant a little forward, tripped, with his hands behind his back and his eyes still a little hawk-like; he tripped through London, towards Westminster, observing' (181). Yet his gaze, despite the hawk-like quality tentatively claimed for it, is not so much penetrating as receptive, experiencing that bombardment of impressions which, for Woolf, constitute the lot of an ordinary mind on an ordinary day:

> And here a shindy of brawling women, drunken women; here only a policeman and looming houses, domed houses, churches, parliaments, and the hoot of a steamer on the river, a hollow misty cry. But it was her street, this, Clarissa's; cabs were rushing round the corner, like water round the piers of a bridge, drawn together, it seemed to him, because they bore people going to her party, Clarissa's party. (182)

The centripetal movement which brings the paragraph to a close is an inner process as well as an observed phenomenon. The creative function of Clarissa's party is to draw people together, and while Peter Walsh witnesses this happening, his own thoughts and feelings are shown drawing themselves around, and focusing on, the central obsession which she represents in his life. Finally the visible world recedes and the inner life takes over:

> The cold stream of visual impressions failed him now as if the eye were a cup that overflowed and let the rest run down its china walls unrecorded. The brain must wake now. The body must contract now, entering the house, the lighted house where the door stood open, where the motor cars were standing, and bright women descending: the soul must brave itself to endure. He opened the big blade of his pocket-knife. (182)

The cold visual impact of the external world is associated with the contracting body and opposed to the vital inner core – first the awakening brain and then the soul nerving itself for its ordeal. The visible emblem of this penetration inward into the unseen life of the subject is the pocket-knife with which the episode concludes. An expression of Walsh's inner anxieties and male assertiveness, it also suggests the process by which Woolf excavates the inner life: 'how I dig out beautiful caves behind my characters', as she puts it in her diary.[4] In the end it is not the hawk-like eye of Peter Walsh that is genuinely penetrating but the tunnelling imagination of the novelist, which, with its constant inclination to transcend the social, is no longer fully represented by the gaze of the *flâneur*.

The importance for Woolf of the strolling figures on the streets like Peter Walsh is that they allow her to explore the rich life of sensations and impressions experienced by ordinary minds on ordinary days in conditions of particular visual variety and intensity. *Mrs Dalloway* brilliantly articulates a Baudelairean sense of the modern as the ephemeral and fleeting, and cleverly exploits the shocks and collisions that Benjamin saw to be the basic experience of life in the modern city (*CB*, 132). One consequence is an essentially passive relationship of perceiving subject to surroundings. So abundant is the stream of fleeting impressions, so incessant the shower of innumerable atoms, that the mind can do little more than yield passively to them. Significantly Walsh's brain begins to awake when the stream of impressions fails him. As an observer of life on the streets he is, indeed, more a *badaud* than a *flâneur*, more a passive receiver of impressions than an active seeker after meaning. That change of emphasis is, as we have seen in Ford and Conrad, characteristic of the aftermath of realism, and Woolf's practice seems to be predicated on the same kind of assumption as Ford's: life does not narrate, but makes impressions on our brains. Where the mind is understood in this way as the receptacle of impressions, and where the detective faculty of the eye is no longer prominent, conventional gender distinctions lose some of their importance, and in *Mrs Dalloway* there is no essential difference between Peter Walsh and Clarissa herself in their role as observers of the urban world. The *flâneur* can equally well be a *flâneuse*.[5]

The stream of visual impressions, whether cold or animated by Clarissa's love of the spectacle of London life, does not itself yield meaning. As Woolf maintains when writing about Proust, 'the mind cannot be content with holding sensation after sensation passively to itself; something must be done with them; their abundance must be shaped'.[6] In the shaping process undertaken by the novelist, Peter Walsh's emblematic pocket-knife plays its part: as a recurrent motif it helps create a pattern of meaning over the span of the narrative. There is, indeed, a double movement in that last paragraph cited above: a movement from outer to inner, and from the stream of impressions to a device which plainly reveals the patterning process of art. It is a characteristic move, since pattern for Woolf is usually located behind or beneath the surface. In her autobiographical 'Sketch of the Past' she writes of the 'shock-receiving capacity' that makes her an artist, and of her conviction that the shocks she receives are intimations of some order behind appearances which it is her task as an artist to make real by putting into words.[7] Behind the 'cotton wool of daily life' is 'hidden a pattern', she believes. But if this looks initially like a neo-Platonic stance, it finally emerges as an aesthetic one, for she maintains 'that we – I mean all human beings – are connected with this [pattern]; that the whole world is a work of art; that we are parts of the work of art'.[8] The pattern behind the flux of appearances and the stream of impressions is ultimately the pattern of art.

This pattern, which it is the task of the writer to disengage from the contingencies of quotidian life, is to be discerned by the reader rather than the characters of the fictional world; but the latter do experience a fleeting intimation of it in those moments of illumination or epiphany that are a familiar motif in the modernist novel. Peter Walsh's experience in Bloomsbury is typical: 'really it took one's breath away, these moments; there coming to him by the pillar-box opposite the British Museum one of them, a moment, in which things came together; this ambulance; and life and death' (168). The context of his *flânerie* through the streets of London is significant for underlining both the accidental and the dynamic nature of the experience. A chance occurrence, like an unexpected encounter in the street, it is not sought, and the course it takes lies beyond his control. One conventional view of such moments invokes the notion of 'spatial form' and interprets them as occasions when time yields its meaning by being suspended.[9] But the suspension is so fleeting that it is the dynamic quality of the experience that receives the final emphasis, reinforced in this instance by Woolf's characteristic recourse to the implied image of the wave: 'It was as if he were sucked up to some very high roof by that rush of emotion, and the rest of him, like a white shell-sprinkled beach, left bare' (168). The similes suggest that the suspended moment of high emotion is simply the instant before the wave breaks, and that the coming together of things in this way presupposes their falling apart again. The underlying pattern intimated by Woolf's recurrent wave metaphor is, indeed, dynamic rather than static, and in *Mrs Dalloway* it is served and supported by the movement of characters through the London streets. *Flânerie* is both a means of dramatically illustrating the mobility of consciousness and an instrument of artistic patterning.

Modernism's most sustained effort at penetrating the phenomenal surface, the cotton wool of daily life, to reach the deeper truth of art is, of course, Proust's *A la recherche du temps perdu*. There the tunnelling activity of the creative imagination and the kind of receptivity to impressions seen in Peter Walsh and Clarissa are both invested in the same person, the narrator himself. In Proust's novel the divergence of the casual and penetrating, the receptive and interpretative aspects of the *flâneur*'s vision, which we have observed in other early modernist works, is related to different phases of the narrator's existence. He lives his life as a *badaud*, so to speak, and finally comes to redeem it through the creative detective work of the artist. In the crucial premonitory moments of his youth, such as his experience of the steeples of Martinville, the visible world offers teasing clues to a deeper, hidden significance which it is to be the writer's task to reveal. The form and sunlit surface of the steeples create an impression which he feels impelled to explore:

> En constatant, en notant la forme de leur flèche, le déplacement de leurs lignes, l'ensoleillement de leur surface, je sentais que je n'allais pas au bout de mon impression, que quelque chose était derrière ce mouvement, derrière cette clarté, quelque chose qu'ils semblaient contenir et dérober à la fois.[10]

> In ascertaining and noting the shape of their spires, the changes of aspect, the sunny warmth of their surfaces, I felt that I was not penetrating to the full depth of my impression, that something more lay behind that mobility, that luminosity, something which they seemed at once to contain and to conceal.[11]

And it is in exploring and articulating his own reactions that he begins to discern the deeper meaning of the experience. To penetrate the visible surface of things – and the surface of the steeples is described as splitting open like the bark of a tree under his self-scrutiny – is in the end to descend into the private world of the perceiving subject. The typically modernist move inward is again associated with physical movement, for he observes the steeples from a moving carriage. This mobile, street-level perspective, reminiscent of the *flâneur*'s, governs his first attempt at writing, in which the metaphorical texture of Proust's mature style is embryonically anticipated by a proliferation of carefully contrived similes to describe the shifting appearance and position of the steeples as the carriage first approaches, then moves away from them down a winding country road (1, 181–2).

This assimilation of the mobile perspective into the artistic process can be seen again in the great coda to *Du côté de chez Swann* (1, 421–7), where the adult narrator strolls through the Bois de Boulogne on a bright November morning. Moved by an urge to see for himself the beauty of the turning leaves in the sunlight, he first notes the way in which autumn alters the visual composition of the Bois, clearly separating into differently coloured sections what in summer appears to be a single homogeneous green entity. The distinct elements do not destroy the sense of a composite whole but change its appearance, and Proust's description brings out the rich variety and splendour of the colours on display. But the desire to see gives way to a bodily desire for the unseen, for the 'chef-d'œuvre des belles promeneuses' (1, 424), the beautiful strolling women who are framed by the trees in the Allée des Acacias for a few hours each day. At this point the narrator's *flânerie* turns inward and backward and becomes a meditation which proceeds by a series of metonymical shifts from trees to dryads, to women, to the happy days of his youth, and finally to an idea of perfection represented by Mme Swann and her equipage in times gone by. Where the description of the trees in their autumn colours invoked analogies with artistic composition and made allusions to actual paintings, such as Michelangelo's *Creation*, the elegiac meditation on the lost world of Mme Swann exploits a specifically literary past. Shocked by the sight of motor cars and modern dresses in place of the elegant carriages and costumes of the past, he declares his inability to compose these scattered and random details of the present into a picture, while at the same time elevating Mme Swann into a mythical figure whose carriage horses resembled the cruel steeds of Diomed and whose passing seems to have a contingent cause in the death of the gods. Likening the Bois de Boulogne to Virgilian groves – 'les bosquets virgiliens' (1, 427) – the narrator implicitly casts himself as Aeneas descending to an underworld inhabited by a few ghastly shades of the feminine beauty he had admired in his youth. The *flânerie* has taken him from the seen to the unseen, from admiration of nature's present richness to melancholy awareness of the impoverished human present, and from perceiving the patterns of the visible world to creating those of a lost realm of myth. The mobility of the stroller is elided into the mobility of the creative imagination, and the gaze of the *flâneur* yields to the mind's eye of the introspective artist.

The eloquent lament at the depredation of time which ends this episode, and the whole volume, proclaims the visible, material world of houses, roads, and avenues to be as fleeting as the years themselves: 'et les maisons, les routes, les avenues, sont fugitives, hélas! comme les années' (1, 427). The stroll through the Bois de Boulogne thus has the effect of first affirming and then questioning the importance of visual appearance and the faculty which perceives it. Reality for Proust, as the final volume of *A la recherche* spells out (3, 882), does not reside in the appearance of things, however solid they may seem, but at a depth where that appearance counts for little; hence his scornful dismissal of the notion that the novel should aspire to a cinematographic vision (3, 883, 889). A true seeing, and a novelistic art worthy of the name, look inward into the mind and memory of the perceiving subject. This focus distinguishes it from the visual and imaginative power claimed by the prototypically realist *flâneur*–narrator in Balzac's *Facino Cane*, whose gaze goes beyond external details to seize the lives of other individuals. Balzac's power is the realist's power of empathy, Proust's the introspection of the modernist, descending 'within himself', as Conrad famously put it in the preface to *The Nigger of the Narcissus*, to find there 'the terms of his appeal'.[12] This creates a different kind of epistemological problem, which lies not in the insecure basis of what the narrator claims to know of others but in the general validity of what he comes to know of himself. A suspicion of solipsism haunts Proust's work and modernist fiction in general. Woolf voices it concisely in the questions she puts to herself in her diary when working on *Mrs Dalloway*: 'Have I the power of conveying the true reality? Or do I write essays about myself?'[13] It is to counter such doubts that Proust pursues a strategy of postulating general laws on the basis of subjective experience – a strategy visible in the mythical elevation of Mme Swann in the passage above, where an impersonal pattern of myth is projected on to a deeply personal sense of loss.

The disjunction of the inner life and the outer here recalls Nietzsche's definition of the predicament of modern man, and it generates a typically modernist irony; an ironic vision which holds in focus, and in a relationship of mutual interrogation, both the disconnectedness of phenomena and the possibility of their artistic ordering. Rather like the way in which Woolf's wave metaphors imply resolution and dissolution in the same moment, Proust's *flânerie* moves back and forth between images and implications of composition and fragmentation. From admiring the Bois de Boulogne as a composite whole, 'un assemblage composite', he comes to yearn for the 'chef-d'œuvre' of beautiful strolling women framed by the trees, and then, confronted by the spectacle of modern life, despairs of composing its random details into a whole even as he begins to construct on another level an elegiacally harmonious picture of Mme Swann and the past. Temporal loss and artistic redemption, the contingent and the necessary, are encompassed in one sinuous movement of the imagination which prefigures on a small scale the achievement of the whole novel.

The ironic modernist vision presupposes a degree of detachment from the quotidian world which exceeds anything to be found in the realist novel. However excluded they may feel, Balzac's *flâneur* figures are implicated in the spectacle of fashionable society by the force of their desires; and even so subtle an explorer of the inner life as Henry James registers the lure of the commodity and commercial display, which cause Strether to 'want things he shouldn't know what to do with'. No such material wants trouble Proust's narrator or Woolf's characters, who circulate freely on a level inwardly remote from the circulation of cash and commodities, from the whole traffic and commerce of daily life. Bond Street, where Clarissa Dalloway goes to buy her flowers and which she finds fascinating, holds itself superciliously aloof from all such vulgarity: 'its shops; no splash; no glitter; one roll of tweed in the shop where her father had bought his suits for fifty years; a few pearls; salmon on an iceblock' (13). Her acknowledged 'passion for gloves' (14) is an incidental aside that plays no part in the life presented in the novel. And although Proust analyses the obsessive and fetishistic nature of love, he pays no attention to the fetishism of the commodity. Such aloofness is not simply the arbitrary privilege of wealth and class – although it may be that too – but a matter of artistic orientation. The alienated condition which Balzac dramatically explored is now, it seems, taken for granted, and modernism's commitment to the higher, or deeper, truth of art is predicated on a fundamental estrangement and a deliberately adopted distance. As a recent critic has put it, in modernism a metaphysics of depth is associated with an aesthetic of detachment.[14]

This detachment confirms Nietzsche's diagnosis of the modern gulf between inner and outer, but it also involves a more radical distancing of the historical than he envisaged. The protagonist of modernist fiction is rarely a strolling spectator of history since history barely enters his purview. For Proust history is subordinate to a personal sense of time lost. Despite the background presence and destructive impact of the Great War in both *A la recherche* and *Mrs Dalloway*, history is effectively marginalized. Where Flaubert in *L'Education sentimentale* showed an individual on the margins of history, consuming the spectacle it afforded in the way Nietzsche deplored, Proust and Woolf locate history on the margins of individual lives whose central concerns lie elsewhere. Even in *Ulysses*, where Joyce's generous and capacious imagination embraces the popular culture and commercial life of Dublin as well as the sights, sounds, and smells of the city's streets, the larger movements of history – that nightmare from which Stephen Dedalus is trying to awake – register only on the fringes of Leopold Bloom's mobile mind. When he stands in front of a shop window and starts looking at field glasses the ensuing train of associations includes a reflection on the course of contemporary commercial history:

> Must get those old glasses of mine set right. Gœrz lenses, six guineas. Germans making their way everywhere. Sell on easy terms to capture trade. Undercutting. Might chance on a pair in the railway lost property office. Astonishing the things people

leave behind them in trains and cloakrooms. What do they be thinking about?[15]

The historical detail takes its place as just one of the odd pieces of information in a mind as full of random objects as the lost property office, and Bloom's thoughts continue in characteristic fashion by tracing a widening arc which eventually takes in the sun, the moon, and the universe: 'Gasballs spinning about, crossing each other, passing. Same old dingdong always' (212). Moving swiftly from visual instruments to a cosmic vision, the passage illustrates how Joyce's peculiar inclusiveness tends to dwarf the merely historical into insignificance.

The novel which both marginalizes history and most clearly takes issue with that procedure in the ironic manner of modernism is Thomas Mann's *Der Zauberberg* (*The Magic Mountain*, 1924). In transporting the average young German Hans Castorp from his bourgeois Hamburg home to an Alpine sanatorium, Mann displays the modernist configuration of metaphysical depth and aesthetic detachment. The remoteness of the setting provides the conditions in which the lineaments of a whole culture can be defined and the meaning of life interrogated. Set apart from history and governed by its own peculiar sense of time the Berghof sanatorium allows Hans to transcend the limitations of his conventional bourgeois upbringing, but at the same time it presents an intensified image of the historical world of the European bourgeoisie, its values, assumptions, and ideological conflicts. Mann's novel sustains this ironic doubleness, demonstrating the power of fiction to transcend the historical and create an autonomous world of the imagination, while insisting ultimately on its inescapable historical grounding. Thus Hans Castorp's metaphysical vision in the snow at the moral climax of the novel is balanced by the narrator's historical vision of Hans on the battlefield of the Western Front at its conclusion: the harmonious vision of love and beauty, achieved in full awareness of death and destruction, and the discordant vision of death and destruction in which love and beauty are no more than a desperate hope have to be read against each other. Both visions imply the detachment of the perceiving subject – Hans in the blizzard has gone beyond the Berghof to the very frontiers of existence – but the narrator's view of Hans in the closing pages is marked by a self-critical awareness which excludes any sense of superiority. Repeatedly referring to himself as a shadow, and implicating the reader in his shadowy security – 'and we are shrinking shadows by the way-side, shamed by the security of our shadowdom'[16] – he self-consciously stresses the insubstantiality of fiction in the face of the brutal conflicts of history. He, and we as readers of fiction, may be like strolling spectators, but Mann makes painfully plain the limitations of that privileged role, for only with embarrassment can such history as this be treated as spectacle. The modernist writer may aspire to a vision that transcends the historical world, but for Mann the harmonies and orderings of fiction have finally to be read in the light of all that resists them.

In Sartre's *La Nausée* (*Nausea*, 1938) the ironic awareness of the limits and possibilities of fiction to be found in Mann is intensified into a thoroughgoing scepticism which signals a move beyond modernism. This scepticism focuses particularly on the way narratives, whether literary or historical, structure experience and on the power of sight to make sense of the world. In the 'undated sheet' which begins the novel a blank, where one would expect to find the word 'see', indicates the need for another term to describe the way Roquentin apprehends things; and in the climactic scene with the chestnut tree in the park 'seeing' again proves inadequate to define the intensity and complexity of his experience; and he dismisses vision itself as an abstract invention, a simplified idea. The visual sense is displaced from the central position it occupied in the realist novel. And yet Roquentin's relationship to the world is essentially that of an outsider who observes, and in that respect his experience harks back to realism as well as pointing forward to the postmodern.

His Sunday stroll on the rue Tournebride is a final example of *flânerie* transposed into a modern mode. The interpolated passage from *Eugénie Grandet* which he reads in the café at the end of his morning walk invites us to read the whole scene in relation to Balzacian realism, as a 'scene of provincial life' ironically reworked to bring out the contrast between Balzac's ordered, novelistic bourgeois world and a contemporary perception of bourgeois reality.[17] But continuity is as prominent as contrast, since Roquentin is not only sardonically distanced from what he observes but also as confidently knowing as any Balzacian narrator in defining and interpreting it. He may, like Balzac's Lucien de Rubempré on the Champs-Elysées, feel himself to be separated by an abyss from the social parade he is watching, but the distance is one of mocking superiority rather than painful estrangement. A head taller than the crowd about him – 'je domine les deux colonnes de toute la tête'[18] – he dominates it in more than a physical sense, seeing through its pretentions, seizing on its absurdities of behaviour, and detailing its history. In this episode the visual does yield meaning, and Sartre uses Roquentin's *flâneur* perspective to read the signs of the social world and anatomize it on the basis of appearances with all the assurance and attention to sartorial detail of a Balzac:

Depuis le temps que je viens dans cette rue voir les coups de chapeau du dimanche, j'ai appris à distinguer les gens du Boulevard et ceux du Coteau. Quand un type porte un manteau tout neuf, un feutre souple, une chemise éblouissante, quand il déplace l'air, il n'y a pas à s'y tromper: c'est quelqu'un du boulevard Maritime. Les gens du Coteau Vert se distinguent par je ne sais quoi de minable et d'affaissé. (63–4)

Since I started coming to this street to see the Sunday hat-raising, I have learnt to distinguish between the people from the boulevard and those from the Coteau. When a fellow is dressed in a new overcoat, a soft felt hat, and a dazzling shirt, when he displaces air in passing, there's no possibility of a mistake: he is somebody from the boulevard Maritime. The people from the Coteau Vert can be recognized by an indefinable shabby, sunken look.[19]

The point of such analysis is not, of course, Balzacian; the end it serves is satirical dismissal rather than social understanding; but the means employed owe more to realist practice than the Balzacian intertextuality would at first suggest.

Roquentin's Sunday stroll does not, however, simply recreate a realist mode of perception. The feeling of adventure he experiences as the lights go on in the evening – a feeling of being involved in a meaningful sequence of events – is a version of the modernist epiphany. Briefly the aimless stroller has the sense of heading somewhere specific; the isolated individual on the empty streets of a French provincial town feels that he is marching in step with embattled humanity in Berlin and New York. This sense of life as ordered and meaningful is arbitrary and short-lived, and the exact opposite of his experiences of nausea; but both are functions of his *flânerie*, chance encounters with the unexpected in a peculiarly unstructured mobile existence. The mobile perspective encompasses incompatibles without embarrassment. On the one hand the absurd comedy of bourgeois life on the rue Tournebride is the product of a detached and penetrating vision for which nothing is problematic. Signs do not deceive – 'ces signes ne trompent pas' (69) – and seeing is knowing. On the other this reinstatement of realist convention is explicitly challenged by the experiences of nausea, which seemingly demolish the very idea of a visible world that is stable and knowable. Faced with the pebble, the mauve braces, or the tram-seat, Roquentin is not the sardonic detector of bourgeois bad faith but more like a gaping *badaud*, overwhelmed by what his gaze cannot understand or interpret. Vision fails him and, significantly, he finds relief in sound and language; in the sound of the jazz tune and the dream of writing a novel which, too, would stand apart from the nauseating contingency of existence. In plotting the swing of the perceptual pendulum between two opposite kinds of vision, the penetrating and the penetrated, *La Nausée* shows how that 'joy of watching' (*CB*, 69) which Benjamin saw to be triumphant in the *flâneur* can turn into a nightmare.

Where realism revealed the problematic aspects of vision through undercurrents of ironic implication, Sartre sets out the problem on the surface of his text, as it were, through the juxtaposition of opposites. *La Nausée*, with its discordant elements of the realistic and the surreal, of social satire and philosophical tract, is a work of unresolved antinomies. The resolution that is apparently offered in Roquentin's decision to write a novel is unmistakably tainted with a suspicion of irony, or outright parody, in its proximity to Proust's redemption through art. Sartre's frontal assault on the forms of control and authority enshrined in bourgeois culture can hardly leave unscathed the claims made by the major modernists for the transcendent power of art and the mastery of the creative imagination. In making the seminal work of art in the novel a jazz tune – written by a Jew, sung by a black woman, and heard on a record in a café – Sartre seems deliberately to challenge the notion of art's high calling; and this incorporation of a popular art form is one of the grounds for seeing *La Nausée* as announcing a move to a postmodernist mode of fiction.

Accounts of the postmodernist succession to *La Nausée* tend to a ritual invocation of writers like Beckett, Borges, and Barthelme; but it is to a less spectacularly radical work that we may usefully turn to observe how the novel continues to engage with the problematic perspective of the spectator under the distinctive conditions of contemporary life. The title of Graham Swift's *Out of this World* suggests the privileged but questionable vantage-point of its central character, a photo-journalist who, like Sartre's Roquentin, looks on life from an inner distance. But whereas Roquentin views bourgeois culture from outside with the political reflexes of a 1930s intellectual, casting a jaundiced eye on the getting and spending of consumer society which the nineteenth-century realist had explored from within, Swift's character Harry Beech is the inhabitant and creation of a culture dominated by the image, and his detachment is of a kind conferred by the instrument of his trade. Feeling that 'if you exist in your vision, then nothing can hurt you',[20] he reflects on the way the camera seems to make news photographers 'invisible, invulnerable, incorporeal . . . like those immortal gods and goddesses who flitted unharmed around the plain at Troy' (121). Penetrating this illusion of invulnerability, the novel examines the problematic nature of

Beech's role and of a world which, continuing the development Nietzsche had identified as early as the 1870s, has become an 'exhibition of recorded data', a 'continuously running movie' (119). In pondering the problem of his own medium the photographer raises a general problem of vision and representation:

> The problem is what you don't see. The problem is your field of vision. (A picture of the whole world!) The problem is selection (true, Mr Interviewer), the frame, the separation of the image from the thing. The extraction of the world from the world. The problem is where and how you draw the line. (119)

Under such scrutiny the capacity of the visual image to convey the truth appears highly questionable. As another character in the novel points out, 'an image . . . is without knowledge or memory'; and this gives rise to the crucial question: 'Do we see the truth or tell it?' (76). The question goes to the heart of a culture saturated with images, while the answer implied in the very form of Swift's novel is just as typically postmodern. In making the principal characters tell their own life-stories in their own words he reasserts the value of story-telling as a cognitive act, and in this respect aligns himself with writers like Salman Rushdie and Angela Carter, Primo Levi and Gabriel García Márquez. There may be no master narrative, but truth, if it can ever be found, may be found more readily in the toils of language than in the deceptive clarity of the visual image.

Swift's preoccupations and formal strategies are unmistakably contemporary, but in exploring problems of vision and representation, of seeing and knowing, spectating and consuming, he shows how issues which engaged his realist predecessors still bear on the modern novelist with undiminished urgency. The reader of *Out of this World* may be reminded of Scott's critique of the spectator, Balzac's dramas of alienation in a commodified culture, Dickens's use of the *flâneur*'s mobile perspective, or Flaubert's dissection of a modern sensibility. If Graham Swift can be described as a postmodernist, his novel illustrates the absence of any clean break between postmodernism, modernism, and realism. The history of fiction is not one of sudden ruptures and absolutely new beginnings; it is, rather, the history of a continuous and continuing process of interrogation and innovation in which, to name only the concern of this study, the relationship of the fictional spectator to the world observed defines a persistent problem of vision.

NOTES

1 INTRODUCTION

1 This is, of course, open to debate. There is disagreement about whether the mirror on the wall behind the painter reflects his canvas or the actual figures of the King and Queen. Nevertheless, the important point is that their presence outside the painting as the painter's sovereign patrons is insinuated within it by means of the reflection in the mirror and the reactions of the other figures. See J. Brown, *Velázquez: Painter and Courtier*, New Haven and London, Yale University Press, 1986, pp. 253–64.

2 M. Foucault, *Les Mots et les choses*, Paris, Gallimard, 1966, pp. 19–31. Available in English as *The Order of Things*, London, Tavistock Publications, 1970, pp. 15–28.

3 The figure – he is known to be Don José Nieto – is positioned so that the vanishing point in the painting is located at his bent elbow. See J. Snyder and T. Cohen, 'Critical response. Reflexions in *Las Meninas*: paradox lost', *Critical Inquiry*, 1980, vol. 7, pp. 429–47 (p. 434).

4 W. Scott, 'Review of *Tales of My Landlord* (1817)', in *Sir Walter Scott on Novelists and Fiction*, I. Williams (ed.), London, Routledge, 1968, p. 240.

5 H. de Balzac, *La Peau de chagrin*, Classiques Garnier, M. Allem (ed.), Paris, Garnier, 1967, p. 38.

6 I am not making any precise distinction between these two terms. In the case of Scott's protagonists, for instance, and of Flaubert's Frédéric Moreau in relation to the events of 1848, 'spectator' seems to be the appropriate term; where there is less sense of looking on at a spectacle I tend to use 'observer'.

7 For instance, R. Tallis, *In Defence of Realism*, London, Arnold, 1988, who mounts a spirited attack on its detractors: G. Levine, *The Realistic Imagination: English Fiction from 'Frankenstein' to 'Lady Chatterley'*, Chicago and London, University of Chicago Press, 1981, demonstrates the sophisticated critical self-consciousness at work in the English nineteenth-century novel: C. Prendergast, *The Order of Mimesis*, Cambridge, Cambridge University Press, 1986, shows how the classic texts of French realism encounter the 'limit' of mimesis and subvert received forms of representation: A. Jefferson, *Reading Realism in Stendhal*, Cambridge, Cambridge University Press, 1988, argues persuasively that Stendhal is as self-conscious a writer as any twentieth-century novelist: J.L. Bezier, *Family Plots: Balzac's Narrative*

Generations, New Haven and London, Yale University Press, 1986, examining the role of the father, shows how nineteenth-century texts repeatedly undercut the proffered images of their own authority.

8 J.P. Stern, *On Realism*, London, Routledge, 1972, p. 54.

9 S. Heath, 'Realism, modernism and "language-consciousness"', in *Realism in European Literature*, N. Boyle and M. Swales (eds), Cambridge, Cambridge University Press, 1986, pp. 103–22, puts it well: 'vision, realism's metaphor of reality and its knowledge, cannot contain the fact of realism, its writing, the activity of its production' (p. 112).

10 F.O. Mathiessen, *Henry James: The Major Phase*, London, Cambridge University Press, 1946, p. 32.

11 J. Gribble, *The Lady of Shalott in the Victorian Novel*, London, Macmillan, 1983.

12 A. de Lacroix, 'Le flâneur', in *Les Français peints par eux-mêmes*, Paris, Adolphe Delahays, Paris, 1859, pt. 2, p. 112. As these lines suggest, this sketch of the *flâneur*, which Benjamin drew upon, invests the figure with the same kind of qualities of vision, empathy, and understanding claimed by a realist writer like Balzac, and in the same hyperbolic terms.

13 These are accessible in English in W. Benjamin, *Charles Baudelaire: A Lyric Poet in the Era of High Capitalism*, trans. H. Zohn, London, Verso Editions, 1983. Page references to this translation, abbreviated as *CB*, are given in brackets throughout. For details of the German texts see below, chapter 2, note 3.

14 J.P. Stern, *On Realism*, pp. 122–3.

15 F. Nietzsche, 'On the uses and disadvantages of history for life', *Untimely Meditations*, trans. R.J. Hollingdale, Cambridge, Cambridge University Press, 1983, pp. 57–123 (p. 83). Hollingdale's 'strolling spectator' is a nice translation of Nietzsche's 'herumwandelnden und genießenden Zuschauer': 'Vom Nutzen und Nachteil der Historie für das Leben', *Unzeitgemäße Betrachtungen*, Stuttgart, Alfred Kröner Verlag, 1966, pp. 95–195 (p. 135).

16 H. de Balzac, *Illusions perdues*, Classiques Garnier, A. Adam (ed.), Paris, Garnier, 1961, p. 292.

17 H. de Balzac, *Lost Illusions*, trans. H.J. Hunt, Harmondsworth, Penguin Books, 1971, p. 263.

18 *La Peau de chagrin*, p. 309.

19 G. Lukács, *The Historical Novel*, trans. H. and S. Mitchell, Harmondsworth, Penguin Books, 1969, pp. 35–6.

20 G. Lukács, 'Narrate or describe?', *Writer and Critic*, trans. A. Khan, London, Merlin Press, 1970, p. 116.

21 M.M. Bakhtin, *The Dialogic Imagination: Four Essays*, trans. C. Emerson and M. Holquist, Austin, University of Texas Press, 1981, p. 155.

22 See R. Bowlby, *Just Looking: Consumer Culture in Dreiser, Gissing, and Zola*, New York and London, Methuen, 1985.

23 Heath, op. cit., p. 112.

24 J. Ruskin, *Præterita*, London, Allen, 1907, vol. 1, ch. 6, p. 171.

25 J.-P. Sartre, *La Nausée*, Paris, Gallimard, 1938, p.166.

26 For an account of the pervasive anti-visual discourse in twentieth-century French thought, see M. Jay, 'In the empire of the gaze: Foucault and the denigration of vision in twentieth-century French thought', in *Foucault: A*

Critical Reader, D. Couzens Hoy (ed.), Oxford, Blackwell, 1986, pp. 175–204.
27 By R. Bowlby, op. cit.

2 BENJAMIN'S *FLANEUR* AND POE'S 'MAN OF THE CROWD'

1 See K. Stierle, 'Baudelaire and the tradition of the *Tableaux de Paris*', *New Literary History*, 1979–80, vol. 11, pp. 345–61.
2 W. Benjamin, *Gesammelte Schriften*, R. Tiedemann and H. Schweppenhäuser (eds), Frankfurt am Main, Suhrkamp, 1974–85, vol. 3, pp. 194–9.
3 These essays are to be found, in the order mentioned, in *Gesammelte Schriften*, vol. 5, pt. 1, pp. 45–59; and vol. 1, pt. 2, pp. 511–653. They are all available in English in W. Benjamin, *Charles Baudelaire: A Lyric Poet in the Era of High Capitalism*, trans. H. Zohn, London, Verso Editions, 1983. Page references to this translation, abbreviated as *CB*, are given in brackets throughout.
4 *Gesammelte Schriften*, vol. 1, pt. 3, p. 1105.
5 C. Baudelaire, *Oeuvres complètes*, Bibliothèque de la Pléiade, C. Pichois (ed.), Paris, Gallimard, 1976, vol. 2, pp. 683–724; and *The Painter of Modern Life and Other Essays*, trans. J. Mayne, London, Phaidon Press, 1964, pp. 1–40.
6 See M. Hollington, 'Dickens the *flâneur*', *The Dickensian*, 1981, vol. 77, pp. 71–87.
7 A. de Lacroix, 'Le flâneur', in *Les Français peints par eux-mêmes*, Paris, Adolphe Delahays, 1859, pt. 2, p. 115.
8 H. de Balzac, *La Comédie humaine*, Bibliothèque de la Pléiade, P.-G. Castex (ed.), Paris, Gallimard, 1977, vol. 6, p. 1019.
9 *The Painter of Modern Life*, p. 7.
10 Ibid., p. 9.
11 *Gesammelte Schriften*, vol. 1, pt. 3, p. 1095.
12 E.A. Poe, 'The Man of the Crowd', *Selected Writings*, D. Galloway (ed.), Harmondsworth, Penguin Books, 1967, p. 180. Further page references to this edition are given in brackets.
13 Cited in W. Benjamin, *Charles Baudelaire: Ein Lyriker im Zeitalter des Hochkapitalismus*, ed. R. Tiedemann, Frankfurt am Main, Suhrkamp, 1974, p. 204.
14 Lacroix, op. cit., p. 114.
15 For instance, at the beginning of Rilke, *Die Aufzeichnungen des Malte Laurids Brigge* (*The Notebooks of Malte Laurids Brigge*, 1910), and in the experiences in Frankfurt and Paris of Thomas Mann's Felix Krull in *Die Bekenntnisse des Hochstaplers Felix Krull* (*Confessions of Felix Krull, Confidence Man*, 1954), the early chapters of which were first published in 1922. The only nineteenth-century instance that comes readily to mind is the narrator in the opening pages of Grillparzer's Novelle *Der arme Spielmann* (*The Poor Minstrel*, 1848), but even there the contrasts with writers like Dickens and Balzac are more striking than any affinity.
16 H. Heine, *Lutezia*, in *Werke*, Frankfurt am Main, Insel Verlag, 1968, vol. 3, p. 440.

3 SCOTT AND THE SPECTACLE OF HISTORY

1 *Sir Walter Scott on Novelists and Fiction*, I. Williams (ed.), London, Routledge, 1968, p. 418. Since there is no complete standard edition of the Waverley Novels, and editions are numerous, quotations are identified by chapter only, in brackets in the text.
2 Ibid., p. 240.
3 A. Welsh, *The Hero of the Waverley Novels*, New Haven, Yale University Press, 1967, p. 51.
4 G. Lukács, *The Historical Novel*, trans. H. and S. Mitchell, Harmondsworth, Penguin Books, 1969, pp. 29–69.
5 F. Nietzsche, 'On the uses and disadvantages of history for life', *Untimely Meditations*, trans. R.J. Hollingdale, Cambridge, Cambridge University Press, 1983, p. 83.
6 See J. Millgate, *Walter Scott: The Making of the Novelist*, Toronto, Toronto University Press, 1984, pp. 35–57.
7 P.D. Garside, 'Waverley's pictures of the past', *ELH*, 1977, vol. 44, pp. 659–82 (p. 673).
8 R. Waswo, 'History and historiography in the Waverley Novels', *ELH*, 1980, vol. 47, pp. 304–30 (p. 308).
9 See J. Barrell, *English Literature in History 1730–80: An Equal Wide Survey*, London, Hutchinson, 1983, pp. 176–209. Though Barrell argues, pp. 207–8, that Fielding's characterization of Mr Allworthy in *Tom Jones* shows that he is critically aware of the limitations of the gentleman's vantage point.
10 G. McMaster, *Scott and Society*, Cambridge, Cambridge University Press, 1981, p. 44.

4 BALZAC: THE ALIENATED GAZE

1 H. de Balzac, *Le Cousin Pons*, Classiques Garnier, A.-M. Meininger (ed.), Paris, Garnier, 1974, p. 6.
2 H. de Balzac, *Cousin Pons*, trans. H.J. Hunt, Harmondsworth, Penguin Books, 1968, p. 19.
3 H. de Balzac, *La Peau de chagrin*, Classiques Garnier, M. Allem (ed.), Paris, Garnier, 1967, p. 310. Further page references to this edition are given in brackets.
4 T.W. Adorno, *Noten zur Literatur*, Frankfurt am Main, Suhrkamp, 1963, vol. 2, pp. 19–20.
5 H. de Balzac, *La Comédie humaine*, Bibliothèque de la Pléiade, P.-G. Castex (ed.), Paris, Gallimard, 1977, vol. 6, p. 1019. Further quotations from *Facino Cane* are from this volume of the Pléiade edition, and page references are given in brackets.
6 A. Béguin, *Balzac lu et relu*, Paris, Editions du Seuil, 1965, pp. 153–6.
7 R. Barthes, *S/Z*, Paris, Editions du Seuil, 1970, pp. 96–7: *S/Z*, trans. R. Miller, London, Cape, 1975, pp. 89–90.
8 H. de Balzac, *Le Père Goriot*, Classiques Garnier, P.-G. Castex (ed.), Paris, Garnier, 1963, p. 114. Further page references to this edition are given in brackets.

9 H. de Balzac, *Old Goriot*, trans M.A. Crawford, Harmondsworth, Penguin Books, 1951, p. 28.
10 W. Benjamin, *Understanding Brecht*, trans. A. Bostok, London, New Left Books, 1977, p. 22.
11 H. de Balzac, *Illusions perdues*, Classiques Garnier, A. Adam (ed.), Paris, Garnier, 1961, p. 767. Further page references to this edition are given in brackets.
12 H. de Balzac, *Lost Illusions*, trans. H.J. Hunt, Harmondsworth, Penguin Books, 1971, pp. 299–300. Further page references to this translation are given in brackets.
13 C. Prendergast, *The Order of Mimesis*, Cambridge, Cambridge University Press, 1986, p. 87.
14 S. Buck-Morss, 'Le flâneur, l'homme-sandwich et la prostituée: politique de la flânerie', in *Walter Benjamin et Paris*, H. Wismann (ed.), Paris, Editions du Cerf, 1986, pp. 361–402 (p. 382).
15 H. de Balzac, *Splendeurs et misères des courtisanes*, Classiques Garnier, A. Adam (ed.), Paris, Garnier, 1964, p. 3. Further page references to this edition are given in brackets.
16 T. Eagleton, *Walter Benjamin: or Towards a Revolutionary Criticism*, London, New Left Books, 1981, p. 27.

5 *BLEAK HOUSE*: THE *FLANEUR*'S PERSPECTIVE AND THE DISCOVERY OF THE BODY

1 M. Proust, *Contre Sainte-Beuve*, Biliothèque de la Pléiade, P. Clarac (ed.), Paris, Gallimard, 1971, p. 269.
2 G.K. Chesterton, *Charles Dickens*, London, Methuen, 1913, p. 40.
3 *The Letters of Charles Dickens*, K. Tillotson (ed.), Oxford, Clarendon Press, 1977, vol. 4, p. 612.
4 Ibid., p. 622.
5 C. Dickens, *Sketches by Boz*, The Oxford Illustrated Dickens, London, Oxford University Press, 1957, p. 40. Further page references to this edition of the *Sketches* are given in brackets.
6 M. Hollington, 'Dickens the *flâneur*', *The Dickensian*, 1981, vol. 77, p. 79.
7 C. Dickens, *The Uncommercial Traveller*, The Oxford Illustrated Dickens, London, Oxford University Press, 1958, p. 135.
8 D. Musselwhite, *Partings Welded Together: Politics and Desire in the Nineteenth-Century English Novel*, London, Methuen, 1987, p. 178.
9 Ibid., p. 202.
10 R. Williams, *The English Novel from Dickens to Lawrence*, Frogmore, Paladin, 1974, p. 32.
11 Hollington, op. cit.
12 Hollington, op. cit., p. 84.
13 Hollington, op. cit., p. 85.
14 C. Dickens, *Bleak House*, N. Page (ed.), Harmondsworth, Penguin Books, 1971, p. 65. Further page references to this edition are given in brackets.
15 S. Connor, *Charles Dickens*, Oxford, Blackwell, 1985, p. 65.
16 See V. Blain, 'Double vision and the double standard in *Bleak House*: a feminist perspective', *Literature and History*, 1985, vol. 11, pp. 31–46.

17 *The Letters of Charles Dickens*, W. Dexter (ed.), London, The Nonesuch Press, 1938, vol. 3, p. 791.

18 C. Dickens, *A Tale of Two Cities*, G. Woodcock (ed.), Harmondsworth, Penguin Books, 1970, p. 44.

6 *L'EDUCATION SENTIMENTALE*: THE BLANK GAZE AND THE WEAKENED PERSONALITY

1 G. Flaubert, *Intimate Notebooks 1840–41*, trans. F. Steegmuller, London, W.H. Allen, 1967, p. 27.

2 G. Flaubert, *Correspondance*, Paris, Conard, 1926–54, vol. 5, p. 260. Further references to the volume and page of this edition, abbreviated as *Corr.*, follow quotations in brackets.

3 M. Proust, *Contre Sainte-Beuve*, Bibliothèque de la Pléiade, P. Clarac (ed.), Paris, Gallimard, 1971, p. 299.

4 G. Flaubert, *L'Education sentimentale: Première version*, Paris, Garnier-Flammarion, 1980, p. 54.

5 J. Culler, *Flaubert: The Uses of Uncertainty*, London, Elek Books, 1974, p. 102.

6 C. Prendergast, 'Flaubert: quotation, stupidity and the Cretan liar paradox', *French Studies*, 1981, vol. 35, pp. 270–2.

7 D.A. Williams, *'The Hidden Life at its Source': A Study of Flaubert's 'L'Education Sentimentale'*, Hull, Hull University Press, 1987.

8 F. Nietzsche, 'On the uses and disadvantages of history for life', *Untimely Meditations*, trans. R.J. Hollingdale, Cambridge, Cambridge University Press, 1983, p. 83.

9 G. Flaubert, *L'Education sentimentale*, Classiques Garnier, E. Maynial (ed.), Paris, Garnier, 1961, p. 1. Further page references to this edition are given in brackets.

10 G. Flaubert, *Sentimental Education*, trans. R. Baldick, Harmondsworth, Penguin Books, 1964, p. 15. Further page references to this translation will be given in brackets.

11 Proust, op. cit., p. 587.

12 C. Baudelaire, *Les Fleurs du mal*, Classiques Garnier, A. Adam (ed.), Paris, Garnier, 1961, pp. 103–4.

13 Nietzsche, op. cit., p. 63.

14 Nietzsche, op. cit., p. 63.

15 G. Falconer, 'Reading *L'Education sentimentale*: belief and disbelief', *Nineteenth-Century French Studies*, 1983–4, vol. 12, p. 332

16 Peter Brooks, *Reading for the Plot: Design and Intention in Narrative*, Oxford, Clarendon Press, 1984, pp. 181–3.

17 Brooks, op. cit., p. 181.

18 Nietzsche, op. cit., p. 79.

19 Nietzsche, op. cit., p. 62.

20 Brooks, op. cit., pp. 210–15.

7 VISION AND FRAME IN *MIDDLEMARCH* AND *DANIEL DERONDA*

1 G. Eliot, *Middlemarch*, W.J.Harvey (ed.), Harmondsworth, Penguin Books, 1965, p. 114. Further page references to this edition are given in brackets.
2 J. Wiesenfarth, '*Middlemarch*: the language of art', *PMLA*, 1982, vol. 97, pp. 363–77.
3 H. James, *Literary Criticism: Essays on Literature: American Writers: English Writers*, New York, Library of America, 1984, pp. 961–2.
4 P. Bourget, *Essais de psychologie contemporaine*, 4th edition, Paris, Alphonse Lemerre, 1885, p. 59. A. de Lacroix, 'Le flâneur', in *Les Français peints par eux-mêmes*, Paris, Adolphe Delahays, 1859, pt. 2, p. 114, defines the *flâneur* in similar terms as a dilettante in a positive sense, having 'a necessarily malleable nature, the organization of an artist'; experiencing the whole range of passions; and having not a 'particular taste, but all tastes'.
5 J. Wiesenfarth, op. cit., p. 370.
6 'The Morality of *Wilhelm Meister*', *The Essays of George Eliot*, T. Pinney (ed.), London, Routledge and Kegan Paul, 1968, p. 147.
7 G. Eliot, *Daniel Deronda*, B. Hardy (ed.), Harmondsworth, Penguin Books, 1967, p. 220. Further page references to this edition are given in brackets.
8 H. James, '*Daniel Deronda*: a conversation', *Selected Literary Criticism*, Harmondsworth, Penguin Books, 1968, pp. 65, 76.
9 *The Essays of George Eliot*, pp. 146–7.
10 G. Eliot, *A Writer's Notebook 1854–1879*, J. Wiesenfarth (ed.), Charlottesville, University of Virginia Press, 1981, pp. 109–10.
11 *The George Eliot Letters*, G. Haight (ed.), London, Oxford University Press, 1956, p. 304.
12 *The Impressions of Theophrastus Such*, Cabinet Edition, London and Edinburgh, William Blackwood and Sons, n.d., p. 263.

8 *THE AMBASSADORS* AND *THE GOOD SOLDIER*: AMERICAN OBSERVERS AND THE COMMODITY OF EUROPEAN LIFE

1 H. James, *The Ambassadors*, The World's Classics, C. Butler (ed.), Oxford, Oxford University Press, 1985, p. 55. Further page references to this edition are given in brackets.
2 F.M. Ford, *The Good Soldier*, Harmondsworth, Penguin Books, 1972, p. 45. Further page references to this edition are given in brackets.
3 W. Greenslade, 'The power of advertising: Chad Newsome and the meaning of Paris in *The Ambassadors*', *ELH*, 1982, vol. 49, pp. 99–112.
4 F.R. Leavis, *The Great Tradition*, Harmondsworth, Penguin Books, 1962, p. 178.
5 G. Lukács, *Studies in European Realism*, trans. E. Bone, London, Merlin Press, 1972, p. 6.
6 T. Tanner, 'The watcher from the balcony: Henry James's *The Ambassadors*', *Critical Quarterly*, 1966, vol. 8, no. 1, pp. 35–52 (p. 51).

7 P. Brooks, *The Melodramatic Imagination: Balzac, Henry James, Melodrama and the Mode of Excess*, New Haven and London, Yale University Press, 1976, p. 170.

8 C. Baudelaire, *The Painter of Modern Life*, trans. J. Mayne, London, Phaidon Press, 1964, p. 13.

9 F.M. Ford, *Joseph Conrad: A Personal Remembrance*, London, Duckworth, 1924, p. 182.

10 Ibid., p. 168.

11 F.M. Ford, *Henry James: A Critical Study*, London, Martin Secker, 1913, p. 62.

9 *THE SECRET AGENT*: METROPOLITAN LIFE AND THE PROBLEM OF FORM

1 J. Conrad, *The Secret Agent*, Harmondsworth, Penguin Books, 1963, p. 10. Further page references to this edition are given in brackets.

2 G. Gissing, *Charles Dickens: A Critical Study*, London, Gresham Publishing Co., 1903, p. 29.

3 Ibid., p. 37.

4 For an acute analysis of Gissing's relationship to Dickens and the different way in which he saw London, see J. Goode, *George Gissing: Ideology and Fiction*, London, Vision Press, 1978, pp. 13–40 (p. 34).

5 G. Gissing, *New Grub Street*, B. Bergonzi (ed.), Harmondsworth, Penguin Books, 1968, p. 77. Further page references to this edition are given in brackets.

6 Gissing, *Charles Dickens*, p. 37.

7 R. Williams, *The Country and the City*, Frogmore, Paladin, 1975, p. 282.

8 H. James, *The Princess Casamassima*, Harmondsworth, Penguin Books, 1977, p. 7. Further page references to this edition are given in brackets.

9 Adrian Poole, *Gissing in Context*, London, Macmillan, 1975, p. 41.

10 Ibid., p. 41.

11 T. Eagleton, 'Form, ideology and *The Secret Agent*', *Against the Grain: Essays 1975–1985*, London, Verso Editions, 1986, p. 25. Eagleton's inverted commas register the unease generated by Conrad's ironic discourse.

12 F.E. Hardy, *The Life of Thomas Hardy*, London, Macmillan, 1962, pp. 206–7.

13 G. Holderness, 'Anarchism and fiction', in *The Rise of Socialist Fiction 1880–1914*, H.G. Klaus (ed.), Brighton, Harvester Press, 1987, p. 132.

14 *The Collected Letters of Joseph Conrad*, F.R. Karl and L. Davies (eds), Cambridge, Cambridge University Press, 1986, vol. 2, p. 188.

15 Ibid., p. 343.

16 F. Nietzsche, *The Birth of Tragedy*, trans. F. Golffing, New York, Doubleday, 1956, p. 56. Further page references to this translation are given in brackets.

17 J. Conrad, *The Nigger of the Narcissus*, Harmondsworth, Penguin Books, 1963, p. 13.

10 MODERN METAMORPHOSES OF THE *FLANEUR*

1 V. Woolf, *Mrs Dalloway*, Harmondsworth, Penguin Books, 1964, p. 6. Further page references to this edition are given in brackets.

2 H. Kenner, 'Modernism and what happened to it', *Essays in Criticism*, 1987, vol. 37, p. 101.

3 V. Woolf, 'Modern fiction', *Collected Essays*, London, Hogarth Press, 1966, vol. 2, p. 106.

4 V. Woolf, *A Writer's Diary*, L. Woolf (ed.), London, Hogarth Press, 1953, p. 60.

5 As was certainly not the case in the nineteenth century; see J. Wolff, 'The invisible *flâneuse*: women and the literature of modernity', in *The Problems of Modernity: Adorno and Benjamin*, A. Benjamin (ed.), London and New York, Routledge, 1989, pp. 141–56.

6 V. Woolf, 'Phases of fiction', *Collected Essays*, vol. 2, p. 83.

7 V. Woolf, 'A Sketch of the past', *Moments of Being: Unpublished Autobiographical Writings*, J. Schulkind (ed.), London, Chatto and Windus, 1976, p. 72.

8 Ibid., p. 72.

9 See S. Connor, *Postmodernist Culture: An Introduction to Theories of the Contemporary*, Oxford, Blackwell, 1989, pp. 117–18. The term 'spatial form' was of course coined by Joseph Frank, 'Spatial form in modern literature', *The Widening Gyre*, Brunswick, N.J., Rutgers University Press, 1963.

10 M. Proust, *A la recherche du temps perdu*, Bibliothèque de la Pléiade, Paris, Gallimard, 1954, vol. 1, p. 180. Further references to the volume and page of this edition are given in brackets.

11 M. Proust, *Remembrance of Things Past*, trans. C.K. Scott Moncrieff, London, Chatto and Windus, 1966, vol. 1, pp. 247–8.

12 J. Conrad, *The Nigger of the Narcissus*, Harmondsworth, Penguin Books, 1965, p. 11.

13 *A Writer's Diary*, p. 57.

14 See S. Connor, op. cit., p. 116.

15 J. Joyce, *Ulysses*, London, The Bodley Head, 1960, p. 260. Further page references to this edition are given in brackets.

16 T. Mann, *The Magic Mountain*, trans. H. T. Lowe-Porter, Harmondsworth, Penguin Books, 1960, p. 713. The original text is: 'Und wir sind scheue Schatten am Wege, schamhaft in Schattensicherheit', *Der Zauberberg*, Berlin and Frankfurt am Main, G.B. Fischer, 1954, p. 656.

17 As it is read, with a rather different emphasis, by M. Edwards, '*La Nausée* – a symbolist novel', *Adam International Review*, 1970, vol. 35, nos 343–5, pp. 14–17.

18 J.-P. Sartre, *La Nausée*, Paris, Gallimard, 1938, p. 62. Further page references to this edition are given in brackets.

19 J.-P. Sartre, *Nausea*, trans. R. Baldick, Harmondsworth, Penguin Books, 1965, p. 68.

20 Graham Swift, *Out of this World*, Harmondsworth, Penguin Books, 1988, p. 121. Further page references to this edition are given in brackets.

A SHORT BIBLIOGRAPHY OF
SECONDARY WORKS

Adorno, T.W., 'Balzac–Lektüre', *Noten zur Literatur*, Frankfurt am Main, Suhrkamp, 1963, vol. 2, pp. 19–41.

Bakhtin, M.M., *The Dialogic Imagination: Four Essays*, trans. C. Emerson and M. Holquist, Austin, University of Texas Press, 1981.

Barrell, J., *English Literature in History 1730–80: An Equal Wide Survey*, London, Hutchinson, 1983.

Barthes, R., *S/Z*, Paris, Editions du Seuil, 1970.

— *S/Z*, trans. R. Miller, London, Cape, 1975.

Baudelaire, C., *The Painter of Modern Life and Other Essays*, trans. J. Mayne, London, Phaidon Press, 1964, pp. 1–40.

— 'Le Peintre de la vie moderne', *Oeuvres complètes*, Bibliothèque de la Pléiade, C. Pichois (ed.), Paris, Gallimard, 1976, vol. 2, pp. 683–724.

Béguin, A., *Balzac lu et relu*, Paris, Editions du Seuil, 1965

Bell, M. (ed.), *The Context of English Literature 1900–1930*, London, Methuen, 1980.

Benjamin, A. (ed.), *The Problems of Modernity: Adorno and Benjamin*, London and New York, Routledge, 1989.

Benjamin, W., *Charles Baudelaire: A Lyric Poet in the Era of High Capitalism*, trans. H. Zohn, London, Verso Editions, 1983.

— *Gesammelte Schriften*, R. Tiedemann and H. Schweppenhäuser (eds), Frankfurt am Main, Suhrkamp, 1974–85

Berman, M., *All That is Solid Melts into Air: The Experience of Modernity*, London, Verso Editions, 1983.

Bezier, J.L., *Family Plots: Balzac's Narrative Generations*, New Haven and London, Yale University Press, 1986.

Blain, V., 'Double vision and the double standard in *Bleak House*: a feminist perspective', *Literature and History*, 1985, vol. 11, pp. 31–46.

Bourget, P., 'Du dilettantisme', *Essais de psychologie contemporaine*, 4th edition, Paris, Alphonse Lemerre, 1885, pp. 59–76.

Bowlby, R., *Just Looking: Consumer Culture in Dreiser, Gissing, and Zola*, New York and London, Methuen, 1985.

Boyle, N. and Swales, M. (eds), *Realism in European Literature*, Cambridge, Cambridge University Press, 1986.

Brooks, P., *The Melodramatic Imagination: Balzac, Henry James, Melodrama and the Mode of Excess*, New Haven and London, Yale University Press, 1976.

— *Reading for the Plot: Design and Intention in Narrative*, Oxford, Clarendon Press, 1984.

Buck-Morss, 'Le flâneur, l'homme–sandwich et la prostituée: politique de la flânerie', in H. Wismann (ed.), *Walter Benjamin et Paris*, Paris, Editions du Cerf, 1986, pp. 361–402.

Chesterton, G.K., *Charles Dickens*, London, Methuen, 1913.

Clark, T.J., *The Painting of Modern Life: Paris in the Art of Manet and his Followers*, Princeton N.J., Princeton University Press, 1984.

Connor, S., *Charles Dickens*, Oxford, Blackwell, 1985.

— *Postmodernist Culture: An Introduction to Theories of the Contemporary*, Oxford, Blackwell, 1989.

Culler, J., *Flaubert: The Uses of Uncertainty*, London, Elek Books, 1974.

Eagleton, T., 'Form, ideology and *The Secret Agent*', *Against the Grain: Essays 1975–1985*, London, Verso Editions, 1986.

— *Walter Benjamin: or Towards a Revolutionary Criticism*, London, New Left Books, 1981.

Edwards, M., '*La Nausée* – a symbolist novel', *Adam International Review*, 1970, vol. 35, nos 343–5, pp. 9–21.

Ermarth, E.D., *Realism and Consensus in the English Novel*, Princeton, N.J., Princeton University Press, 1983.

Falconer, G., 'Flaubert, James and the problem of undecidability', *Comparative Literature*, 1987, vol. 39, no. 1, pp. 1–18.

— 'Reading *L'Education sentimentale*: belief and disbelief', *Nineteenth-Century French Studies*, 1983–4, vol. 12, pp. 329–43.

Ford, F.M., *Henry James: A Critical Study*, London, Martin Secker, 1913.

— *Joseph Conrad: A Personal Remembrance*, London, Duckworth, 1924.

Foucault, M., *Les Mots et les choses*, Paris, Gallimard, 1966.

— *The Order of Things*, London, Tavistock Publications, 1970.

Garside, P.D., 'Waverley's pictures of the past', *ELH*, 1977, vol. 44, pp. 659–82.

Gelley, A., 'Represented world, toward a phenomenological theory of description in the novel', *Journal of Aesthetics and Art Criticism*, 1978–9, vol. 37, pp. 415–22.

Gissing, G., *Charles Dickens: A Critical Study*, London, Gresham Publishing Co., 1903.

Goode, J., *George Gissing: Ideology and Fiction*, London, Vision Press, 1978.

Greenslade, W., 'The power of advertising: Chad Newsome and the meaning of Paris in *The Ambassadors*', *ELH*, 1982, vol. 49, pp. 99–112.

Gribble, J., *The Lady of Shalott in the Victorian Novel*, London, Macmillan, 1983.

Hardy, F.E., *The Life of Thomas Hardy*, London, Macmillan, 1962.

Heath, S., 'Realism, modernism and "language-consciousness"', in *Realism in European Literature*, N. Boyle and M. Swales (eds), Cambridge, Cambridge University Press, 1986, pp. 103–22.

Hessel, F., *Spazieren in Berlin*, Leipzig and Vienna, Dr Hans Epstein, 1929.

Hewitt, N., '"Looking for Annie": Sartre's *La Nausée* and the inter-war years', in R. Wilcocks (ed.), *Critical Essays on Jean–Paul Sartre*, Boston, Mass., G.K. Hall & Co., 1988, pp. 209–24.

Holderness, G., 'Anarchism and fiction', in *The Rise of Socialist Fiction 1880–1914*, H.G. Klaus (ed.), Brighton, Harvester Press, 1987, pp. 121–54.

Hollington, M., 'Dickens the *flâneur*', *The Dickensian*, 1981, vol. 77, pp. 71–87.

Huart, L., *Physiologie du flaneur*, Paris, Aubert, 1841.

Jacobs, C., 'The (too) Good Soldier: "a real story"', *Glyph*, 1978, vol. 3, pp. 32–51.

Jameson, F., *The Political Unconscious: Narrative as a Socially Symbolic Act*, London, Methuen, 1981.

Jay, M., 'In the empire of the gaze: Foucault and the denigration of vision in twentieth–century French thought', in *Foucault: A Critical Reader*, D. Couzens Hoy (ed.), Oxford, Blackwell, 1986.

Jefferson, A., *Reading Realism in Stendhal*, Cambridge, Cambridge University Press, 1988.

Karl, F.R. and Davies, L. (eds), *The Collected Letters of Joseph Conrad*, Cambridge, Cambridge University Press, 1986.

Kenner, H., 'Modernism and what happened to it', *Essays in Criticism*, 1987, vol. 37, p. 101.

Knights, L.C., 'Henry James and the trapped spectator', *Southern Review*, 1939, pp. 600–15.

Lacroix, A. de, 'Le flâneur', in *Les Français peints par eux–mêmes*, Paris, Adolphe Delahays, 1859, pt. 2, pp. 112–17.

Leavis, F.R., *The Great Tradition*, Harmondsworth, Penguin Books, 1962.

Levine, G., *The Realistic Imagination: English Fiction from 'Frankenstein' to 'Lady Chatterley'*, Chicago and London, University of Chicago Press, 1981.

Lukács, G., *The Historical Novel*, trans. H. and S. Mitchell, Harmondsworth, Penguin Books, 1969.

— *Studies in European Realism*, trans. E. Bone, London, Merlin Press, 1972.

— *Writer and Critic*, trans. A. Khan, London, Merlin Press, 1970.

McMaster, G., *Scott and Society*, Cambridge, Cambridge University Press, 1981.

Mathiessen, F.O., *Henry James: The Major Phase*, London, Cambridge University Press, 1946.

Miller, J.H., 'Optic and semiotic in *Middlemarch*', in J.H. Buckley (ed.), *The Worlds of Victorian Fiction*, Cambridge, Mass., Harvard University Press, 1975, pp. 125–45.

Millgate, J., *Walter Scott: The Making of the Novelist*, Toronto, Toronto University Press, 1984.

Musselwhite, D., *Partings Welded Together: Politics and Desire in the Nineteenth-Century English Novel*, London, Methuen, 1987.

Nietzsche, F., 'On the uses and disadvantages of history for life', *Untimely Meditations*, trans. R.J. Hollingdale, Cambridge, Cambridge University Press, 1983.

— *The Birth of Tragedy*, trans. F. Golffing, New York, Doubleday, 1956.

Nochlin, L., *Realism*, Harmondsworth, Penguin Books, 1971.

Poole, A., *Gissing in Context*, London, Macmillan, 1975.

Prendergast, C., 'Flaubert: quotation, stupidity and the Cretan Liar paradox', *French Studies*, 1981, vol. 35, pp. 270–2.

— *The Order of Mimesis*, Cambridge, Cambridge University Press, 1986.

Proust, M., *Contre Sainte–Beuve*, Bibliothèque de la Pléiade, P. Clarac (ed.), Paris, Gallimard, 1971.

Stern, J.P., *On Realism*, London, Routledge, 1972.

Stierle, K., 'Baudelaire and the tradition of the *Tableaux de Paris*', *New Literary History*, 1979–80, vol. 11, pp. 345–61.

Tallis, R., *In Defence of Realism*, London, Arnold, 1988.

Tanner, T., 'The watcher from the balcony: Henry James's *The Ambassadors*', *Critical Quarterly*, 1966, vol. 8, no. 1, pp. 35–52.

Waswo, R., 'History and historiography in the Waverley Novels', *ELH*, 1980, vol. 47, pp. 304–30.

Welsh, A., *The Hero of the Waverley Novels*, New Haven, Yale University Press, 1967.

Wiesenfarth J., '*Middlemarch*: the language of art', *PMLA*, 1982, vol. 97, pp. 363–77.

Wilde, A., *Horizons of Assent: Modernism, Postmodernism, and the Ironic Imagination*, Baltimore and London, Johns Hopkins University Press, 1981.

Williams, D.A., '*The Hidden Life at its Source': A Study of Flaubert's 'L'Education sentimentale'*, Hull, Hull University Press, 1987.

Williams, R., *The Country and the City*, Frogmore, Paladin, 1975.

— *The English Novel from Dickens to Lawrence*, Frogmore, Paladin, 1974.

— *The Politics of Modernism: Against the New Conformists*, T. Pinkney (ed.), London, Verso Editions, 1989.

Wolff, J., 'The invisible *flâneuse*: women and the literature of modernity', in *The Problems of Modernity: Adorno and Benjamin*, A. Benjamin (ed.), London and New York, Routledge, 1989, pp. 141–56.

INDEX